50 YEARS

SAGE was founded in 1965 by Sara Miller McCune to support the dissemination of usable knowledge by publishing innovative and high-quality research and teaching content. Today, we publish more than 850 journals, including those of more than 300 learned societies, more than 800 new books per year, and a growing range of library products including archives, data, case studies, reports, conference highlights, and video. SAGE remains majority-owned by our founder, and after Sara's lifetime will become owned by a charitable trust that secures our continued independence.

Los Angeles | London | New Delhi | Singapore | Washington DC

STATE and CIVIL SOCIETY UNDER SIEGE

Thank you for choosing a SAGE product!
If you have any comment, observation or feedback,
I would like to personally hear from you.
Please write to me at **contactceo@sagepub.in**

Vivek Mehra, Managing Director and CEO, SAGE India.

Bulk Sales

SAGE India offers special discounts
for purchase of books in bulk.
We also make available special imprints
and excerpts from our books on demand.

For orders and enquiries, write to us at

Marketing Department
SAGE Publications India Pvt Ltd
B1/I-1, Mohan Cooperative Industrial Area
Mathura Road, Post Bag 7
New Delhi 110044, India

E-mail us at **marketing@sagepub.in**

Get to know more about SAGE

Be invited to SAGE events, get on our mailing list.
Write today to **marketing@sagepub.in**

This book is also available as an e-book.

STATE and CIVIL SOCIETY UNDER SIEGE

Hindutva, Security and Militarism in India

P. M. JOSHY | K. M. SEETHI

$SAGE www.sagepublications.com
Los Angeles • London • New Delhi • Singapore • Washington DC

First published in 2015 by

 SAGE Publications India Pvt Ltd
B1/I-1 Mohan Cooperative Industrial Area
Mathura Road, New Delhi 110 044, India
www.sagepub.in

SAGE Publications Inc
2455 Teller Road
Thousand Oaks, California 91320, USA

SAGE Publications Ltd
1 Oliver's Yard, 55 City Road
London EC1Y 1SP, United Kingdom

SAGE Publications Asia-Pacific Pte Ltd
3 Church Street
#10-04 Samsung Hub
Singapore 049483

Published by Vivek Mehra for SAGE Publications India Pvt Ltd, typeset in 10/13 Berkeley by RECTO Graphics, Delhi and printed at Saurabh Printers Pvt Ltd, Greater Noida.

Library of Congress Cataloging-in-Publication Data

Joshy, P. M., author.
 State and civil society under siege : Hindutva, security and militarism in India/ P. M. Joshy and K. M. Seethi.
 pages cm
 Includes bibliographical references and index.
 1. Civil Society—India. 2. Hindutva. 3. Human security. 4. India—Politics and government. 5. India—Social policy. 6. India—Economic policy. I. Seethi, K. M., author. II. Title.
 JQ281.J67   320.55—dc23   2015   2015029703

ISBN: 978-93-515-0384-2 (HB)

The SAGE Team: Rudra Narayan, Saima Ghaffar, Nand Kumar Jha and Ritu Chopra

Contents

List of Abbreviations

ABVP	Akhil Bharatiya Vidyarthi Parishad
AICTE	All India Council for Technical Education
AIDWA	All India Democratic Women's Association
AIWC	All India Women's Conference
AVP	Arunachal Vikas Parishad
BJP	Bharatiya Janata Party
BJS	Bharatiya Jana Sangh
BMS	Bharatiya Mazdoor Sangh
BSS	Bharat Sadhu Samaj
CAG	Comptroller and Auditor General
CII	Confederation of Indian Industries
CrPC	Code of Criminal Procedure
CSDS	Centre for the Study of Developing Societies
DIA	Defence Intelligence Agency
FDI	Foreign Direct Investment
FICCI	Federation of Indian Chambers of Commerce and Industry
GATT	General Agreement for Trade and Tariffs
ICHR	Indian Council of Historical Research
ICSSR	Indian Council of Social Science Research
IIAS	Indian Institute of Advanced Studies
IMF	International Monetary Fund
IR	International Relations
IRA	Insurance Regulatory Authority
IT	Information Technology
JWG	Joint Working Group
LoC	Line of Control
MF	Ministry of Finance
MGU	Mahatma Gandhi University
MRTS	Mass Rapid Transit System
NATO	North Atlantic Treaty Organization

NCERT   National Council of Educational Research and Training
NDA   National Democratic Alliance
NFIW   National Federation of Indian Women
NGO   Non-governmental Organisation
NHRC   National Human Rights Commission
NREGA   National Rural Employment Guarantee Act
NSM   New Social Movement
OBC   Other Backward Class
POTA   Prevention of Terrorism Act
PUCL   People's Union for Civil Liberties
PUDR   People's Union for Democratic Rights
QR   Quantitative Restriction
RGG   Resurgent Group of Gujarat
RSS   Rashtriya Swayamsevak Sangh
RTI   Right to Information
SAP   Structural Adjustment Programme
SIRP   School of International Relations and Politics
TADA   Terrorists and Disruptive Activities (Prevention) Act
TRIPS   Trade Related Aspects of Intellectual Property Rights
UF   United Front
UGC   University Grants Commission
UPA   United Progressive Alliance
VHP   Vishwa Hindu Parishad
VKA   Vanavasi Kalyan Ashram
VKIC   Vivekananda Kendra Institute of Culture
VKV   Vivekananda Kendra Vidyalaya
VSNL   Videsh Sanchar Nigam Limited
WIA   Women's Indian Association
WTC   World Trade Center
WTO   World Trade Organisation

Preface

The changes that have transpired in the global political and economic scenario since the 1980s have been so profound that their implications for the State, civil society and security are far-reaching. Evidently, almost all Third World countries have been trying to grapple with the challenges emerging from the global political and economic landscape, especially since 1991. Howsoever complex these challenges may be, countries like India witnessed the emergence of several social forces, trends, movements and organisations across a wide socio-political spectrum from the extreme Right to the Left. The revitalisation of the civil society during this period further brought to light the changing contours of development/under-development discourses. Perceptibly, neoliberalism as a policy regime has had a great bearing on India's domestic setting as well as on its economic and security policies. The change of orientation among the major political forces in India could also be discernible when India became fully committed to the neoliberal policy package and globalisation. Consequently, the new path of development, as it evolved since 1980s, raised critical questions about the role of the State and civil society in India. The economic and security strategies under the neoliberal paradigm and the role of the Indian State in sustaining these strategies call for a deeper analysis of their implications. However, the thrust of this study is on the ascendency of the New Right (referred to as Hindu Right) forces in India in the background of the changing paradigm of the State and civil society. The major areas of investigation are the mobilisational strategies and slogans of the Hindu Right forces in the civil society, using security as a critical category of engagement.

The study problematises the changing role of the State and civil society under the neoliberal global setting and examines how the New Right forces have been articulating/re-articulating the notion of 'security' to gain political advantages. It specifically addresses the implications of the ascendancy of the Hindu Right in India as re-articulated through the ideology of Hindutva since 1980s. The emergence of the Hindu Right is also problematised within the larger setting of the crisis of the Indian State consequent upon the liberalisation of the Indian economy and the introduction of the neoliberal policies. These processes have been accompanied by the reactivation of the civil society at different levels. At one level, the State itself has made room for increased non-governmental organisation (NGO) activism and propelled local-level self-governing institutions as important stakeholders of governance and development. At other levels, the process of globalisation and its accompanying problems generated several resistance movements, self-assertion of various identities, etc. Thus, the civil society in India is a complex terrain of activities by various groups, identities, movements, associations and organisations. It is both within and through this realm of activities that the Hindu Right in India has been re-articulating 'security' with its cultural–nationalist ideology of Hindutva.

Obviously, the Hindu Right in India tried to appropriate the currents of social dislocations caused by the neoliberal policies by dividing the society into 'friends' and 'foes'. It has apparently obscured the problems caused by the developmental shift by highlighting a host of imagined 'threats' and 'insecurity'. It may be noted that way back in the 1980s, the assertion of the Hindu Right in India was linked with the process of economic liberalisation. At one level, it tried to offer an 'alternative' to 'Swadeshi' in defence of 'national' industries, and it was made popular through the realm of civil society. The most widely used slogan at this time was 'Hindutva' (the central ideology of the Hindu Right). It was the culmination of a long process of communal mobilisation within the civil society, which made its beginning way back in the 19th century. What facilitated the process was a host of developments such as the decline of the 'Congress system', the full-fledged integration of the Indian economy into the world capitalist system, the Shah Bano controversy, the attempts to implement the Mandal recommendations, the Ram Janmabhoomi–Babri Masjid issue, call for the abrogation of Article 370 and Uniform Civil Code. All of them had provided enormous political space for the Hindu Right to assert. By politically appropriating the situation, the Bharatiya Janata Party (BJP), the political dispensation of the Hindu Right, became the leader of the ruling coalition (National Democratic Alliance—NDA) at the centre. During the first term/spell of the NDA rule (1997–2004), the BJP-led coalition pursued a full-fledged neoliberal policy and vigorously implemented globalisation programmes. Meanwhile, as a result of high pressure from the Hindu Right organisations, the NDA government sought to reinvigorate a militaristic State by undertaking a series of nuclear tests and declared India as a nuclear weapon State. During the Kargil war (between India and Pakistan) in 1999, the NDA government and the Hindu Right organisations mobilised public opinion in their favour by resorting to vigorous campaigns in the civil society. However, the inability of the BJP government to adequately address the basic issues of the people reflected in the 2004 election results. The study also makes an assessment of the electoral debacle of the BJP in the 2004 Parliamentary elections. After a decade, under the leadership of Narendra Modi, the BJP-led NDA government came to power with a stunning victory in the 2014 Parliamentary elections. This book argues that the electoral success of the BJP in 2014 has to be understood in the background of the changing dynamics of the State–civil society relations in India under neoliberal conditions. The revitalisation of the civil society under the neoliberal regime has provided a better environment for the Hindu Right organisations to penetrate into the society through their organisational networks. The Hindutva forces have been using the civil domain to execute their cultural agenda, which crystallised the 'self' which very much helped the BJP to consolidate the majority Hindu votes.

There is an impressive array of literature on State, civil society and security from different perspectives and contexts. These include philosophical writings, critical–rational readings, Marxist, neo-Marxist writings, liberal and neoliberal perspectives, etc. There are also several books written on the Hindu Right in India. Besides original works by the Hindutva ideologues, there are books written by quite a number of writers from Walter to Subhash Gatade. However, there is hardly any work linking State, civil society and security within the framework of engaging the Hindu Right in India. The significance of the book lies in establishing linkages between the State, civil society and security, on one hand, and the Hindu Right ascendancy in India, on the other.

The study emerged as part of the doctoral work by Dr P. M. Joshy at the Mahatma Gandhi University, Kerala. The work has been thoroughly restructured and updated. It comprehends and brings forth the complex relations between the State and the civil society in the mainstream discourses and elucidates the changing notions of State, civil society and security under neoliberal conditions and with the ascendancy of the New Right forces across the world. It also explicates the historical evolution of the State and civil society in India and brings out its trajectory during the colonial and postcolonial periods. It critically unfolds the nature of the Indian State and civil society under neoliberalism with the assertion of the Hindu Right forces. The study traces the genealogy of Hindutva and analyses it within the framework of the New Right ideology. It elaborates the mobilisational strategies of the Sangh Parivar and its notion of security and also analyses the implications of the policies of the NDA headed by the BJP.

The study is premised on the assumption that State and civil society are interrelated as well as interrogated realms, and the notions of the State, civil society and security have undergone significant changes during the neoliberal era. As far as India is concerned, State–civil society relations appear to have shown a complex pattern, different from the experience of the advanced capitalist countries. The Hindu Right in India initially used the challenges of economic liberalisation for mobilisation, but became a votary of the same paradigm later. The ideology and strategies of the Hindu Right seem to have focused on new sites of 'insecurity,' thereby deploying 'hard' options of security. The Hindu Right in India has used the civil society to mobilise people along cultural–nationalist framework deploying its own discourses on security/insecurity and the NDA government led by the BJP tried to legitimise the Hindutva notion of security through its policies.

This book has been divided into six chapters. The first chapter deals with theoretical questions on State, civil society and security. It starts with an analysis of the historical evolution of the concepts of State, civil society and security in the liberal and neoliberal discourses as well as in the Marxist, neo-Marxist, post-positivist traditions. The second chapter focuses on the evolution and trajectory of the State and civil society in India. It analyses the whole range of issues of development and security during colonial and postcolonial times. The third chapter is an attempt to trace the genealogy of the Hindu Right in India. It provides a compre-hensive discussion on the ideology, strategy and the working of various Hindu Right organisations in India. The chapter also focuses on how the Hindu Right has been penetrating into the civil society with a view to crystallising the 'self' and the 'other.' The fourth chapter offers a comprehensive analysis of the assertion of the Hindu Right and its securitisation of the social and cultural issues. This chapter also examines the policies and programmes of the NDA government, especially their economic, security and educational policies. The fifth chapter covers the whole range of development from the 'electoral debacle' of Hindutva politics (2004) to the 2014 Parliamentary elections. The sixth chapter provides a summary, findings and observations.

Acknowledgements

This book draws on our constant engagement with theoretical as well as empirical sources on State and civil society in India. It is the result of several years of consultation, travel and meetings with concerned scholars and intellectuals. While it is not possible to name the whole lot of people and institutions, we would like to mention the faculty and researchers of the School of International Relations and Politics (SIRP), Mahatma Gandhi University, for their warm support and encouragement for the completion of this work. We thank them all. We are also indebted to Dr A. K. Ramakrishnan, Professor, Centre for West Asian Studies, Jawaharlal Nehru University, New Delhi, and Dr K. N. Harilal, Professor, Centre for Development Studies, Thiruvananthapuram, who were of immense help in this research. We must also thank the late Dr Asghar Ali Engineer for his valuable suggestions in the course of the work.

We gratefully acknowledge our gratitude to Prof. Muzafar Azadi (Mysore University), Dr Jose George (Mumbai University) and Dr Shaji Varkey (Kerala University) for their critical comments and suggestions. We also express our gratitude to Prof. Mohanan B. Pillai, Pondicherry University, who has given an academic space to Dr Joshy (through an ICSSR Project), which helped us in many ways to complete this study.

The libraries of Mahatma Gandhi University, Kottayam; Jawaharlal Nehru University, New Delhi; Centre for Development Studies, Thiruvananthapuram; University of Kerala, Thiruvananthapuram; Central University, Pondicherry; have been the main sources of information and data. The primary sources used in this study have also been collected from the Bharatiya Vichara Kendram, Thiruvananthapuram. We thank the staff and research personnel of these institutions. We are also thankful to Shri P. Parameswaran, Director, Bharatiya Vichara Kendram for sharing his thoughts.

We also place on record our gratitude to the members of our families for their patience, positive thinking and helping mind. We extend our thanks to Smt. Mini (Mrs Seethi) and Smt. G. Sreedevi (Mrs Joshy) for their constant help and encouragement, and our gratitude also goes to Appu, Kunjunni (sons of Prof. Seethi) and Shivanand Joshy (son of Dr Joshy) for their lovely support. Last, but not the least, we would like to express our thanks to our colleagues and friends, Dr Raju Thadikkaran, Dr A. M. Thomas, Dr M. V. Bijulal, Dr C. Vinodan, Dr R. Girish Kumar Mrs Sonia George, Mrs Rekha Raj, Fr. John Thomas, Mr K. T. Rejikumar, Mr Reghunath, Mr Sudheep (Mahatma Gandhi University); Dr P. Deepa, Dr Renjith (Pondicherry University); Dr Dimpi V. Divakaran (PGMM Government College, Kerala); Mr Biju Mathew (Don Bosco College, West Bengal); Dr M. R. Biju, Dr P. Maya, Abhilash T, Suja Karapath (S.N. College Kollam, Kerala); and P. R. Prathibha (S.N. College Cherthala, Kerala) for their warm support in the completion of this book. We also extend our deep gratitude to SAGE Publications, particularly to Mr Rudra Narayan Sharma, Ms Saima Ghaffar and Mr Nand Kumar Jha for their valuable suggestions and constant help in the completion of this book.

P. M. Joshy and K. M. Seethi

1

State, Civil Society and Security: Theoretical Questions

The State and civil society are the critical realms of socio-political activity. The nature and engagements of (as well as the relations between) the State and civil society vary across time and space, and between regions and countries. Complexities abound with regard to the conceptualisation and interpretations of the State and civil society (Chandhoke 1995, 2003; Cohen and Arato 1992; Hall 1995; Jessop 1990; Kaviraj and Khilnani 2001; Keane 1988; Pierson 1996). Many of the contemporary studies on the State and civil society focus on how the State as an agency faces critical challenges under neoliberal conditions. There are also studies dealing with how and why the State retreats from the social security realms and how the residual space has been made available for free individual self-regulation and NGO activism in the civil society (Diaz 1993; Fukuyama 2001; Seethi 2009b; World Bank 1999). Over the years, the concept of civil society itself has undergone various interpretations and achieved different meanings. In liberal understanding, civil society has been seen as a realm that protected the rights of the individual from the arbitrary power of the State. However, during the last three decades, civil society has been made out as a space detached from the State. There are also efforts to transpose the State in the Third World from its developmental practices (Blaney and Pasha 1993; Rudolph 2000; Wickramasinghe 2005). In the name of 'good governance', 'radical democracy', 'grass-roots development' and 'people's participation', a large array of NGO network is being deployed as civil society (Ayers 2006; Williams and Young 1994; World Bank 1997, 2000). It is with this new version of civil society that the neoliberal policies have been implemented across the world.

Paradoxically, the 'shrinking' State has also been too much militaristic in implementing laws and treaties of the market. Here, both the State and civil society tend to generate insecurity complexes. While the civil society is being appropriated by the neoliberal institutions for developmental purposes, say as an 'alternative' to the State, many undemocratic/revivalist/ fundamentalist forces have been making inroads through this sphere. Many of them sought to gain political strength using tradition, culture, religion, etc., by putting across sensitive issues for mobilisation (Tetreault and Denemark 2004). All these trends might affect the democratic processes in countries where cultural diversity is critical and complex. The liberal spirit behind seeing civil society as "an essential pre-requisite for democratisation" is being threatened today with the very manipulation of civil society by the neoliberal institutions on one hand and the revivalist/ fundamentalist forces on the other. By arguing that civil society is an 'alternative' to the State, neoliberals try to undermine its role in the larger context of democratic practices. This chapter seeks to examine the historical evolution of the concepts of State and civil society by analysing the important theoretical narratives on the theme. It also tries to outline the discourses on security in relation to the State and civil society.

State and Civil Society: Liberal Readings

The historical evolution of the concepts of State and civil society in liberal discourses is being associated with the development and expansion of capitalism in the West. It was accompanied by the Western Enlightenment paradigm, which celebrated 'rational equality' of human beings (Jacob 2000; Williams 1999) and a shift from theocentric view to a humano-centric view about man and society. The new inventions in science and technology questioned the very rationality of the old order. The gradual shift from feudalism to capitalist mode production and the emergence of a new middle class reconfigured the power equations in Western societies. It was viewed as a shift from the 'insecure' social conditions to a 'secure community', in which people were guided by modern rationality. The vernacular statist institutions also evolved in this setting.

The West—as a system of states and economies—evolved hand in hand. The absolutist/authoritarian States can be considered as the precursors of the modern State. Absolutism arose in the 16th- and 17th-century Europe. It was an admixture of both the archaic as well as the modern elements and facilitated the rise of capitalism on one hand and maintained the feudal structures on the other (Anderson and Hall 1986: 21–40). Perry Anderson sees it as "a redeployed and recharged apparatus of feudal domination." He notes: feudalism was "demarked by the unity of economy and polity distributed in a chain of parcellized sovereignties." With the coming of money rents, this unity became "weakened and it paved the way for 'free labour' and the 'wage contract'." The weakening of the feudal structures contributed to the upward mobility of the sovereignties towards a centralised militarised system—the absolutist State (Anderson 1979: 18–19; Gellner 1983, 1994a).

The introduction of Roman law provided sufficient space for free capital growth in town and country. The basic feature of this law was its separation of the 'private' from the 'public'. The right to property was protected under the private law. In accordance with the public law, the administrative power was centralised (Anderson 1979: 25–28). The absolutist States protected the feudal privileges as well as the interests of the "nascent mercantile and manufacturing classes" (Anderson 1979: 40; Williams 1999). As Christopher Pierson notes, "Absolutism is perhaps best seen as a transitional form, albeit one that spanned several centuries" (Pierson 1996: 45). The transition from feudalism to capitalism was a gradual process. In the process, the State became more and more dependent on the civil society, for getting economic support for the smooth implementation of its policies (Mann 1986: 512). At the same time, the powerful sections in the civil society hoped to shape State action to suit their own interests, because of its capacity to provide a coordinating framework for the new emerging capitalist economy (Gellner 1994b; Held 1996: 83). This mutually dependent alliance system shielded the protectionist self-development of native capitalism in the mercantile period.

The revolutions in Europe marked the end of the absolutist regimes in the West, which shifted the balance of power away from monarchy and aristocracy to the commercialised gentry and merchants. The newly emerged capitalist State enunciated the rights of the upper and middle ranks of the society to participate in power along with the rulers.

This was formalised within the constitutional system (Anderson and Hall 1986: 35–40). In fact, the transition from absolutism to a contractual state led to the releasing of the capital for self-development without any constraints from the State. The separation of the 'civil' from the 'political' became the hallmark of the time. Coincidently, the liberal discourses on State and civil society took progress along with these developments (Gaus 1983; Kymlicka 1989). However, there is no pure doctrine of liberalism. The liberal notions are overlapping with other ideologies. But there are some core ideas, which work differently in distinct contexts (Vincent 1995: 24–27). David Held sees liberalism as an attempt "to define a private sphere independent of the state itself, that is, the freeing of civil society from political interference and the simultaneous delimitation of the states' authority" (Held 1998: 13). The separation of the private from the public and the freeing of the economy are the basic features of an advanced capitalist system. In its classical period, liberalism overemphasised individualism. The influence of Descartes was prominent during this period. Bertrand Russell puts it: "Descartes' fundamental certainty, 'I think, therefore I am', made the basis of knowledge different for each person, since for each the starting point was his own existence, not that of other individuals or of community" (Russell 1979: 579). So each individual was regarded as an abstract entity.

Social Contract theorists like Hobbes and Locke offered the basic premises for the development of the concepts of State and civil society in their modern liberal version. In the Contractualist tradition, the separation of the 'civil' from 'political' seems to be ambiguous. The civil society was deliberately used to distinguish a particular form of social and political organisation from the state of nature (Chandhoke 1995: 80). The individuals created civil society in order to get out of the problem-ridden state of nature. The civil society is a rational order compared to the uncivil conditions of the state of nature. In order to overcome the insecure conditions of civil society, people created the sovereign—the State. The fundamental nature of the 'state of nature' in the analysis of Hobbes and Locke made differences in their political conclusions about the State. The life in the Hobbesian state of nature was: "Solitary, poor, nasty, brutish and short" (Hobbes 1991). But, to Locke, the state of nature was a 'state of perfect freedom' and individuals were within the bounds of the 'law of nature', and 'reason' taught them to obey the laws. They were the products of one omnipotent (Locke 1960: 269–71). So, in the Hobbesian state of nature, people needed an all-powerful overarching authority to maintain peace and security. But, to Locke, the State was limited, and was only an agency for preserving 'civility' in the civil society.

Hobbes's position regarding the State and society was a mixture of both liberal as well as illiberal elements (Held 1998: 14–16). In his analysis, individuals were mere abstract entities. Hobbes portrayed the State as a machine and not the end of an individual. On the contrary, the individual was the end of the State (Hobbes 1991; Wayper 1974: 63). In a market society, Hobbes's autonomous men may become a threat. In order to control the self-seeking market men, he advanced the notion of sovereign. These self-seeking, self-moving market men were the rising bourgeoisie (Mc Clelland 1996: 270). He was also influenced by the rival fanaticisms of his time (Russell 1979: 539). That is why he supported an all-powerful State—the absolutist monarchy.

The Social Contract theorists agreed on the importance of 'consent' in the making of 'civil/political' society. Giving 'consent' is a rational deci-sion because the individual gets security of his life and property only in a 'civilised' community. The civil society is characterised by the civilised behaviour of an individual. They develop mutual respect and obligation. For the preservation of civility in civil society, people created political authority through consent. Civil society was co-terminus with political society, but the latter was possible only when civility in human relations was ensured through a contract. Conversely, civility could be maintained only when political authority enforced it. In the Social Contract tradition, the primacy of rights separated the civil domain from the political, and which restricted the power of the sovereign. The basic end of the political authority is the protection of the natural rights of the individual. These rights are natural, so no authority has the right to deny them. In this understanding, State and civil society are dialectically linked (Chandhoke 1995: 80–85).

The Lockean idea of limited government and the autonomous develop-ment of an individual have been taken up by the utilitarians. According to them, a government should be accountable to the people. They imaged the State as an 'umpire' in economic matters. But whenever laissez-faire appeared to be inadequate to make the possible outcome, or any threat arose from the individuals, groups or classes, strong State intervention was justified (Held 1998: 23–25). Thus, the aim of the State was to maintain peaceful conditions for easy economic transactions. John Stuart Mill puts it: "the only purpose for which power can be rightfully exercised over any member of a civilised community, against his will is to prevent harm to others" (Mill 1991: 14). According to Mill, political institutions are made by the people and their existence depends upon the human will. He put forward three conditions for the better functioning of political institutions. These are: (a) the consent—the people for whom the form of government is intended must be willing to accept it, or at least not so unwilling as to oppose an insurmountable obstacle to its establishment; (b) active participation—they must be willing and able to do what is necessary to keep it standing; and (c) rational behaviour of the people—they must be capable of fulfilling the conditions of action and the conditions of self-restraint (ibid.: 207–08). Mill considered the representative form of government as the best political authority for a civilised community.

But Mill was also sceptic of modern State. He had in mind the dangers of the overpowering modern democratic State, or the majority tyranny and the levelling spirit of democracy, which lead to intolerance of social experimentation and personal eccentricity. This sentiment was shared by Tocqueville also. He put across three basic ideas for controlling and keeping the State power accountable to the people; the separation of powers, periodic elections and the social associations (Deakin 2001: 86–87). The associational life of an individual in civil society stretches in a wide canvas. It brings forth the active individual participation in public matters, the sustainability of democratic values and the considerable check on the governmental power. He believed that the free associations would link private interest with the general. According to Tocqueville,

> it is difficult to draw a man out of his own circle to interest him in the destiny of the State, because he does not clearly understand what influence the destiny of the State can have upon his own lot. But if it be proposed to make a road cross the end of his estate, he will see at a glance that there is a connection between this small public affair and his greatest private affairs; and he will discover, without its being shown to him, the close tie, which unites private to general interest. (Tocqueville 2000: Chapter 4)

From the 17th century onwards, a lot of voluntary associations mushroomed in the West. 'Self-help' was the motive behind joining an association. Religions also formed associations in order to integrate the followers. Because of the large-scale exclusions, women also formed their own associations. Later on, such movements extended themselves to the lower strata of the population (Frevert 2005: 65–67). In his analysis on American democracy, Tocqueville said that democracy was closely associated with political liberty. This could be attained only through the 'equalisation of social conditions'. But such an egalitarian society could be safeguarded only through the institutional models that had developed in America. He warns, "If these free institutions are destroyed, this will lead to despotism" (Tocqueville 1997: 31; 2000). Tocqueville's work was an antidote to the emerging individualism of his time. The tension between the demands of free democratic politics prompted him to develop the techniques of political citizenship as against the negative social effects of commercial society (Welch 2001: 235). And also, the associational life in the civil domain would integrate the individuals out of their primary attachments (Warren 2001: 42). However, Tocqueville was not arguing that associational life was an alternative to the political. He said that it was an inception to the political life. This was obviously an antidote to the emerging individualism of the industrial capitalism.

According to Hegel, "Civil society exists between family and the state." In the civil society

> universal and particular have fallen apart, yet both are still reciprocally bound together and conditioned. While each of them seems to do just the opposite to the other and supposes that it can exist only by keeping the other at arm's length, none the less each still conditions the other. (Hegel 1897: 182–84, 1952)

The particular ends of the individual cannot be attained without the help of the universal. As Hegel points out, "Individuals can attain their ends only in so far as they themselves determine their knowing, willing, and acting in a universal way and make themselves link in this chain of social connections" (Hegel 1897: 187).

Frederick Beiser viewed, "What is most striking about Hegel's treatment of civil society is his balanced appraisal of it, his attempt both to preserve and to negate it" (Beiser 2008: 244). According to Hegel, the domain of civil is also a sphere of self-centricism and exploitation. He had rejected the classical economist position of the self-regulation of the market and stressed the importance of State in this realm. To Hegel, the realm of economy and civil society are the same. The exclusionary nature of the market prevents the vast sections of the people from enjoying the freedom of civil society. These excluded sections may pose a threat in the society. So, he argued for the regulation of the market in order to reduce the socio-economic and moral consequences emerging out of it (Chandhoke 2003: 122–23). Hegel stressed that there should be a balance between the individual interest and social interest. In his own words,

> the individual must certainly have a right to earn his living in this way or that, but on the other hand the public also has a right to earn his living in this way or that, but on the other hand the public also has a right to expect that necessary tasks will be performed in the proper manner. Both viewpoints must be satisfied, and the freedom of trade should not be such as to prejudice the general good. (Hegel 1897, 1952)

Roughly, Hegel's idea of free market and administration of justice resembled that of the classical liberals like Locke and Smith, but he varied from them in case of the importance of State in society. To Hegel, the State—an instrument to transcend the self-regulation—is necessary to lessen the tension between the general interest and the private interest (Femia 2001: 13). Here, Hegel stands for an ethical society upon a commercial society (Jones 2001: 114). According to Hegel, "Civil society is a set of social practices which are constituted by the logic of the capitalist economy and which reflect the ethos of the market, but which have an existence distinct from the economy" (Chandhoke 2003: 117). Chandhoke notes, "Hegel gives us a picture of civil society that is shot through with shades of grey" (ibid.: 124). But in Hegel's analysis the working class remains in the dark side of the capitalist system (ibid.: 136). However, in order to secure and maintain the system, he called for State regulation.

It is clear that there exists a historical nexus between the Western liberal State, civil society and capitalism. Liberalism has been characterised by its defence of the private realm from the arbitrary power of the State. The differences within the liberal discourses, over a period of time, were on the question of the intensity of the State regulation on society, in accordance with the demands/interests as well as the strategies of the world capitalist system. In its classical period, liberalism sought to demand/support for more individual autonomy and very less State regulation.

In its welfare capitalist phase, there was more State intervention in societal matters, quintessentially a State-guided society. When it comes to the neo-liberal epoch, the State has been rolling back from social security/welfare realms. With the shrinking of the role of the State as a major provider, individual self-regulation and NGO activism became prominent. In the liberal lineages, the State is not a static entity because its root lies in the society. The liberals generally viewed the realm of civil society a 'buffer zone', which is protecting the individual from the arbitrary power of the State. This line of thought presupposes that modern State has a natural tendency of overpowering. The role of civil society is to check this tendency and protect the individual. Hence, the State and civil society are dialectically linked, which ensures a somewhat systemic balancing of both.

According to Max Weber, "State is a human community that (successfully) claims the monopoly of the legitimate use of physical force within a given territory" (Weber 1958). The modern States are said to be successful in maintaining legitimacy among their people. Weber continues, "Like the political institutions historically preceding it, the state is a relation of men dominating men, a relation supported by means of legitimate (i.e., considered to be legitimate) violence" (ibid.: 33–34). Indeed, the State has been trying to make the whole society act in accordance with its 'line of thought', whereby the use of force is a legitimate source of power. It could be understood only by analysing the relationship between State, society and the capitalist system.

Weber recognised the State as a superior power entity. While Marx viewed it as a bourgeois enterprise, a product of capitalism, Weber rejected this class-State linkage. To him, classes cannot be reduced to the realm of mere economic relations. It is only one factor in the distribution and struggle for power. But there are umpteen number of factors, broadly called the nationalist sentiments, playing a crucial role in the creation and mobilisation of political power. To Weber, State is not a product of capitalism, but a promoter of capitalism. He notes that

> the modern state is a compulsory association which organizes domination. It has been successful in seeking to monopolize the legitimate use of physical force as a means of domination within a territory. To this end the state has combined the material means of organization in the hands of its leaders, and it has expropriated all autonomous functionaries of estates

who formerly controlled these means in their own right. The state has taken their positions and now stands in the top place. (Weber 1958: 37)

Accordingly, the State is an overarching authority, which has been legitimately dominating the society and for this motive (domination) it has taken over the privileges of the autonomous actors who were dominating the society, and the State became ascendant to the supreme authority in the society. On a Weberian account, questions like what makes the modern State so distinct from other State forms may yield a somewhat concrete answer: "the centrality of societal power and the legitimate use of physical force." Weber writes, "Bureaucracy … is fully developed in political and ecclesiastical communities only in the modern state, and in the private economy, only in the most advanced institutions of capitalism" (ibid.: 40). Here he tests the Marxian notion of the historical connection between the State and capitalism: "State is a product of capitalism." According to Weber, capitalism fosters the expansion of more rational administration bureaucracy (Held 1993: 63). Both the State and capitalism evolved on a parallel line. At last, the State had become the overarching authority over the total means of political organisation. He also contends the view of abolishing private capitalism. This would lead to the merging of the bureaucracy with the capital and result in the bureaucratisation of the top management of the nationalised or socialised enterprises. The market is the key countervailing power to the State (ibid.).

The period between 1870 and 1914 witnessed profound social changes in the West. With the boom in industrialisation, a mass society came into existence. This displaced the dominant liberal paradigm resulting in new forms of social and political organisation. The emerging pressures prompted the State to intervene in the social realm. Since then the State shifted its role from an 'umpire' on individual matters to an activated agency—a shift from 'laissez-faire' system to a 'Welfare State capitalist' system. During this period, the Western liberal states took a 'consensual path' in order to deal with the varied interests, especially the interests of the dominant propertied class on one hand and the proletariat, on the other. Along with these developments, the fundamental liberal notions about the individual and State also changed. Andrew Vincent notes: "from the late 1880s onwards, liberalism has been changing its direction from the classical 'atomism' to 'social individualism', which gave equal weight to the individual and the community. Its resonance extended up to the 1970s" (Vincent 1995: 30–50). During this period, the concept of civil society lost its glamour in academic as well as political discussions. Sunil Khilnani notes:

> Central to classical western political theory, the concept of civil society was largely moribund during the days when models of state-led modernisation dominated both liberal and Marxist conception of social change and development. It was recovered during the late 1970s and 1980s, as these models disintegrated. (Khilnani 2001: 12)

Critical Reflections: Marxian/Neo-Marxian Readings

It is also important to look at the critical responses to the debates on State and civil society in the context of the theories of capital accumulation. Marx viewed the State as a product of society in a particular stage of its transition. In the *Communist Manifesto*, Marx and Engels described the modern State as "a committee for managing the common affairs of the whole bourgeoisie" (Marx and Engels 1848). He argued that the State and its officials tend to exploit and oppress the civil society on behalf of certain particular sectional groups (Marx 1843: 44–45). Marx put the State at the super-structural level and viewed it as the system of property relations and the ruling class struggle (Marx 1857). Engels argued that the State is an institution to regulate the struggle between the two opposing classes through oppression and concessions and it moderates the class struggle without altering the ruling class domination (Engels 1884: 154–63). The central idea is that the State is an instrument of the ruling class, which protects the dominant class interests. The workers, women and children were excluded from this arena of power sharing.

Marx endorsed a vital role for civil society in the historical development of mankind, and contended that it cuts across both the State and the nation (Marx 1967: 469). However, he rejected the existence of civil society as an independent sphere, but saw its origin in the class relations and in the political economy (Marx and Engels 1962: 362). He saw civil society not primarily as an arena for voluntary meetings between groups and individuals, but for exploitation, and due to its inherent inequality based on various roles within the capitalist system, it could, according to Marx, never develop into a sphere that strengthened the social fabric. While other thinkers saw civil society as a place of refuge from the exploitive relations of the family and the economy, Marx saw it largely as a mirror of these exploitations, and unlike Hegel, did not see the State as a remedy for the inequalities and possible unrest in the civil society. The State is—according to Marx—not universal, as it is influenced by the capitalist power structure and would therefore, reinforce rather than resolve conflicts within civil society. While denying the positive role of civil society suggested by Tocqueville and others, Marx nevertheless saw civil society as a part of social and political changes. This change would, however, not come about through interaction within civil society, but through a revolutionary change within both the political and the economic spheres (Femia 2003: 138; Seethi 2009b).

Marx viewed civil society as bourgeois society and the State as an extension of it controlled by the dominant class. He placed civil society in the substructure (Marx 1843: 44–45) and claimed that the realm is basically exclusionary and exploitative that caused the total alienation of the working class. This is in contrast to the liberal view, which generally regarded civil society as a realm of high emancipatory potential. Marx observed that the capitalist system itself is self-contradictory, and that a major chunk of the population, that is, the workers, women and children were excluded from its developmental concerns. A Marxian sociologist notes that

> behind the factor of rule of law, voting rights and the slogan of liberty, equality and fraternity was the economic exploitation and alienation of the working classes that made a mockery of all these high sounding terms and phrases. The ideology of liberalism blurred the vision of the workers who could not see liberty as liberty to die of starvation. (Sheshadri 1979: 64)

The ideology of liberalism produces nothing other than ensuring the 'legitimate' sustainability of the modern capitalist system.

Habermas tried to synthesise both Weberian and Marxian notions regarding the modern State. His analysis is set in a frame—the question of 'legitimation'. He notes: "The functions accruing to the state apparatus in late capitalism and the expansion of social areas treated by administration increase the need for legitimation" (Habermas 1975; Connolly 1984: 145). The bourgeois revolutions caused the flourishing of a mass democracy in the West. The State becomes a coordinating force for the varied interests of various capitalist forces. He pinpointed three interest areas of the State to make consensus on the competing demands—these are individual capitalism, state capitalism and generalisable interests. And the increased State activity is the net result of a like in the need for legitimation, which seemed disproportionate as concerned with the ruler and the ruled (Connolly 1984: 146). Thomas Mc Carthy pointed out that the stability of the capitalist social formation would depend on the "continued effectiveness of legitimation that could not withstand discursive examination." The problem, however, is how to distribute socially produced wealth inequitably and yet legitimately (Mc Carthy 1984).

Antonio Gramsci—an Italian Marxist thinker—extended the Marxian notion that the State is a coercive instrument of dominant class (Gramsci 1998). He goes further and said that the very process of domination is not achieved through coercion alone, but also through the active 'consent' of the masses. Gramsci's theory of the State came out of a proper understanding of the relationship between the State and civil society (Mukherjee and Ramaswami 2000: 371). He had rejected the 'economism' of the conventional Marxism in all its forms (Merrington 1977: 140–75), and explained how both the State and civil society played a constitutive role in creating/maintaining the ruling class hegemony. Gramsci fixes the civil society and the political society/State at the superstructural level, and the 'intellectuals' in the society are the 'mediators' (Gramsci 1998: 12; Merrington 1977). The intellectuals ensure the 'spontaneous' consent of the people, while the State "legally enforces the discipline on the masses, those who hesitate to give consent" (Gramsci 1998: 12). Here, the State and civil society play a rhythmic role in maintaining the ruling class domination. It is a mutual balancing system and if any systemic failure occurs, the rule would be through coercion alone. "The moment of force is a sign of great weakness; normally the hegemonic equilibrium is characterized by a combination of force and consent, which balance each other reciprocally, without force predominating excessively over consent" (ibid.: 154). Gramsci viewed that the "organic crisis," that is, "the conflict between the represented and the representatives" is a crisis of ruling class hegemony, quintessentially, the crisis of the State (ibid.: 210).

Conceptually Gramsci's definition of the State may appear to be ambiguous and wavering. In his notes on 'Political Struggle and Military War' Gramsci made a comparison between the Russian and the Western States. In the West, contrary to Russia, "the state was only an outer ditch, behind which there stood a powerful system of fortresses and earth works" (Gramsci 1998: 238). Gramsci writes that

> every state is ethical in as much as one of its most important functions is to raise the great mass of population to a particular cultural and moral level, a level (or type) which corresponds to the needs of the productive forces for development, and hence to the interests of the ruling classes.... In reality, a multitude of other so-called private initiatives and activities tend to the same end-initiatives and activities which form the apparatus of the political and cultural hegemony of the ruling classes. (ibid.: 258)

In another instance, Gramsci stated, "Hegemony over its historical development belongs to private forces, to civil society which is 'state' too, indeed is the state itself" (ibid.: 261). In these statements, one can see varying positions of Gramsci. Sometimes it is political society and civil society, and then a balance between the civil society and the political society, and in certain respects the State and civil society are one and the same. In short, on a Gramscian account, the State is "the entire complex of political and theoretical activity by which the ruling class not only justifies and maintains its domination but also succeeds in obtaining the active consent of the governed" (Femia 1981: 28). So, in this analysis, the State is symbiotically related to the civil society and each cannot be analysed in isolation.

In his analysis of the European State and civil society, Gramsci brings in the ruling class domination and views: "Civil society consisted of private institutions like schools, churches, clubs, journals and parties which were instrumental in crystallizing social and political consciousness" (Gramsci 1998). He elaborated on how these institutions in the civil society created ruling class hegemony. The institutions in the civil domain seemed quasi political and most often, political parties broke these civil–political distinctions, and functioned as a mobiliser of social power into political power. The institutions in civil society reproduced the existing dominant values and had a great influence on public policymaking. These influences were channelised through the political parties. They played a vital role in shaping social and political consciousness. Broadly speaking, the Marxian notion of civil society explained the exclusionary nature of that realm and Gramsci elaborated on how this realm sustained the ruling class domination legitimately (Merrington 1977).

Nicos Poulantzas's analysis on the State is a departure from the conventional Marxist position. He focuses on political and ideological struggles and rejects all forms of instrumentalism in analysing the modern State and viewed that State is a complex social relation. According to him, classes cannot be seen as simple economic forces existing outside the State and controlling it as a passive instrument for its own interests. The class struggle is not impounded to the civil society, but it is reproduced within the State apparatus. He saw the State as a social cohesion and by way the capital accumulation could be pursued unrestricted (Poulantzas 1968: 44–50; 1974: 78–81). Accordingly, the State played a vital role in unifying the bourgeoisie and ensuring its domination. Quite distinct from the widespread Marxist view regarding the class unity that a class unity is related to the shared position of that class in the economic system, Poulantzas argued that class unity depended upon the existence of the particular forms of organisation and representation (Barrow 1993: 9–12; Poulantzas 1968: 188–89).

The ideological hegemony of the ruling class is ensured by the leadership of the popular classes by the dominant classes or power bloc (Poulantzas 1968: 130–41; also see Barrow 1993; Gramsci 1998). For the domination of the dominant bloc, it needs the support of the dominated classes such as the peasantry, urban petty bourgeoisie, various sections of the working class, the social forces such as the ethnic minorities, religious sections and so on. This has been done by slot in certain interests of such sections into the dominant ideology. The entire State apparatus as well as the practices such as universal suffrage, competing parties, the separation of powers and Parliamentary government provides flexibility to the power bloc to maintain social cohesion, thereby ensuring conditions for sustained capital accumulation (Poulantzas 1968: 277–307).

Like Gramsci and Poulantzas, Lukacs (1993) also contributed to rethinking classical Marxist position on State and civil society. The Critical Theorists of the Frankfurt School had drawn heavily from the perspectives of Lukacs (particularly his writings on Hegel) and Gramsci on the relevance of civil society and culture (Seethi 2009b). Max Horkheimer,

Friedrich Pollock, Theodor Adorno, Erich Fromm, Herbert Marcuse, Jürgan Habermas and others offered critiques of the State under both capitalism and Soviet socialism. They tried to analyse the ever-expanding role of the State, the growing interlocking of the base and superstructure, the spread of culture industry, the development of authoritarianism, human rights violations, social movements, etc. (Horkheimer 1972; Held 1980). A major theoretical contribution from the Critical Theory tradition was the concept of 'public sphere' developed by Jürgen Habermas (Habermas 1989; Seethi 2009a). For him the coffee clubs, salons and small discussion groups were instances of inclusive literary public spaces wherein equality, critique, accessibility and reflexivity prevailed. The public sphere, to be located in civil society, was a realm where people could discuss matters of mutual concern, and learn about facts, events, and the opinions, interests and perspectives of others in an environment free of coercion or inequalities. To Habermas, the civil society comprised "those more or less spontaneously emergent associations, organisations, and movements that, attuned to how societal problems resonate in the private life sphere, distil and transmit such reactions in amplified form to the public sphere." Its core "comprises of a network of associations that institutionalizes problem-solving discourses on questions of general interest inside the framework of organized public spheres" (Habermas 1997: 367). Thus, neo-Marxists, in particular Critical Theorists, offered powerful insights that "transcended the conventional paradigm of state and civil society" (Seethi 2009b).

Broadly speaking, the perspectives on the State vary from the 'state centrists' to the 'society centrists'. The statist perspectives are too obsessed with equilibrium, order and the formal functions of the State and dismantled the change and transformation from below (Chandhoke 1995: 57). Nordlinger asserts, "The state is conceptualized as a closed off entity; bounded, shielded from society, its reference point is its own officials—there is neither need for, nor a disposition towards private tutoring" (Nordlinger 1989: 56). Durkheim conceptualises State as a special organ whose responsibility is to work out certain representations which hold good for the collectivity. These representations are distinguished from the other collective representations by their higher degree of consciousness and reflection (Giddens 1986: 40). All these definitions are state-centric. Chandhoke viewed that "the state is simply social relations, in as much as it is the codified power of the social formation" (Chandhoke 1995: 49). Here she stressed upon the dialectical relationship between the State and society and its considerable separation.

The State and society can also be distinguished. As a source of power, the society pioneers the State, and has an influence on the State. Unlike society, the State is the sole authority to enact and enforce laws for the collective interest and which monopolises the means of coercion within its territory. And also, through its political practices, the State fixes unstable powers in the society (ibid.: 66–70). In this understanding, the State is a supreme power entity, which is under the twists and turns of the societal power. However, the State is not a static entity. Joel S. Migdal notes that the State is not a fixed ideological entity. Rather it embodies an ongoing dynamic, a changing set of goals, as it engages other social groups (Migdal 2001). The State also implies the conflicting societal interests and their mutations between the identities in a frame of both national and global capitalism. In short, the State is an ensemble of societal power relations in a given territory. The institutional practices broadly distinguish the public from the private. The interplay of these spheres of activities results in the mobility of the whole system. The system has been revolving around the centripetal force of the international capitalist system. It is within this State–society frame that the role and dynamics of civil society needs to be studied.

In the liberal discourses, the domain of civil society is open to all those who are ready to obey the terms and conditions of it. As far as the civil domain remains as a realm of unequal power-sharing or a sphere of exploitation and oppression, there would be responses from the victims of exploitation. Most often these responses are absorbed or appropriated by the political/religious/cultural mechanisms in the society and thereby perpetuate the existing order. The responses sometimes turn violent. The role of the State generally is to deal with those 'uncivil elements' either through 'coercion' or through 'consensus' (Rhoads 1990: 256–305). The strategy of consensus is a somewhat diluted form or 'civilised' form of coercion. This is wrapped by the dominant values and their interpretations, and may be justified in the name of 'development', or 'security' or their umpteen forms.

The rejuvenation of the concept of civil society in the last quarter of the 20th century was associated with the 'activist' assertions in many parts of the world (Elliot 2003: 1). Charles Taylor says that the notion of civil society "expressed a programme of building independent forms of social life from below, free from state tutelage" (Taylor 1997). He defined the civil society as "webs of autonomous associations, independent of the state, and these have an effect on public policy" (Elliot 2003: 44; Taylor 1997). Michael Walzer notes that

> only a democratic state can create a democratic civil society; only a democratic civil society can sustain a democratic state. The civility that makes democratic politics possible can only be learned in the associational networkers; the roughly equal and widely dispersed capabilities that sustain the networkers have to be fostered by the democratic state. (Walzer 2003: 79)

To him, civil society means "the space of un-coerced human association and also the set of rational networkers formed for the sake of family, faith, interest and ideology" (ibid.: 64).

According to John Keane

> civil society is an ideal typical category … that both describes and envisages a complex and dynamic ensemble of legally protected non-governmental institutions that tend to be non-violent, self-organizing, self-reflexive and permanently in tension with each other and with the state institutions that frame, construct and enable their activities. (Keane 1998)

The libertarian Cato Institute in Washington, D.C. defined the concept of civil society as fundamentally reducing the role of politics in society by expanding free markets and individual liberty (Edwards 2004).

According to Neera Chandhoke

> civil society is a sphere which is flanked by the domain of particularistic loyalties and the state. It is a complex structure consisting of rights bearing individuals, associational life, and the construction of a critical rational discourse on the modes of social and political organization. It is important because it *offers the possibility of democratization*. (Chandhoke 1995: 51)

The process of democratisation seems a mission of civilising. Chandhoke observes that "there is nothing intrinsically democratic about civil society. Civil society has to be rendered democratic in and through sustained engagement with undemocratic groups" (Chandhoke 2007a). The process of democratisation also may bring forth conflicting values and violent responses. The Western-oriented individualistic approach on society and polity may cause chaos in non-democratic countries. This individualistic conception of modern politics is the net result of modern capitalism. Capitalism reduced an individual to the level of a commodity. The abstraction of the individual from his social surroundings is one of the objectives of modern capitalism. The liberals generally advocated associational life in civil domain in order to curb the ill-effects of this system.

Neoliberalism, State and Civil Society

Much before neoliberalism emerged as a new version of liberal ideology, many libertarians had argued for a 'minimal state'. They held that many of the powers of the modern Welfare State "are morally illegitimate." Institutions of the State violate the rights of citizens when they punish or threaten to punish individuals. The State also violates the rights of citizens when they force, or threaten to force, individuals to transfer their legitimately held wealth to the State in order to provide for pensions, to help the needy, or to pay for public goods etc. Robert Nozick asserted that nothing more than the maintenance of peace and security of individuals and property by the State can be justified (Nozick 1974: 149). Friedrich August von Hayek had already reflected on this theme of 'minimum' dispensation (Hayek 1960). This line of thinking has gained a lot of attention since the 1980s.

The disintegration of the Soviet Union and the Socialist Bloc created necessary conditions for the minimalist school to assert its position. This also became inevitable for legitimising the process of globalisation. The situation was gently used by the right-wing forces in many countries. They created a general feeling that there was no alternative to the liberal ideology and institutions. This was the time when the neoliberal global institutions were trying to incorporate the Third World economies into the world capitalist system. Richard Falk notes that

> the historical unfolding of economic globalization in recent decades has been accompanied by the ascendancy of a group of ideas associated with the world picture of neoliberalism. This ideological outlook as 'the Washington

Consensus' ... accurately highlights the 'made in the USA' package of the neoliberal scheme of things. This neoliberal scheme points to the general direction of autonomous markets and facilitative states. (Falk 1999: 1)

Globalisation has changed the conventional understanding of the nation-state category. The international politics during the Cold War was dominated by the realist worldview by which the nation-states were the major actors in an 'anarchical' international system (Morgenthau 1985). With the emergence of a US-led 'new world order' accompanied by neo-liberal global regimes, the scholars and statesmen declared the 'retreat' of the nation-state and its inability to tackle the emerging problems. As Ernst-Otto Czempiel writes:

> we have to give up the notion and the concept of the state as well as the terminology that is traditionally connected to it.... There are no 'states' acting in the transitional world; there is no use preserving in terminology what can no longer be found in reality. (Sorensen 2004: 2)

The advances in science and technology, no doubt, reduced 'time and space'. People-to-people interactions increased and large-scale migrations across the national borders created hybrid cultural formations and new spaces of interactions. In this globalised scenario, the conventional State faced threats from different quarters. The State reduced its role in society, giving way to the informal networks and market in accordance with the provisions of the 'Washington Consensus'. This changing scenario marked the conventional sovereign State as inadequate to tackle the complex problems that were becoming more and more global and trans-national. This situation has been portrayed by many as 'the retreat of the state' (Strange 1996).

Contrary to the liberal view of the role of the State, the realists still portray the State as a sovereign entity which has been determining the boundaries of the non-State actors. George Sorensen sums up the realist arguments regarding the State action in the following way:

> States are unitary and coherent actors. Strong states (i.e., great powers) have a robust portfolio of power resources. Most important in this respect is a high level of military power relative to other states. Governments are constrained by the international system, but such constraints may not be strong enough to affect the great powers. Governments are autonomous

in relation to their own societies; that is, they are able to act freely on their behalf. (Sorensen 2004: 16)

Sorensen notes the liberal arguments against the backdrop of the realist views on the State:

> The state was never a strong, unitary, coherent and autonomous actor for liberals; it was always a guardian of individuals and groups in civil society and, therefore, strongly influenced by these 'non-state actors.' In recent decades, transnational and transgovernmental relations have increased significantly and this has accentuated the erosion and dispersion of state power. (ibid.: 17)

So both the 'state centrists' as well as the 'retreat' scholars draw two parallel lines, which never intersect. One is obsessed with the inevitability and capability of the State to control power resources, while the other views the State as a guiding authority on individual matters and the guardian of the civil society generally. Georg Sorensen explains the 'transformation' of the modern State to a postmodern statehood. In his own words, "The transformation from modern to postmodern statehood implies a more prominent role for non-state actors than was the case under the conditions of modern statehood" (ibid.: 179). The peculiar feature of the postmodern statehood is the multi-level governance system. In this system, apart from the conventional nation-states, the influence of IGOs, the expanded role of UN institutions, the expansion of transgovernmentalism, mushrooming of NGOs and its widening influence across the national borders created a complex governing system (ibid.: 60–61). So, naturally, the space of the State activity got reduced.

Sorensen shares an in-between space of the realist and the liberal positions. The State centrists and the 'retreat scholars' exhibit two different dimensions of the same picture. But, both are not sufficient enough to understand the exact picture of the 'state transformation'. Actually, the State has got strengthened in some areas, while being weakened or shrunk in other areas. Sorensen viewed that the widened economic activities across the national borders and the extended activities of the non-State actors put the State under pressure. State's management of the national economies considerably decreased. At the same time the States attempted to compensate for their decreased national capacities for regulation by increasing their international capacities for regulation through cooperation with other States (Sorensen 2004: 37). The States also started playing a crucial role in order to provide favourable conditions for market operations (ibid.: 37–38). Thus, the State has been an 'introvert' in matters of social security and 'extrovert' in cases of making and implementing stringent laws for the smooth functioning of the market. So a shift from the Keynesian Welfare State to the neoliberal State changed its role, and the State became too much militaristic. A. K. Ramakrishnan writes:

> There is ambivalence in neoliberalism as far as the role of the state and the provision of security is concerned. It wants the state to be weak for the operation of the market but wants to be strong for ensuring laws and conditions for free markets. The privileging of the non-state realm of markets as against other major national and international actors in neoliberalism boils down to an imagination of free competition and freedom from the state. But in the process, a weak public authority that cannot ensure freedom and security fully result in the ensuing legitimation crisis, the state in security terms becomes more militaristic and at the same time, less powerful as far as its provider role is concerned. (Ramakrishnan 2004: 64)

The new-found role of the State as a facilitator of global finance has implications for common people. The changed equation between the State and civil society in a globalised environment has inevitably generated new patterns of security threat. Indeed, globalisation is equated with Westernisation. As such resistances are underway in the non-Western societies against the unilateral imposition of Western values. Meanwhile there are attempts towards cultural hybridisation and the resulting assertions of New Right forces (like the Hindu Right in India) that tend to undermine the process of democratisation. These forces have been appropriating the civil society by penetrating into it. The changing notion of civil society under neoliberalism is, thus, providing a fertile ground for the assertion of such forces.

Neoliberals considered the civil society to be a non-violent response against the authoritarian regimes. The net effect of the civil society mobilisation was the collapse of many authoritarian States (Chandhoke 2007a: 607). However, the very notion of civil society became trampled over years. Chandhoke identified three reasons for the 'flattening' of the concept. First, the close relation between the civil society and the collapse of the authoritarian States was used by the multilateral and donor agencies to superficially view it as a technique for democracy. Second, civil society was interpreted as an alternative to the derailed party system. Third, in accordance with the post-'Washington Consensus' the State shrunk, and the remaining space was allotted to NGOs in the name of civil society (Chandhoke 2007a: 608). However, the very notion of civil society is viewed as an essential pre-condition for deepening and widening of democracy though the question remains whether the entire activities in the name of civil society necessarily lead to consolidation of democracy.

The World Bank-sponsored structural adjustment programmes (SAPs) demanded the active involvement of civil society in the implementation of the economic packages. The 1997 *World Bank Report* by the World Bank was specifically devoted to 'State and Civil society'. It emphasised the importance of strengthening the statist institutional mechanisms in terms of providing adequate support to the smooth functioning of the market. The then-president of the World Bank introduced the report titled *The State in a Changing World*: "Development requires an effective state, one that plays a catalytic, facilitating role, encouraging and complementing the activities of private business and individuals" (World Bank 1997). The report promoted the contracting out of delivery of social services to NGOs. It specifically mentioned the importance of NGOs in the emerging developmental scenario. According to the report

> the emergence of private and NGO alternatives to public provision can help meet gaps in the supply of public goods, as well as provide those goods and services that individuals are willing to pay from out of their own pocket. NGOs can be both partners and competitors in the delivery of public services. And when backed by citizen voice, they can exert useful pressure on Government to improve the delivery and quality of public services. (ibid.: 116)

The neoliberal appropriation of civil society has been aimed at the weaving of an apolitical realm, which ultimately promulgates a 'consensual pattern' of capitalist development, ensuring the better integration of the world capitalist economy. There is also a concerted attempt to transpose the State. The role of the State has been reduced to a mere facilitator for world financial capital (Below 1955).

According to the neoliberal perspective, "Civil society consists of associational life—a non-profit, voluntary 'third sector'—that not only restrains state power but also actually provides a substitute for many of the functions performed by the state" (Kaldor 2004: 9). The transfer of power and functions of the State to the civil society organisations is the dictum of the 'Washington Consensus'. The term Washington Consensus was initially coined in 1989 by John Williamson to describe a set of specific economic policy prescriptions for the Third World countries promoted by Washington-based institutions such as the International Monetary Fund (IMF), World Bank and the US treasury Department. It became associated with neoliberal policies in general and was drawn into the broader debate over the expanding role of the free market constraining upon the State. Chandhoke pinpointed the political meaning of Washington Consensus: (a) the State, particularly in the Third World countries should withdraw from the social sector; (b) the market should be freed from all constraints and people in the civil society should organise their own social and economic reproduction instead of depending on the State (Chandhoke 2002a: 43). The Washington Consensus, thus, underlined the pre-eminence of the market over the State. The post-Washington Consensus packages, however, sought to replace the State by the civil society organisations. The consensus opined that only through a strong civil society under the guidance of NGOs we could foster Democracy (ibid.: 43–45).

The shift from Keynesian welfare economism to the Washington Consensus-based structural adjustment was considered as the essential pre-requisite for 'strengthening' and 'deepening' democracy in the Third World. The rollback of the State from social sectors and market in the name of furthering democracy yielded to the intrusion of non-State actors in the remaining space. This was conceptualised by donor agencies such as civil society, which primarily introduced non-governmental agencies or the voluntary sector (Chandhoke 2002b). This large array of NGO networks across the national borders smoothened the process of globalisation. Thus, the neo-Tocquevillean notion of civil society offers a picture where State has a very limited role (Ayers 2006; Williams and Young 1994; World Bank 1997, 2000).

The neoliberal version of civil society is different from the conventional–liberal understanding of civil society which viewed it as a realm to protect the individual rights by restricting the overpowering of the State. However, the neoliberal view tries to transpose the State in their discussions on civil society. By considering the position of John Locke and Hegel,

Gurpreet Mahajan notes that a civil society "exists for the sake of securing the rights of men, and within it the actions of the sovereign are supposed to create conditions by which individuals can enjoy their rights and liberty fully." As a result, "a political society in which the basic rights of citizens are not recognised or given priority by the sovereign does not constitute a civil society." Mahajan continues, "Civil society is also a kind of political society in which the principle of 'primacy of rights' distinguishes the civil society from other forms of political society" (Mahajan 1999: 170). In response to Mahajan's position, Andre Beteille writes, "Politics alone cannot change a society fully. A certain kind of state is inevitable but it is not sufficient. For analytical purpose, there is no need to assign pre-eminence to state or any other institutions of society. The differentiation and integration are complementary" (Beteille 1999: 2589). It is true that civil society cannot sustain itself without the rule of law. The State is the guarantor of rule of law in a society. The basic presuppositions of the civil society are the separation of functions between the State and itself. At the same time, the State also needs sufficient support from the civil society for its projects. If it lacks, no State can perform in the long run. So, the civil society and State are symbiotically related.

Under neoliberalism, the conventional liberal notion of national civil society has also been transcended to its new form—global civil society. Martin Shaw notes:

> In the second half of the twentieth century, much of the nation-state frameworks of civil society have been transformed. During the cold war, both the state and civil society underwent changes in the West. National forms were maintained, but they lost much real significance. There was a huge internationalisation of western military, economic, cultural and ideological power. Western states increasingly shared frameworks for organising their monopoly of violence and their management of economic life. They created the conditions for massive process of economic and cultural globalisation. In this context the old national civil society declined. (Shaw 1999: 271–72)

With the advancement of globalisation, many of the local/national problems have assumed global ramifications. In this scenario, the national and inter-governmental bodies seem to be inadequate to tackle the issues. It is here that a global civil society is supposed to have transnational capabilities (Etzioni 2004: 341). However, the leading advocates of global civil society described it as a 'fuzzy' and 'contested' concept (Giddens 2001). There is still confusion hanging over the concept about what it is? John Keane defines it as "a vast interconnected and multi-layered social space that comprises many hundreds of thousands of self directing or non-governmental institutions and ways of life" (Keane 2001: 23). It has been reported that a fifth of today's international NGOs were formed after the 1990s (James 2004). This is inextricably linked with the ascendancy of the neoliberal global regime. From a neoliberal point of view, a global civil society is capable of providing adequate 'governance' to the people, an area where the conventional States are said to have failed. Thus, it has the power to transpose the conventional understanding of State system, in which the nation-states were the major actors. The shift of emphasis from the State to the NGOs in the name of civil society has been portrayed as the best way to foster democracy in the Third world. This view is based on the assumption that a democratic culture can be developed and sustained through informal networks and associational life even without support from the State (Fukuyama 2001; World Bank 1999).

The neoliberal attempts to globalise the neo-Tocquevillean notion of civil society tend to dismantle the complex relations between the State, religion and the voluntary sector. According to Tocqueville, in America the religion and the political system are complementary, not contradictory. The religion also "facilitates the use of free associations" (Tocqueville 1997: 36–37). In America, the government is the major source of funding to the domestic communitarian bodies, without which it cannot function properly (Etzioni 2004: 349). So this dependency must be kept in mind when we extend these types of models to the international realm.

Most often the global civil society visionaries discard the political economy aspect from their discussions. It undermines the realities of power and hegemonial relations at the international level. The global political economy is not governed in a democratic fashion. The current global governance reflects the interests of a narrow section of humanity, in which the majority are excluded. Inevitably, associational life only fosters the structures of the existing hegemonial relations (Pasha and Blaney 1998: 432–33). The gap between the haves and have-nots has been widening at the national as well as international levels. According to Mac Ewan, "In spite of the tremendous rise in production, rapid technological change and greater increase of life expectancy, the 'development gap' appears as large as it was 100 years ago. The lack of change is certainly remarkable" (Mac Ewan 1999: 1). So without reducing the inequalities, without providing a somewhat equal accessibility of participation to whole members of this planet, the discussions on global civil society seem quite beside the point.

Alternative Readings: Postmodern–Neoliberal Nexus

The concepts of State and civil society also came in for critical evaluation in the post-positivist traditions of social theory, as represented in the post-modern/post-structural literature since the 1970s (Seethi 2001, 2009b). The writings of Michel Foucault, Derrida, Deleuze, Lyotard, Baudrillard, Fredric Jameson and others have thrown open critical questions concerning the very foundation of modernity, liberalism and socialism (Jameson 1992; Harvey 1989; Lyotard 1984). According to postmodernists, the claims and promises of both liberalism and socialism, with respect to 'emancipation', 'liberation', 'development', human rights, etc., are no longer sustainable. The significance of postmodernism in understanding the dynamics of State and civil society is to be seen in its critique of 'modernity' and all 'grand narratives' (Foucault 1988: 16–46) of the past. Foucault questioned the state-centric notions of power and stressed on the 'capillary flow of power' in the societal body (Foucault 1979). He insisted that the studies of power should begin from the 'micro-physics of power', which are the specific forms of exercise in different institutional sites. He viewed that the disciplinary techniques of the modern State originated from these local centres and they were later taken up and integrated into the global strategy of bourgeois domination (ibid.). Unlike the statists, the Foucauldians put forward a bottom-up approach. In fact, these perspectives ignore the complex, contradictory and constitutive relationship between the State and society.

Akbar S. Ahmed argues that postmodernism is reinvigorating many ethno-religious forces all over the world. However, he writes, "While noting the fragmentation of social and political ideas and shifts in thought, postmodernists fail to link this process with the revival of ethnicity and religious fundamentalism." The identity assertions are augmented with the media revolution. These types of revivalist assertions challenge the modernist conceptions of large state structures (Ahmed 1993: 13–14). Similarly, a discussion on postmodernism and the assertion of the ethno-religious forces is not complete without considering its linkage with neoliberal/New Right thinking. As Seethi notes, "The post-industrial capitalism generates new forms of diversity, plurality and creativity. They are increasingly susceptible to commodification and commercialisation" (Seethi 2001: 310). At the same time, postmodernism provides an epistemic support to the assertion of many marginalised sections and the assertions of such sections threaten the existing power equations. This is in striking contrast with the emergence of Islamic fundamentalism in many countries in West Asia and South Asia, and Hindutva in India. Such forces have gained considerable leeway in the civil society of these countries, which amounted to silencing the critical social engagements.

Apart from the neoliberal version of civil society, the new communication networks bring forth a notion of global public sphere where non-instrumental communication can take place. The 'migratory quality of experience' unites the people at various international forums in their fight against the 'globalised evils'. The social movement approach sees global civil society as mainly progressive, because it does not "seek to replace one form of power with another;" instead its objective is to 'whittle down' the capacity of concentrated centres of power (Stammers 1999: 1006). Like the neoliberal version of global civil society, this approach also tries to bypass the State. The States are regarded as the central barriers to the emancipatory political practice (Chandler 2004: 314). Social movements are different from the conventional political parties: "they are networks of interaction between different actors" (Della Porta and Diani 2000: 16). It appears to be an attempt to depoliticise the movements and also to depoliticise the realm of civil society.

The social movement perspective viewed the realm of civil society as 'apolitical'. For Mary Kaldor, "anti-politics is the ethos of civil society" (Kaldor 2004: 57). Rajni Kothari considers it as a "whole new space," which is "essentially a non-party space." The role of this space "is to deepen the democratic process in response to the state that has not only detached the poor and the oppressed but has turned oppressive and violent." It is to "make them part of the political process" (ibid.).

The struggles of the marginalised sections to get a space in the civil domain are historical, and the 'new social movements' (NSMs) exhibit new dimensions to these struggles. Their slogan is that it is possible to change the existing power equations without capturing the political power. State is the codified form of power in a given territory. So without changing this political power equation, it is difficult to change the state–society relations. The vertical social mobility has its strengths as well as weakness. Under the banner of NSMs, many historically undermined problems came to the central stage. However, it amounted to undermining the possibility of a class movement by the workers. To a great extent, these movements scattered the working class and created a structured apolitical realm, which was easily vulnerable to neoliberal appropriation.

There has been perceptible intellectual bias in the liberal discourses, especially in the Social Contract traditions, regarding the birth of civil society and the State. In their discussions, the notion of security is enmeshed in the idea of civil society. A shift from the state of nature to the civil society implies a shift from insecurity to security, danger to safety, disorder–order, and anarchism-to-statism, and ultimately a transfiguration of 'uncivil' conditions to a 'civilised society'. The civil society is a rational order, where the individuals share certain common values which are mutually beneficial. The basic assumption of liberal thinking is that the spread of this value system all over the world will eventually lead to peace and stability. Today, the liberals generally accept the Kantian notion of 'transnational peace' as the end of history. Unlike Rousseau, Kant believed that the war between the sovereign States at the international state of nature would lead to 'perpetual peace'. The violence and conflicts are inherent in the spread of Western Enlightenment across the world. Kant resembles the State at the international realm with the human beings in the state of nature. The people envisaged civil society in order to get out of the problem-ridden state of nature; likewise, the challenge of the sovereign States is to create an 'international civil society' (Buchan 2002: 407–27).

After a long period of retreat, the end of the Cold War gave a space for the liberals to reclaim their legacies. Fukuyama claimed the end of Cold War as the triumph of 'ideal state' and the 'liberal capitalism' (Fukuyama 1992). He revived the liberal internationalist view regarding international peace that the spread of 'legitimate political order' would eventually bring an end to international conflicts. This neo-Kantian position saw the liberal state as a model for the rest of the world. The liberals claimed that the illiberal states were responsible for war. The militaristic and undemocratic States created war in order to increase their control over the citizens (Burchill and Linklater 1996). The basic assumption of this view was that the liberal States were peace loving and had a 'normative superiority' over the illiberal states (Buchan 2002: 409–10). He noted the main variants of this normative explanation—shared norms between liberal representative states (ibid.: 414). The liberal State contained an 'independent' civil society/civilised condition, which would restrict the State to get into war. But in an 'illiberal' State, the lack of civility in social relations generated war.

Francis Fukuyama who shared the non-statist view saw civil society as "a complex welter of intermediate institutions, including businesses, voluntary associations, educational institutions, clubs, unions, media, charities, and churches." A thriving civil society depended upon people's habits, customs and ethics—attributes that could be shaped only indirectly through conscious political action and must otherwise be nourished through an increased awareness and respect for culture (Fukuyama 1995: 4–5, 360). For Fukuyama, civil society was the whole private sector (including business) outside government. He contended that the capitalist economy had been evolving toward a moral (civil) order. The early Scottish philosophers of the Enlightenment "all hoped that the destructive energies of a warrior culture (lords, barons, monarchs) would be channelled into the safer pursuits of a commercial society, with a corresponding softening of manners." Fukuyama was hopeful for the continued evolution of society. He argued that human beings do not act like rational 'utility maximisers' in any narrow sense, and they are invested in economic activity with "the moral values of their broader social life." In effect, a civil society and a private economy belong together; the capitalist system advances civil society. In other words, the free market economy stabilises and develops civil society. Fukuyama said that the left-wing version of civil society was about mobilising a grass-roots movement to stop Wal-Mart or lobby Congress. The right-wing version was about how civic groups are antidotes to big government (Fukuyama 1999).

The 'normative superiority' of the liberal States over the illiberal ones is based on the understanding that the liberal States contain a vibrant civil society, which restricts the States' war-making capacity. Those States share common norms and values, which prevent them from fighting each other. A common value system includes the sharing of certain economic values and interests. According to the liberals, especially in its classical and neoliberal persuasions, the State should be minimal in the market. The role of the State is to make adequate conditions for free market operations. As a scholar observes:

> The state must act as a 'housekeeper': it must provide only necessary background conditions for capitalism to develop. These essentially comprise the creation of private property rights, a conducive system of law and company law, a police force and an army/navy to ensure order and security. These institutions effectively create 'confidence' without which the smooth running of the economy will be impossible. (Hobson 2000: 71)

Thus, the liberals, especially in their neoliberal version, suggested a militaristic state in matters of law and security in the market. Contrary to the liberal notion of 'free trade' and 'minimal state', the so-called 'illiberal' states were said to be following 'protectionism' in economic matters. Liberals claimed that, "Interventionist (authoritarian or despotic) States had a natural propensity towards tariff protectionism which, in undermining exacerbated tensions and jealousies between States, led to tariff wars and eventually military conflict" (ibid.: 169). Thus, the idea was that the liberal notion of free trade strengthened co-operation and friendship between the peoples of various liberal States and this intermeshing of civilised people/civil societies across the national borders brought forth an 'international civil society' which ultimately created a 'liberal peace zone'. Kant had viewed it as a 'confederation of republican states' (ibid.: 70), and the role of the liberal State was to take initiatives to create an 'international civil society' (Buchan 2002; Luke 1991; Richard Falk 1991).

Ascendency of the New Right: World Mapping

The term 'New Right' is used as a descriptive term for various forms of conservative, right wing or self-proclaimed dissident oppositional movements and groups that emerged in the second half of the 20th century. They were ideologically committed to neoliberalism as well as being socially conservative. Key policies included deregulation of business, a dismantling of the Welfare State, privatisation of nationalised industries and restructuring of the national workforce in order to increase industrial and economic flexibility in an increasingly global market (Green 1987; Gunn 1989; Levitas 1986). The nature and operations of the New Right groups and organisations differ from country to country. So are the strategies employed and realms of articulation and mobilisation. Religion, race, ethnicity, etc., are the most widely used categories for mobilisation and articulation, and civil society is the terrain of activities through which the right-wing forces attempt to gain legitimacy (Tetreault and Denemark 2004).

Since the 1970s, the British–American governments were forced to reconstitute their (developmental and security) strategies in both national and international spheres of action. It may be noted that since the 1940s, the US had been experiencing undisrupted growth rate in its economy. The collapse of currency stability in 1971 and the oil crisis of 1973 caused recession in the US economy which threatened the stability of the Western economy in general. Both the British and American governments adopted two strategies: to rebuild a new alliance at the international level in defence of the West, to change the balance between the State and society and reinvigorate their national culture (Gamble 1988: 1–3). In fact, the crisis in the Fordism led to the post-Fordist restructuring of the world capitalist economy. Fordism refers to the simultaneous growth of productivity and consumption. The Amsterdam School viewed post-Fordism as the decline of Fordism. The 'Reaganomics' in the US and 'Thatcherism' in Britain were reactions to the crisis of Fordism. In this scenario, the financial interests overshadowed those of productive capital, brought decline in the State intervention, freed the market and returned to the conservative values. This change was generally viewed as the triumph of neoliberalism. H. Overbeek notes that neoliberalism "is at once directed towards disarticulating the old formation which is in crisis, that is, towards deconstructing corporatism and the Keynesian welfare state, and towards the formation of a new configuration, the construction of a post-Fordist accumulation regime" (Overbeek 1990: 19). Gamble viewed that the decline of Fordist accumulation regime, the decline of American leadership in international affairs and the crisis of social democracy led to the ascendancy of the New Right (Gamble 1998: 1–3). Lisa McGirr sees New Right as emerging in reaction to the left-oriented social movements of the 1960s (McGirr 2001).

Milton Friedman and Peter Bauer influenced the policies of Thatcher and Reagan administrations. Friedman emphasised the replacing of the Keynesian Welfare State with an activated financial market. According to them, the chief aims of the monetary policy were to promote price stability and to preserve the gold standard; "the chief criteria of monetary policy were the state of the 'money market', the extent of 'speculation' and the movement of gold" (Friedman 1963, 1968: 5). This was an inception to the New Right thinking. According to this, government interference in the market would distort the very balance of demand and supply. It emphasised *laissez faire* in the market. According to Friedman, the government should only focus on matters of defence, law and order, necessary public works, etc. (Friedman 1962, 1980).

Gamble says that "a wide range of groups and ideas make up the New Right and there are many antennal divisions and conflicts" (Gamble 1998: 27). He continues, "As a political program, the New Right is identified with opposition to state involvement in the economy." They are fierce critics of Keynesian policies of economic management, and high public expenditure on welfare. But the New Right politicians are also renowned as advocates of "national discipline and strong defense." The peculiar feature of the New Right is the convergence of the traditional liberal defence of the free economy with the traditional conservative defence of State authority (ibid.: 28–29). As a doctrine, "Conservatism has always been characterized by its emphasis upon the conditions that are required for the establishment and maintenance of social order. These conditions include the need for authority, hierarchy and balance." In fact, the conservatives are highly critical of the liberal doctrines of individualism. But in order to counter the advanced form of liberalism and the social democracy in Europe, the conservatives joined the neoliberals. They identified social democracy as their common enemy. The conservative New Right strongly believed that the dismantling of many aspects of social democracy was inevitable to curb the expansion of communism. The motif behind the creation of a grand military alliance that is the North Atlantic Treaty Organization (NATO), in the post-war years was to curb the expansion of the Soviet communism (ibid.: 54–57). At the domestic level, for example in the US, a 'threat' from the left meant threat from the blacks.

Roger Eatwell pointed out that many of "the left hold that overt, or more usually covert, racism has further helped right wing parties" (Eatwell 1989: 5). Gamble notes, "The most urgent task which the conservative New Right identified in the 1970s was to reverse the drift towards chaos and authoritarianism by restoring authority at all levels in society" (Gamble 1998: 58). These strands—the conservative New Right thinking and the neoliberal one—led to the emergence of Thatcherism in Britain and Reaganomics in the US (Green 1987; Gunn 1989; Levitas 1986).

As in the US and Britain, the conservative movements got intensified in many parts of the world. Edelman argued that the conservative reactions were the outcome of growing social tensions, rapid cultural change, the advance of democratisation and such related progressive movements (Edelman 2001: 293–94). Diamond viewed that "to be right-wing means to support the State in its capacity as enforcer of order and to oppose the State as distributer of wealth and power downward and more equitably in society" (Diamond 1995: 9). The conservative right movement varied from country to country. It could be seen in both the East and the West. In France, Italy, Germany, Greece, UK, USA, Australia, Thailand, New Zealand, Romania, Netherlands, South Korea, Ukraine and India, the New Right movements could be seen in different forms.

In Thailand, during the 1970s, the State intervened in the civil society and created a right-wing movement. The village Scouts (Wild Tiger Cubs) is considered as the largest right-wing movement in Thai history. It was founded in 1971 under the support of the Ministry of the Interiors' powerful Border Patrol Police. The ultimate end of this State-sponsored social movement was to contain communism (Bowie 2005: 47). During the 1970s and 1980s, the Labour Party in Australia initiated New Right policy reforms based on social conservativism, on one hand, and liberal economy, on the other. The politicians favouring New Right reforms were labelled as 'dries' and those who were opposing (means those who were supporting the Keynesian economism) were called the 'wets' (Moore 1995; Saleam 2010).

The Italian New Right has a more critical and constructive perspective regarding the Western modernity. It focused essentially on culture, rather than direct political action. It often indicated a willingness to search for a new synthesis and tried to reconcile contradictory positions, such as anti-egalitarianism and libertarianism. Italian New Right culture was heavily influenced by the late fascist experience. For an entire generation of veterans, the loss of the war resulted in a feeling of isolation and alienation from political life. In this context, the ex-fascists founded a party, the MSI. The MSI and its cultural organs (such as the *Centro Studi Ordine Nuovo*) seemed unable to find new life in post-World War Italy. In this context, the ideas of the far right, especially the ideas of Julius Evola (1898–1974) had considerable impact. He was influenced by Eastern traditions and his philosophy was based on the rejection of linearity in history and on the assumption of its cyclical character. His cyclical vision of history postulated the deterioration of a spiritually superior stage to one of decadence, where only a small elite stood out within a world in ruins. This vision had a powerful and reassuring impact on a generation that had lost a war and felt estranged in a modern mass society characterised by the reduction of qualitative aspects of life to vulgar economic values (Sacchi 2006).

The French New Right was born in 1968. It was less concerned with the tradition and stressed on the libertarian values. The French New Right today strongly supports clear and strong identities favouring cultural difference. It is against racism and also stressed that struggle against racism was not negating the concept of race, nor by the desire to blend all races into an undifferentiated whole. Rather it is meant for the refusal of both exclusion and assimilation: neither apartheid nor the melting pot; that means the acceptance of the other as 'other' through a dialogic perspective of mutual enrichment. The New Right is against immigration because according to them it would spare individuals from being cut off from their cultural roots. It upholds differentialist feminism, the feminine rights like the right to virginity, to maternity, to abortion, etc. It gives prominence to participatory democracy and celebrates local community life rather than homogenising civil society. It also stands for a federal Europe (Piccone 2006). Paradoxically, the position of the French New Right has identifiable features with the postmodernist perspectives.

New Discourses of Security

In the 1990s, the notion of security assumed a new dimension with the advent of globalisation. The concept of human security gained considerable attention during this period (Acharya 2001; UNDP 1994). This underlined a shift from the State-centric notion of security to a global, individualistic version of security. The human security approach implied that the individual was at the core of any security perspective. Satisfaction of individual needs at different realms of life was central in such approach (Ramakrishnan 2004: 68). An individual was facing so many threats from different quarters and the conventional State was said to be incapable of providing security to all (Chen et al. 2003). The attempts to transpose the State centrism in security thinking generated new meanings and spheres of action. According to Glasius, human security

> is a term with which global civil society activists can confront the current preoccupation of governments and public opinion with terrorism, entering the security debate with strategies that go beyond repression. This could be more realistic and productive than just lamenting the current security paradigm. (Glasius et al. 2006: 31)

An examination of the challenges emerging from the increased globalisation are perhaps relevant (Cha 2000: 391–403; Clark 1999; Scholte 2000).

The Cold War scenario was dominated by the realists who stood for a strong 'state', the basic unit of an 'anarchical' international system. Here the Hobbesian notion has apparently been deployed in the realm of international system, where all States are in a state of war. The actions of such States are justified on the ground of national interest (Buzan 1987). For several decades, the cold war ideology "served to eclipse the distinction between the state, popular interests and the multiplicity of values, claims and identities of a state's citizenry." When it came to considering security, State and society were considered as one. As Poku notes,"Issues like internal conflicts, interstate migratory flows and environmental problems were more or less subsumed under the security policies and interests of nation-states" (Poku et al. 2005: 9). This State-centric notion of security has been challenged by the widened process of globalisation. The increased interdependence brought in a somewhat sensitive relation between the 'local' and the 'global'. Anything that happens at the 'local' has serious repercussions on the 'global' and vice versa. On issues like migration, environment, etc., the realists call for a beyond-State approach. Ethical and moral standards are important in order to deal with such issues. Consequently, the realist proposition of national security has been challenged on a human security angle today. The conventional notion of national security does not touch every sphere of individual action, while at the same time a major chunk of the population is marginalised due to increasing stresses. The security of one State is tantamount to the insecurity of the people of other States (Poku et al. 2005: 10–21). Thus, the human security frame "acknowledges that the security of citizens is not always bound up with the security of the state." At times, the State itself may threaten its citizens. It also acknowledges that in the 21st century, the State may not always be able to keep its citizens secure, and other actors, at the local, regional and global levels, should share responsibility for human security (Glasius et al. 2006: 108). Here the notion of human security is enmeshed in the neoliberal paradigm. The individual-centred idea of human security seems to be hybridised with the proposed non-state developmental pattern of neoliberalism. But, in reality, neoliberalism tends to undermine human security.

Thus, the notion of human security is basically individual-centric. The neoliberal ideas seem to be the core of the process of globalisation. The globalisation brings forth an individualistic culture, where the individual has been compartmentalised from his social surroundings. The advancement of information technology (IT) provides wide networks of interactions among the individuals. But such interactions may be formal and egoistic. This makes a somewhat insecurity complex among the individuals and that may lead to many societal problems. In so far as neoliberalism contributes to uneven socio-economic development, a major chunk of population has been marginalised from the mainstream socio-economic path. This generates social tensions and thereby new security problems. The process of globalisation, thus, not only brings forth hybrid cultural forms but it also results in aggressive responses.

The whole matrix of relations in a society is structured on a legitimate ground, the security. McSweeney notes: "The verb to 'secure' was first predicated of people. It became attached to states" (McSweeney 1999: 17). According to Michael Dillon, security became the predicate upon which the

> architectonic political discourses of modernity were constructed; upon which the vernacular architecture of modern political power exemplified in the modern state, was based; and from which the institutions and practices of modern (inter) national politics, including modern democratic

politics ultimately seek to derive their ground and functional legitimacy.
(Dillon 1996: 13)

The notion of security perpetuates its alter-ego, the danger. People are
used to both tangible and intangible measures to secure from 'threats'.
McSweeney says that "we imagine security as an 'inner experience but
which makes an undefined 'other'" (McSweeney 1999: 13). This 'self/
other' dichotomy perpetuates conflicts and chaos. The capitalist system
and its rational institutional mechanisms made the binaries, civilised or
uncivilised. The coercive instruments of the State have been deployed to
deal with these 'uncivil' elements.

The global interconnectedness has changed the importance of security from its State-centric approach towards a humanocentric one. The
Brandt Report of the 1980s stated, "An important task of constructive
international policy will have to consist in providing a new, more comprehensive understanding of security, which would be less restricted to
purely military aspects" (ibid.: 52). McSweeney notes, "...security relates
to a *quality of a relationship*, grounded in human needs, which encourages
confidence in the participants that their legitimate values are protected
in a manner compatible with the capacity of others to do likewise" (ibid.:
100). Here, he identifies security with a negotiable realm. He stressed the
role of identities in this spectrum. "Identity is not a fact of society, it is a
process of negotiation among people and interest groups" (ibid.: 73). In
his opinion, the identities are not the cause of the security problem, but
the effect of it. The historical representations attached to the identities
make unequal footing in their negotiations. To a greater extent, their assertions are treated as 'security threat' and dealt with severely. The process
of globalisation brings forth a world of insecurity complexes, struggles
and uncertainties.

Identity and Security

Though security is a core concept in the theory and praxis of national,
regional and international politics, it is also viewed in the context of
local, inter-local and trans-local relations. In the positivist paradigm,

security is assumed to possess an ontological and epistemological certainty where the sources of insecurity as well as the referent of security are givens. Conventional International Relations (IRs), therefore, focus on a State-centric, power-oriented and militaristic discourse of security. With its focus on power, politics and anarchy as fixed—mainstream IR reads narrowly into the role of ideology as manifested in the concepts of State, national interest and nationalism. Neither does it pay attention to the ways in which anarchy or insecurity may be constructed or how the roles of ideology, culture, history or State practices themselves may produce anarchy in IR (Das 2002: 76–89).

The critical constructivists address the above concern. Problematising the conventional assumption that IR is in a state of perpetual anarchy, the critical constructivists instead view security as what David Campbell calls 'representations of danger' (Campbell 1998: 1–13). For the critical constructivists, objects of insecurity and insecurities are not ontologically separate things. Rather, they are mutually constituted in a variety of ways that may privilege a certain conception of identity over others. Operating within a framework of meanings, assumptions and distinctive social identities, the representation of the 'other', their identities and what constitutes insecurity 'imaginaries' are left open to the dynamics of interpretation, whereby relations of identity may also be produced, enforced, and reified in a conflictual manner (Muppidi 1999: 124). Furthermore, construction of identities influencing security dynamics may not simply be confined to rigid interstate dynamics, but may also be mediated by "complex network of social relations, cultural traditions, and political structures..." involving State security elites themselves (Niva 1999: 152). Thus, critical constructivists assume that all social (in)securities are culturally produced (Weldes et al. 1999: 1). Central to the concept of postcolonial insecurity is what Sankaran Krishna calls postcolonial 'anxiety', defined as an ideological drive of postcolonial State leaders to achieve successfully the "modern enterprise of nation-building" (Krishna 1999: xvii–xix). Central to the metaphor of creating a nation as something "ever in the making but never quite reached" is the idea of nationalism (Das 2002).

Thus, in the new literature of IRs (Campbell 1998; Krause and Williams 1997; Lipschutz 1995; Weldes et al. 1999), security is conceptualised as a productive discourse that brings forth insecurities to be operated upon. It also defines the identity of the object to be secured. This contests the dominant conceptual paradigm of security that sees insecurities as essential variables, while focusing attention on the acquisition of security by given entities. It underlines the processes through which something or someone (the 'other') is discursively formed as a source of insecurity against which the 'self' needs to be secured (Anand 2005: 203–15). Thus, discourses of insecurity are about 'representations of danger' (Campbell 1998; Dillon 1996). Insecurities are inevitably 'social constructions' rather than givens—threats do not just exist out there, but have to be produced. All insecurities are, thus, culturally shaped in the sense that they are produced in and out of "the context within which people give meanings to their actions and experiences and make sense of their lives" (Weldes 1999: 1). Insecurities and the objects that suffer from insecurities are mutually constituted. That is, in contrast to the received view, which treats objects of security and insecurity themselves as pre-given and natural and as separate things, we treat them as mutually constituted cultural and social constructions and, thus, products of processes of identity construction of self–other. The argument that security is about representations of danger and social construction of the 'self' and the 'other' does not imply that there are no 'real' effects. What it means is that there is nothing inherent in any act or being or object that makes it a source of insecurity and danger (Anand 2005: 203–15).

Dibyesh Anand argues that security is linked closely with identity politics. How we define ourselves depends on how we represent others. This representation is, thus, integrally linked with how we 'secure' ourselves against the 'other'. Representations of the 'other' as a source of danger to the security of the 'self' in conventional understandings of security are accompanied by an abstraction, dehumanisation, depersonalisation and stereotyping of the 'other.' The 'other' gets reduced to being a danger and hence an object that is fit for surveillance, control, policing and possibly extermination. This logic of the discourse of security dictates that the security of the self facilitates and even demands the use of policing and violence against the 'other.' This is demonstrated through the case of the Hindu Right's politics of representation, which legitimises anti-Muslim violence in the name of securing the Hindu 'self' at various levels. 'The Muslim' as such is a threat not only to the Hindutva but also to the international security. These representations of 'danger' to the security of the Hindu body politic facilitated the 'politics of hate' in India. This is done through the realm of civil society in an aggressive manner using a wide network of organisations as well as the media.

According to Anand, 'Muslim' as an object of insecurity in the discourse of the Hindu Right organisations inhabits the levels of the personal, local, national and international. Here the 'Muslim' is discursively constructed as a site of fear, fantasy, distrust, anger, envy and hatred, thus generating desires of emulation, abjection and/or extermination. His argument is that these desires are not confined to the subscribers to Hindutva but are prevalent in the wider society among those describing themselves as Hindu. The Hindu Right assertion is not an inevitable result of these prejudicial desires but scavenges upon them and, in turn, fuels and fossilises them. The desire of emulation, abjection and extermination is inextricably linked to certain threatening representations of 'the Muslim' (Anand 2005: 203–15). Anand points out that "Hindutva's 'politics of representation' is one replete with myths and stereotypes." For instance, Anand shows, how Hindutva discourses

> construct a myth of the Hindu self as virtuous, civilized, peaceful, accommodating, enlightened, clean and tolerant, as opposed to 'the Muslim' other, which is morally corrupt, barbaric, violent, rigid, backward, dirty and fanatic. The myth borrows from various stereotypes and motifs that are prevalent in India and elsewhere, including the West. (ibid.; see also Das 2002)

Thus, the articulation, representation and mobilisation of 'threat' and 'security' are carried out through the realm of civil society and, in most cases, the State reinforces such perceptions of 'threat' and 'security' through the media and other agencies in the civil society.

2

State and Civil Society in India: The Historical Experience

The State and civil society in India are often characterised as complex realms of socio-political engagement given the very nature of their origin and development under colonial and postcolonial conditions. While the State in India had been undergoing changes during the colonial days, the civil society had become vibrant in the context of the challenges of modernity and the rising tempo of nationalism. The State had the pressure of colonial administration and all its requirements, but the civil society in its multitudes developed its own concerns and responses from different vantage points. These concerns and responses were manifested in the anti-colonial struggle, nationalist aspirations, anti-caste or socio-religious reform movements, civil liberty activities, etc. In the postcolonial conditions, the State and civil society further went through a variety of experiences largely because of the new challenges of State-building and nation-building. It is within this complex setting of State–civil society engagements that the study of the Hindu Right becomes relevant. This chapter, therefore, aims to analyse the trajectories of engagements of the State and civil society under the structural compulsions of colonial and postcolonial India.

Precolonial/Colonial Experience

The value of the concepts of State and civil society in a Third World context has been heavily criticised, as arguments against the universal applicability of the concepts developed within Western political philosophy have been raised (Blaney and Pasha 1993; Rudolph 2000; Wickramasinghe 2005). It is said that the very idea of a civil society, and also its proposed role in the development and consolidation of democracy is confined to a unique West European (and possibly North American) experience (Berglund 2009). In order to validate this, it is necessary to understand the respective developments of the State in both the West and in the Third World. The modern State was in the West paradoxically developed simultaneous with a civil society, a process covering centuries, which included a gradual shift towards a more powerful and efficient State, but also towards a stronger and more independent civil society. In the Third World the power of the precolonial State was, in most cases, not absolute in the same sense as in the West, with influential religious and traditional power structures often outside the immediate reach of State power. Every Third World society and every democracy has its own special construction of State–civil society relations, and almost all States have had a colonial history that influenced these relations. While differing from country to country the colonial period meant a serious break with traditional political organisation, and although such breaks are not necessarily negative for the development of democracy, the close relation between the economic sphere and the State proved fatal for the development of both political democracy and civil society.

Olle Törnquist outlines how a symbiotic relationship between politics and economy developed, where the State dominated the economic sphere and where economic success came through political power rather than skilful use of labour and capital. The domination of the colonial powers stopped the growth of a domestic capital making the middle class necessary to challenge both the State and the feudal order, and capitalism was, instead, introduced by external forces and controlled by an alliance between the colonial State and the ruling feudal classes. The middle classes outside the domination of the feudal system were very weak, as was the basis for a strong civil society. Although capitalism expanded in some areas, the expected process of social and political modernisation failed to show, largely because of the strong connection between the political and the economic sphere, and the feudal system was instead of being replaced, incorporated in the colonial capitalism. The symbiotic relation between politics and economy continued in the postcolonial period too. State-led modernisation plans became the order of the day, with a major role for the State within the economy and with continuously-weak domestic capitalists. Also in this new setting, the road to economic power ran through the political elite and through the State. The symbiosis of the political and economic spheres is one example of how State–civil society relations developed differently in the Third World, which has consequences on how the civil society theory can be applied (Törnquist 1999: 9–14). The relatively slow and—at least partly—peaceful growth of civil society and the development of civil and political rights in Western Europe have little or no correspondence in postcolonial States (Berglund 2009).

Mobilisation within the civil society in India was evident already in the colonial period, but the formation of both State and civil society in India was different from that of Western Europe (Kaviraj and Khilnani 2001). While the modern State in the West developed simultaneously with civil society—a process covering centuries and including a gradual shift towards not only a more powerful and efficient State but also towards a stronger and more independent civil society—the development of civil society in the rest of the world did not follow the same pattern. The powers of both the precolonial and the colonial State were not absolute: the State coexisted with influential religious and traditional power structures outside its immediate reach and the effects of these alternative power structures were evident also in the formation of the civil society. One example is the tendency of the British colonial State to respect religious differences and to divide the population according to faith. In the Indian case, this practice led to a strong position of the native religious elites and the strengthening of religious identity in both the private sphere and in civil society (Ali 2001).

It seems to be relevant here to explain some aspects of the nature of Indian State in the precolonial era and also its mode of governance in the society. The political arrangements in the traditional India appear to have been stretched over three distinct levels. The micro foundations of power lay in the structure of village communities over which regional kingdoms exercised a real and proximate political authority. Power at the level of the village community was exercised through the logic of the caste system (Dumont 1970). Historically, the Aryans had compartmentalised the Indian social system into four 'varnas': Brahmin, Kshatriya, Vaisya and Sudra in accordance with the four functions that were allotted to them respectively, knowledge: production and interpretation of the existing knowledge system; defence: the psychical protection of the people belonging to the other three *varnas*; wealth: trade and commerce; labour: the physical labour to the above three *varnas* of the social hierarchy (Kothari 2006: 21–31). This division was based on the principle of purity or pollution.

According to Manu's code of law (Olivelle 2005: 91), the duties or functions—broadly called 'dharma'—are societally assigned to an individual and she or he has no choice at all to take decision on his own matters as concerned with the work or has no right to cross-cut this pre-fixed social boundary. The individual freedom, mobility in its modern sense, was unknown and this system continued to be the core of the Hindu social order. The *varna* classification is a generalised one within which there existed umpteen numbers of castes (*jatis*) and sub-castes. This made the Indian social system more complex, which resisted any generalisation. Indeed, to a greater extent, this system of stratification made the Indian society static for a long period of time. This was the prime instrument of exclusion, which froze the intellectual and social development of the communities that were historically marginalised from the mainstream path.

Given the nature of this system, the State could not act as the symbol of society as a whole. The State itself was subject to the systemic control (Kaviraj 2000: 39–40). Unlike the territorial division of the modern nation-State, in the traditional Indian State, each significant practice had a territorial structure specific to itself. Religious and economic domains demonstrated greater stability in comparison to the 'high mortality' of ruling dynasties and their general fragile States. The precolonial type of authority was not an authority for appeal against widespread structural injustice or oppressions of social process. The State had neither the great advantages nor the great responsibilities of being the universal institution, which assumed at least symbolic responsibility for society's general good or evil (ibid.: 41–42). Both the Mughals and the British did not alter the system much. The society was under various conflicting power centres and was hierarchically ordered. The British pursued a policy in which the colonial administration linked the governmental authority with those power centres and avoided a direct link between the colonialists and the people in general. The colonial reluctance to intervene in the 'private' slowed down the possibility of social transformation.

The British colonialism introduced a new type of regime, which favoured wealth compared to the previous one (Dumont 1997: 54). The contact of the Indian society with the colonial power was a contact of two very different principles of construction of society and State. The colonialists dealt with the system with the support of their rationalist discourses and gave primacy to commerce and economic control. In the traditional Indian social thinking, commerce and economic activities were politically insignificant. The State only 'squeezed' the economy rather than restructuring it. The State and society were in a harmonious relation and the State never altered the Hindu social order. The Mughals also did not disturb this social system. They had established a 'subordinate empire' on the top without altering the caste-based village structure on the ground. But the British colonialism destabilised this dualism (Kaviraj 1997: 143–152). Nicholas Dirks notes that

> colonialism changed things both more and less than has commonly been thought. While introducing new forms of civil society and separating these forms off from the colonial state, colonialism also arrested some of the immediate disruptions of change by preserving many elements of the old regime. (Dirks 1997: 164)

The power under colonialism was public. The British had created a public sphere which they filled with the European model of institutions and laws (Kaviraj 1997: 143). This rule of colonial difference was challenged by the nationalists (Chatterjee 1994: 10). However, the colonial State was marginal and remained as a thin stratum of institutions, which focused on the maintenance of colonial order and the extraction of the public revenue (Kaviraj 1997: 44). The overall practices of the British colonialism in India reveal some kind of an externality in their dealings with the natives, which was quite contrary to the rationalist or humanist discourse that they used for legitimating their authority in the colony. The colonialists did not make any attempt to radically change the society but followed a tricky business of extraction and accumulation.

However, the impact of colonialism was multifaceted. Most importantly, it altered the peaceful coexistence of different communities. Historically, Indian society was complex and in their day-to-day experiences in the precolonial India, people had developed a composite culture. It had gone beyond the Bhakti-Sufi tradition. Neera Chandhoke notes,

"The inhabitants of Indian society during the course of working and living together or through the practice of everyday life had developed a common transcendent culture that both merged as well as surpassed the best of component cultures" (Chandhoke 2003: 199). The political practices under the colonial rule fragmented the society along the lines of caste and religious differences. There were no communal conflicts reported before the 19th century except two incidents, one in 1710 and the other in 1740. From 19th century onwards, we can see a chain of communal riots and caste wars. In a multi-religious society like India where the relation between religion and politics was a complex one and the internal compositions of religion and modern politics were contradictory, this is not surprising.

A synthetic culture existed in the precolonial era. However, this did not mean that there had existed an egalitarian society in India. Compared to the 'modern' Indian society, it was relatively peaceful. Andre Beteille notes, "The organizing principles of Indian social life mainly came from Hinduism. The tolerance of diversity is an ethical basis of Hinduism. But this tolerance of diversity cannot be equated with the individual freedom and equality" (Beteille 2005: 367–68). The individual was chained to the prescribed duties and obligations and 'rights' were unknown to them. The State did not have much role in the society except for police function. The self-maintaining moral order of the caste system subordinated the status of the State in the pre-modern India (Kaviraj 2000: 40). The notable feature of the precolonial State–society relation was the "interweaving of change and changelessness." The political boundaries may change but the basic structure of the society remained static (ibid.: 42). Jayaprakash Narayan notes that the insularity of society from the State, ensured that the "vertical fragmentation of society continued and institutions remained static and frozen" (Narayan 2003: 78–79). This social system had been persisting without much alteration.

Colonial Modernity and Nationalisms

The British ruled India not only by coercion alone but also by the power of their rational discourses, which enabled them to sustain psychological domination among the natives. It should be noted that in the post-Mughal period, the Indian society was obsessed with certain practices of the religious belief system; specifically, Hinduism was beset with idolatry, polytheism and superstition. These practices were challenged by various unorthodox sects which emerged in almost all parts of India. The Satnami, Appapanthi and Shivanarayan sects in Uttar Pradesh; the Karthabajas and Balramis in Bengal; the Charanadsis in Rajasthan; and others denounced the degenerated practices of the Hindu religion, especially its caste distinctions. The 19th-century intellectuals generally believed that the superstitious belief systems and social practices of the Indian society were a stumbling block on the path of progress. While opposing the hegemonic values of the Indian feudal society, the intellectuals accepted the inevitability of the Western bourgeois order for the development of the Indian society (Panikkar 1995: 3–8). The Hindu religious reformers strongly opposed the superstitious belief system of their religion. This response emerged from the Western critique of the 'Orient' that it was a superstitious social formation. Indeed, the intellectuals were fascinated by the Western 'security community.' The newly emerged intelligentsia generally believed that the acceptance of Western Enlightenment values was the only panacea to shift the 'insecure' Indian social system into a 'secure community.'

The Western Enlightenment project was a 'security project.' The gaze of Enlightenment viewed the rest as 'inferior' and they had to follow the West for developing a 'rational' socio-political order. The emerging modern nation-State in the West was viewed as a symbol of security and development. The modern nation-State was a product of Western modernity, accompanied by the emergence of a capitalist system, the advanced form of social and sexual division of labour, and the transition from a theocentric world order towards a humanocentric order. Modernity is thus inextricably interlinked with reason, rational behaviour of the individual and primacy of 'science' over all other 'traditional experiences.' All this was to liberate man from the superstitions. The discourses of modernity were the legitimising factor behind the colonisation of the eastern societies by the West. The Western Enlightenment project divided the world into two—the 'civilised' West and the 'uncivilised' East. The discourses were based upon the assumption that the West was a rational socio-political order and the rest were guided by unreason and superstitions. So the

West believed that it had a legitimate role to 'civilise' the rest, the so-called 'White man's burden.'

In India, the British colonial authorities maintained their hegemony over the inhabitants through various ways. Besides the civilian and military superiority, the colonialists also employed the power of rational discourses. They introduced railways, scholastic institutions, judicial system, defence infrastructure, etc., to facilitate the better extraction from the colony (Nehru 1993: 291–92). However, all these developments created a feeling of urgency to transform the Indian society from its age-old traditions into modern. Most importantly, the influences of Western education in the colonies produced a new set of intelligentsia who strongly supported the inevitability of the Western Enlightenment values. Indeed, to the British, the assertion of the native intellectuals was an essential prerequisite for legitimising their regime in the colony. The educational policy of the British was to fulfil the administrative needs of the empire in India and also to sustain an ideological hegemony over the natives. While the educational programmes were oriented to the regeneration of the country, the Indian intellectuals pursued an educational strategy, which promoted education through the medium of the vernacular languages. This new educational system gave primacy to science education, and was the result of the growing awareness among the intelligentsia about the need of science for the progress of the country (Panikkar 1995: 7–12).

However, while supporting the Western rationality and its emancipatory role in the Indian society, the English-educated intelligentsia never switched off their tradition. They were highly influenced by the spirituality of their saint tradition and its humanism. Partha Chatterjee viewed that by dividing the world of social institutions and practices into the spiritual and material, the anti-colonial nationalism created its own domain of sovereignty within the colonial society, well before it began its political battle with the imperial power. The 'outside' was the realm of 'material', in which the West proved its superiority and the 'inner' was the sphere where the Indians preserved the distinctness of their 'spiritual' culture (Chatterjee 1994: 6). Thinkers like Vivekananda, Dayananda Saraswati and many others strongly supported the inevitability of the Western technology for the progress of India and at the same time, they emphasised the importance of re-invoking the old rational tradition of Hindu religion. The reformist movements were aimed to regenerate the Indian society to the ages of an imagined past. They condemned the religious practices of their time because of their superstitious biases and celebrated a rationalist tradition which was competent with the present variety of Western rationalist order (Nehru 1993: 335–39).

Bengali literary figure Bankim Chandra Chatterjee viewed that the British domination in India was the net result of its 'cultural failure' and he identified two reasons. Firstly, Indians were lacking a natural desire for liberty and secondly, the lack of solidarity among the Hindu folk (Chatterjee 1986: 54–56). Mahatma Gandhi offered a different reason that it was not because of the cultural weakness of India that India was under colonialism but because the Indians were so fascinated by the glitte of the Western civilisation that they had become a subject people (ibid.: 85–86). In his *Hind Swaraj*, Gandhi severely criticised the modernist version of civil society in India which brought forth total subjugation of the Indians to the West. He made a civilisational critique of the modern Western civilisation and emphasised the importance of re-invoking the Indian way of life and society (Chatterjee 1986: 85–86; Gandhi 1938).

The civil society in India evolved during the colonial period. It was embedded in the idea of 'nation' and 'nationalism.' There are three 'master narratives' in Indian nationalism. One is secular nationalism propagated by the Indian National Congress; the other is religious nationalism which consisted of mainly two streams: the Hindu nationalism and the Muslim nationalism. There is another version namely, the caste-based assertions of the deprived sections. The first stream was more coalitional across caste and religious divisions. The second stream was radical and it used religious identity as the source for mobilisation. The caste-based identity assertions were basically against the existing exploitative Hindu social system—so naturally against the second stream—and also it was a search for an alternative social order based on the principle of equality and social justice (Varshney 2002: 55–59). These movements were both a response to the colonial gaze and a product of colonial influences. The caste-based assertions challenged the Hindu social system and its discourses on the relationship between man and man. The Congress's position was a Western secularist version of social mobility and national construction, which was not at all anti-religious, but stressed the importance of detaching the State from religion. The secular nationalism became the dominant ideology of nation-building in India. The national resistance movement, spearheaded by the Congress, was the main source of civil society activity in the early 20th-century British India. When the Congress developed into a mass movement, large segments of the population were for the first time drawn into political and social activism. While the struggle was basically anti-colonial, the movement held within itself many forms of activities which would continue as independent sections of civil society, one case in point being the women's movement. Partly outside of the Congress, other forms of social movements too gained in strength during the first half of the 20th century.

Associational Life and Anti-colonial Movements

The introduction of Western education in India generated a modern-ist version of associational life and civic engagement. On one hand, it reproduced the regime legitimacy and on the other hand, the very structure generated a number of critical discourses within and outside the realm of dominant civic engagement. The nationalist movement in India emerged as a response to the contradictory economic or political stand of the colonialists. The colonial policies generated greater frustra-tion among the newly emerged middle class, who were fascinated by the emancipatory potential of the Western modernity, which was so obsessed with the rational equality of all human beings. But under colonial rule, the Indian middle class experienced a subordinate status in comparison to the colonial elites. They questioned this self-contradictory stand of British colonialism.

The British colonial authorities followed a representational mode of governance and ruled out the possibility of a direct relationship between the individual and the State. Amir Ali notes, "National rituals in Europe emphasized common values and 'traditions.' They stressed upon a history that defined participants as like in their relationship to the State. On the contrary, imperial rituals in British India stressed the diversity of impe-rial rule" (Ali 2001: 2420). The colonialists pursued a policy that linked the centres of power in the society with the colonial administration and consequently the feudal elements in the society got prominence under the colonial rule.

During the anti-colonial struggle, the nationalist elite established a modern associational life in India. Partha Chatterjee noted that it "emerged in accordance with the wishes of the nationalist elites during the anti-colonial struggle. They sought new ethical life in congruence with the Western society" (Chatterjee 2002: 176). The national civil society was established well before the rise of mass nationalist movement in the early 20th century. The elites were highly critical of the inconsistencies of the colonial State to cope with the modern standards of a liberal constitutional State (ibid.: 75). The self-contradictory stand of colonialism had generated greater frustration among the newly emerged 'middle class' (Chatterjee 1994). They turned against the colonial rule. But the role of the masses seemed out of question because the anti-colonial movement turned to be a massive struggle only in the early part of the 20th century, especially under the leadership of Mahatma Gandhi. Chatterjee notes the following:

> Even as the associational principles of secular bourgeois civil institutions were adopted in the new civil society of the nationalist elite, the possibility of a different mediation between the population and the state was already being imagined, one that would not ground itself on a modernized civil society. (Chatterjee 2002: 175)

This eventually led to the establishment of a superficial democracy.

From the 19th century onwards, struggles by untouchables and other deprived sections were underway against the existing exploitative system. This included the Mahar and non-Brahman movement of Maharashtra, the non-Brahman movement of Madras, Ezhavas of Kerala, the Chamars of Chhattisgarh area, the Namashudras of Bengal, etc. These movements recognised the modern Western view of democracy and the equality of man (Zelliot 2001: 33–47). Though they were basically against the existing social evils of the Hindu belief system, they also challenged the hegemonic nature of the religious reformist movements in British India. The religious movements like Brahma Samaj, Arya Samaj, Prarthana Samaj and the Theosophical Society promulgated a version of Hinduism, which was based upon the principle of harmoniously integrated *varnas*. It was reformative but not for any radical changes in the society (Nehru 1993: 335–39). The reformers, however, legitimised the emancipatory potential of 'true' Hinduism and argued that untouchability was the product of the 'perverted' Hinduism. This was challenged from different quarters, especially the movements by the untouchables and other deprived sections. A large number of people who were under the lowest grade of the caste hierarchy in the Hindu social order converted to Buddhism. There were such movements in many parts of India. Pandit C. Ayodhya Dasa (1845–1914), known as Iyothee Thass, forerunner of B. R. Ambedkar, started a neo-Buddhist movement in Tamil Nadu. He was in search of a new religion based on liberty, equality and fraternity. He viewed that social emancipation was only possible through the Buddhist religion. He started the South Indian Sakya Buddhist Association and converted many Dalits to Buddhism (Samel 2004: 182–83). The 'Self Respect' movement by Periyar E.V. Ramasamy is another example. The reformist movements under the guidance of Sree Narayana Guru, Ayyankali and Sahodaran Ayyappan in Kerala are other instances noted in the history of modern India. These reform movements, on the whole, sought to ensure vertical social mobility in India.

The Western-educated Hindu middle class in the urban areas revolted individually or formed associations in their protest against the existing unjust social order. C. H. Heimsath classified these associations into three types: general (voluntary) associations, caste-reform associations and religious-reform bodies (Heimsath 1964). Social reform associations came into existence at the provincial and local levels. Some of these associations focused on social issues like widow remarriage and child marriage, while others protested against the religious authorities, superstitions, caste restrictions for crossing the sea, etc. Most of them were loose organisations whose activities were largely restricted to arranging programmes, conferences, passing resolutions, etc. Some reformers acted within their caste and formed caste associations. This was aimed to fight against the unacceptable practices of the caste system. Reformists like Raja Ram Mohan Roy formed the Brahmo Samaj and protested against the practice of 'Sati' in the Hindu society. The Prarthana Samaj by M. G. Ranade in Bombay and the Arya Samaj by Dayananda Saraswati played a decisive role in the 19th-century reform efforts. Social reform movements among the Muslims began with the Aligarh Movement led by Syed Ahmad Khan. In south India (Kerala), it was initiated by Vakkom Moulavi (Miller 1976). The movements within the Muslim community were the result of growing realisation that called for use of the modern education and technology in a competitive socio-economic order.

In 1927 the All India Women's Conference (AIWC) was formed, influenced by the 19th-century reform movements. It was associated with the nationalist movement and later on, it became a part of the Congress party. During the colonial period, the organisations that addressed social issues and sought changes in the status of women were closely associated with the nationalist movement. After independence, the AIWC was incorporated into the Women's Indian Association (WIA) and was succeeded by the National Federation of Indian Women (NFIW). The Indian women's movement became particularly visible after the 1970s (Subramanyam 2004: 635). However, AIWC was preceded by the birth of several women's associations. In Bengal, the Brahmo Samaj organised the Brahmika Samaj in 1856. The Arya Nari Samaj and the Bangla Mahila Samaj represented different factions in the Brahmo Samaj. These were followed by a variety of local associations influenced by the revivalist ideas in the early 20th century and many magazines for women (Dalits Intellectual Collective 2009: 32–33). After 1910, a number of national and provincial women's associations came into existence. It should be noted that these associations were initiated more by women without much influence from male social reform organisations. The first was Sarla Devi's Bharath Stri Mahamandal founded in 1910, followed by the WIA in 1917 by Annie Besant, Dorothy Jinarajadasa and Margaret Cousins. Then came the National Council of Women in India—a pro-British, social service-oriented elite organisation founded in 1925—by Lady Aberdeen, Lady Tata and others and linked provincial welfare charity organisations. The AIWC represented the association for Indian women in the colonial period. They organised campaigns on various issues in support of the Sarda Act against child marriage, for women's suffrage against purdah, etc.

It may be noted that a number of women's organisations and associations emerged in the post-independence period and some of them were associated with various political parties (Katzenstein 1989: 55). The Communist Party of India-led NFIW, the Communist Party of India (Marxist)-led All India Democratic Women's Association, Naxalite-inspired Progressive Organisation of Women, Naxalite students group in Hyderabad, Stri Shakti Sanghatana and Janata Party-led Mahila Dakshata Samiti were some of the prominent women's organisations associated with the political parties (ibid.: 55–56).

In the following decades, a lot of autonomous women's organisations and associations mushroomed in different parts of the country. These organisations did not formally have any party affiliation though there were no restrictions to the individual members to have party affiliation. In Delhi in 1979, a small group of women started the publication of *Manushi* (both Hindi and English). In 1982, 'Saheli'—an organisation for women—was formed, which was concerned with issues like dowry death and domestic violence. 'Ankoor' (with adult education); 'Jagari' (with the collection of feminist documentation, film and literature); 'Kali for Women' (devoted to the publication of original feminist literature and analysis); 'Stree Sangharsh' (street plays about dowry murders, etc.); 'Forum Against Oppression of Women'; 'Vimochana' and 'Street Jagrata Samiti' in Bangalore; 'Pennorima Iyakkam' in Tamil Nadu; 'Chingari Nari Sangathan' in Ahmedabad; and 'Anweshi' in Kerala were some of the women's organisations that emerged in different parts of India.

The peasant movements were also decisive in the political history of India. During the colonial period as well as in the postcolonial period, the peasants revolted against the existing exploitative system. The so-called Sepoy Mutiny of 1857, the Moplah rebellion of 1836 and 1896, and the Santhal and Munda revolts of the 1890s were the major peasant movements in the colonial era. At the end of the colonial rule, two major peasant movements emerged—Tebhaga movement in Bengal in 1946–47 and the Telengana uprising in Andhra in 1946–48. There were also a large number of minor peasant revolts reported during the colonial period (Viswanath 1990: 118). Kathleen Gough discovered 77 major and minor peasant revolts during the colonial rule (Gough 1974).

The Congress linked some localised peasant movements like the Bardoli Satyagraha in 1928 and the non-rent campaign with the broad national movement for independence (Low 1977). However, the Congress never encouraged any movement that sharpened the conflict between the landlords and tenants (Pandey 1977). The role of the Kisan Sabha was noticeable in organising various agrarian movements, especially in Uttar Pradesh, Bengal, Bihar and Punjab during the 1920s (Rasul 1974). The role of the leftist parties in organising various movements in the society was also decisive. Movements like the Telengana uprising (Ram 1973), the Tebhaga movement (Bandyopadhyaya 2001), the Naxalite movement

(Mukherji 1987), the land grab movements of the 1960s and the agricultural labours movements in Kerala since 1940s were remarkable.

The movements by the tribals added new dimensions to the existing struggles. While the peasant movements remained purely agrarian as peasants lived off land, the tribal movements were both agrarian and forest-based. There was also the ethnic factor; the tribal revolts were directed against zamindars, moneylenders and petty government officials not because they exploited them but also because they were aliens. During the 19th century, the British had come into conflict with various tribes in different parts of the country when they annexed tribal kingdoms and imposed British administrative system in those areas. The identity crisis led to revolts against the existing colonial domination and in the postcolonial period, the statist interferences in the name of development and nation-building brought about the same situation and their struggles got intensified.

Like the tribal movements, the Dalit movements in India also emerged in response to the socio-economic–cultural differences existing within the system. Leaders like Jyotirao Phule represented a very different outlook on India—different from all the upper caste elite thinkers of the so-called Indian renaissance. The elite expressed an ideology of 'national revolution.' It was the nationalism of a class combining bourgeois and high caste traditions. Phule represented the ideology of the social revolution with a peasant and anti-caste outlook (Omvedt 1971). In states like Kerala, there were many movements against social discrimination and exploitation. Organisations like Sree Narayana Darma Paripalana Yogam, Kerala Pulayar Maha Sabha; upper class organisations like Nair Service Society and Namboodiri Kshema Sabha; and various Christian and Muslim organisations were instrumental in the emergence of modern Kerala.

Most of the reform movements in the 19th century were basically socio–religious. B. R. Ambedkar's perceptions were a turning point in the history of assertion of the deprived sections. A leader of the Mahar community and the inspiring source of Dalit assertion in India pointed out that political means are the best way to raise status and effect improvements than employing religiously-oriented methods (Larbeer 2003; Zelliot 2001: 11). Indeed, the assertions of the deprived sections in the society were mainly aimed to get a space in the mainstream civil domain, that is, shifting from a feudalistic exploitative system towards a society based on social equality and justice. This perception was based on the principles of Western modernity and the deprived sections on the whole anticipated emancipation through modernity. The influence of the Western missionaries is noted here. On one hand, the movements were against the existing hierarchically ordered Hindu social system and on the other hand, they supported the dominant national movement. The mainstream nationalist movement was aimed to establish a modern version of an independent nation-state and civil society. These movements had progressed simultaneously. However, many extremist religious movements also progressed along with this.

During the colonial as well as the postcolonial period, the Congress used secularism as an ideology in order to accommodate different sections of the populations. However, the Congress was not a complete success in accommodating the diverse sections. The nationalist movement, in fact, progressed along the majoritarian lines also which brought forth many contradictions, exclusions and insecurity complexes in the society. In spite of its secular character, most of its leaders also used majoritarian norms and symbols for mobilising the mass. Mahatma Gandhi is an example. Gandhi used the Hindu tradition against the colonialists but he was not against any other religion. The Congress, while sustaining secular lines, urged for reconstructing the tradition-bound Indian society along the line of Western modernity. In order to attain that type of 'security community' India had to be liberated from the British rule. However, Gandhi's position was one of challenging the leaders like Nehru. He had clear-cut differences on matters of tradition, development, social mobility, etc. In fact, the religious premise of Gandhi's thinking and the use of religious norms for mobilisation had become inaccessible to certain sections in the minority communities in India. Jinnah and his Muslim League viewed Gandhi's method as 'Hinduisation' of the nationalist movement. Nehru and other secular leaders also felt uncomfortable with Gandhi's method. The Urdu–Hindi controversy in 1872 in the central provinces (King 1994) and the Cow Protection Movement by Dayananda Saraswati were issues that alarmed the Muslims. During the nationalist struggle, these problems became acute. Sajal Nag observed that

> the Muslim politicians feared that Hindu majoritarians which would emerge
> from the introduction of elections would further curb what many felt was an

essential part of their religion. The growing assertion of the Hindus as the dominant community through various symbolic agitations also provoked a kind of insularity as well as stubborn collective self-assertion from the Muslim. (Nag 1999: 87)

The minority assertions, especially from the Muslim community, were not a reflection of the will of the whole Muslim population in India; rather they reflected the interests of an elite class within the Muslim community. The Muslim elites, especially the north-Indian landed elite, had always been preoccupied with the defence of its sectional interests (Ahamad 1997: 21). In fact, before 1940s, there was no indication of a separate nation for Muslims, neither from the League nor from any significant number of individuals from that community. Jinnah's presidential address to the Muslim League became a turning point. He viewed that Islam and Hinduism were two nationalities and because of this reason, India was always divided into 'Hindu' and 'Muslim' segments (Hasan 1997: 60). The events since 1940 eventually made the partition inevitable. However, the partition riots further led to polarisations in society. Using this, the Hindu Rightist forces in India also began to take advantage.

Indian Capitalist Class and Anti-colonial Struggle

The nature of Indian State and its path of development are critical factors in understanding the potential and limitations of the role of civil society. The development of capitalism in India is therefore a major factor. As mentioned earlier, colonialism and the advent of European capital was a crucial factor in the development of capitalism in India (Buchanan 1934; Pavlov 1999; Shah 1990). In the course of colonialist expansion, an economic condition was created to facilitate the formation of capitalist relations in India on a massive scale (Pavlov 1999). This was of considerable importance for the development of Indian capitalism. Initially, the British policies tended to impede the expansion of Indian domestic market that led to the underdevelopment of productive forces, and the capitalist classes in the country (Bagchi 1991: 8–9). The crisis of the British empire following the outbreak of World War I and the growth of Indian nationalism in India provided new opportunities. The colonial administration was forced to change its policy and granted a measure of financial autonomy to India to protect some existing Indian industries against foreign competition (Bagchi 1982: 91–93). The colonisers were thus ready to build railways and establish a few industries. They also initiated commercialisation of certain agricultural products in their own interest. However, the limitations of the colonial office to control all activities pertaining to trade and other business compelled them to create a subservient class of bureaucrats and other officials in India who would serve them effectively.

Meanwhile, a few Indians had already made use of the business opportunities thrown open to them and began their career as traders. The Indian traders could not totally ignore their Indian identity. Alongside the British trade associations, many Indian trade associations were formed in the 19th century itself. The Indian businessmen, however, did not confine themselves to mere trade and commerce. They gradually began to engage themselves in the industrial field. To further their interests, they even organised themselves into associations such as the Bombay Mill Owners' Association (1875) and the Ahmedabad Mill Owners' Association (1891). The economic nationalism that shook the country during the early nationalist phase gave an impetus to many nationalist-minded Indians to start their own industries (Srikanth 1994: 338–39).

The withdrawal of the British East India Company from commercial activity in 1833 had already prompted the native businessmen to organise an institution, which would represent their business interest to the government. In 1833, the Calcutta Chamber of Commerce and in 1836, the Bombay and Madras Chamber of Commerce were formed. Nationalist leaders like M. G. Ranade took initiatives to organise the industrial association of Western India. Since 1905, the Congress started conducting Indian Industrial Conferences along with its annual sessions. R. C. Dutt, Madan Mohan Malaviya, Lajpat Rai and others were the eminent nationalists who associated with the conferences. The efforts culminated in the formation of the Indian Federation of Indian Chamber of Commerce in 1927. It was later changed to Federation of Indian Chambers of Commerce and Industry (FICCI). It was recognised by the British government. The leaders of the Indian national movement were aware of the importance of the emerging capitalist class and also the leaders of this class had shown greater interest in political affairs (Mukherjee 2002: 34–39).

The position of the Indian capitalists was strategic. Aditya Mukherjee notes the following:

> The Indian capitalist class's strategy vis-à-vis imperialism was certainly one which remained within the bourgeois framework but was not at any point anti-national i.e., seeking and supporting social, economic and political concessions or reforms, wrested from or offered by the colonial government, or its preference for legal and constitutional opposition as against revolutionary, extra-legal opposition cannot be understood per se as its surrendering to imperialism. If it supported the colonial government on certain specific issues, this was in the nature of a *tactical support to reforms within the system while maintaining a strategic opposition to the system as a whole.* (Mukherjee 2002: 51)

It may be noted that after World War I, significant changes were underway in the Indian economy that enabled the Indian capitalist class to grow and establish a considerably large independent economic base for capitalist accumulation (Mukherjee and Mukherjee 1990: 78). Despite several setbacks, especially during the period of the Great Depression, the Indian entrepreneurs made considerable progress. They established many factories in different parts of the country. Their progress can be seen from the fact that the number of Indian group companies had increased during the period from 172 to 366 (Markovitz 1985). The growing need of industrial finance and the indifferent attitude of the British government compelled Indians to start their own banks and insurance companies. The Indian industrial capitalist class had its "gestation in a laboratory of economic change, peculiar to itself, imposed by the colonial power." Its emergence followed "complex interactions between the colonial power and the trading, landed and usurious components of the propertied classes that attained an established status" during the period (Satyamurthy 1994: 134).

However, the Indian capitalists had already become well aware of the importance of protective development of Indian capital under the shield of the State. The dependence on the foreign capital was the net result of the lack of basic industries, and the newly emerged class urged for a State-supported development. The aspiration for self-development had prompted the capitalists to actively support setting up a national State. However, without having support from the feudal elements in the society, a successful struggle against the colonialists was not possible. The nexus between the emerging bourgeoisie and the nationalists determined the future course of India's development. It may be noted that earlier, the Indian capitalist class did not take keen interest in the nationalist struggle started by the nationalist intelligentsia. Once the capitalist class strengthened its position, it began to play an active role in the freedom struggle and by the mid-1930s, it became the most influential class on the anti-imperialist front. The capitalist class could easily exercise its influence on the Indian National Congress and became a decisive factor at the time of the transfer of power. The Indian business groups drew closer to the Indian National Congress, which was emerging as a mass movement aimed at putting an end to the British rule. For its part, the Congress was committed to a policy of rapid industrialisation, which it believed would benefit the capitalist class too (Nehru 1993: 403).

The capitalist class in India had clearly recognised a critical role of the postcolonial State in India for capitalist development. During the early 1930s and 1940s, a strategy of economic development was evolved within the Indian National Congress, which envisaged planned development as a critical factor. Even in the 1930s, the Economic Affairs Committee of the Congress had admitted the possibility that the State might not be in a position to own all the crucial means of production. The perspective of the Indian business class in respect of a planned economy on the lines proposed by the Congress was reflected in the speech of A. R. Dalal, the President of the Indian Chamber of Commerce in 1939. He said that the steps taken by the Congress in establishing a planning committee to survey and prepare the ground for the formation of an all-India scheme for India's economic regeneration was a move in the right direction (Ray 1979: 333). During this time, the leading Indian industrialists expected that the economic policy of the Congress would enable them to break out of the constraints imposed by the imperial framework of the economy.

In 1944, the leading men of Indian business and industry met in Bombay and proposed what was known as the 'Bombay Plan' for the development of India. The Plan clearly recognised the necessity of active participation of the State in promoting industry. State ownership and State management of key sectors were accepted by them. The State intervention was welcomed as it would not bring about any radical changes in the relations of production (Thakurdas et al. 1944). Regarding the Bombay

Plan, Jawaharlal Nehru wrote that "revolutionary changes" were inherent in it and that it was "a welcome and encouraging sign of the way India must go." The Plan was "based on a free India and on the political and economic unity of India" (Nehru 1993: 501). The post-independence political economy of India obviously reflected this thinking.

The Nature of the Indian State and Development Paradigm

The Indian State was however not a mere product of capitalism. Unlike in the West, the emerging State undertook the task of social transformation (Kaviraj 1997: 73), in accordance with the provisions of the newly enacted Constitution. The fundamental nature of class configuration in the Indian society forced the State to follow a well-balanced strategy in its dealings with the socio-economic power centres. The State facilitated the capitalist development on one hand, and to a greater extent preserved the pre-capitalist forces, on the other. This 'passive revolution' was the net result of the varied alliances made by the nationalists with the bourgeoisie and other dominant as well as subordinate classes, in their struggle against the colonial rule. This strategy was aimed to contain the class conflict (Chatterjee 2000: 130–34). However, in this transformative process, the State 'slowed down' the social and land reforms (Palshikar 2004: 148–49). Under the provisions of the Indian Constitution, the land reforms and agricultural policies were assigned to the states, while the central government's power was assigned to the rural sector (Hassan 2000: 17). In this scenario of power sharing, the central government gradually withdrew from the task of social transformation and focused on the strengthening of the national bourgeoisie. The post-independent State followed the proposals of the 'Bombay Plan', which demanded replacing of the foreign capital to national bourgeoisie (Patnaik 2000: 142). This new institutional and policy change integrated the bourgeoisie as a national class, and provided sufficient space for the autonomous development of capitalism with State patronage. At the same time, the national State allowed the pre-capitalist forces to sustain their autonomous existence without much alteration.

The political economy of the Indian State, as it has historically evolved, was an important factor in determining the economic and trade policies of post-independence governments. However, scholars still differed on questions concerning the nature of State and its development dynamics. The debate on the mode of production in India, initiated later, had thrown open many critical questions about the nature of Indian State and its developmental path (Patnaik 1990; Chattopadhyay 1972). Pranab Bardhan argued that the industrial bourgeoisie was the 'dominant propri- etary class' and the 'principal beneficiary' of State policies in India. This class supported the government policy of encouraging import-substituting industrialisation, quantitative trade restrictions providing automatically protected domestic markets and of running a large public sector provid- ing capital goods, intermediate products and infrastructural facilities for private industry (Bardhan 1998: 40–41). Budhadev Bhattacharya asserted that the transfer of political power was from the imperialist rulers to the newly constituted ruling party representing the interests of the Indian capitalist class which marked the beginning of the domination of the Indian bourgeoisie over the politico-economic structure in the country (Bhattacharya 1990: 141). Describing the "autonomy of the Indian State" as a "striking and unique fact," Achin Vanaik argued that there was no major capitalist country in the Third World, which had a more powerful State than India's or an indigenous bourgeoisie with more autonomy from foreign capital (Vanaik 1990: 15).

According to Bardhan, in the first decades after 1947

> the state elite in India enjoyed enormous prestige and sufficiently unified sense of ideological purpose about the desirability of using state inter- vention to promote national economic development—it redirected and restructured economy, and in the process exerted pressures on proprietary classes. However, over the years, the autonomous behaviour of the State was reflected more often in its regulatory rather than its developmental role. (Bardhan 1998: 38–39)

At the time of independence, the basic infrastructure necessary for development was very weak. The private sector did not have the ability to undertake any large-scale industrialisation on its own, particularly in the basic industries. The Indian capitalist class did not have adequate finance, technology and expertise to establish large-scale industries, which needed long gestation periods. This class was thus well aware of its limitations. As discussed earlier, even before independence, the Indian capitalist class provided general guidelines for planned economic development to be implemented after independence. Both the National Planning Committee set up by the Indian National Congress and the Bombay Plan prepared by the leading Indian industrialists underlined the need for active participation of the State in promoting Indian industry (Nehru 1983a: 111, 114). The extent to which the State could play a dominant role in the process of development depended upon the constellation of class forces in the post-independence period. The main issue was whether the apparatus of State power should be directed towards building an indigenous capitalist class (Sobhan 1984: 247). However, the State became the principal instrument to mobilise domestic resources, foreign aid and loans, and to provide the necessary guarantee to foreign capital, to retain their investments and make new investments in the domestic economy. This reflected the Keynesian approach to the role of the State in the capitalist development (Keynes 1957).

The notion of Welfare State was thus put in place to legitimise the capitalist path of development. The successive governments in India acclaimed the concept of mixed economy in high terms. Commenting on the subject, Jawaharlal Nehru said that those countries which did not want either of the two (capitalist or socialist) extremes "must find a middle way." In that middle way, there was bound to be more emphasis on some factors than on others but obviously a middle way or a mixed economy was inevitable. He said that the private sector in India did not have the strength or capacity to undertake large-scale industrialisation and hence, "the State inevitably has to take them up" (Nehru 1983b: 45–48). Reflecting the Keynesian approach to capitalist development strategy, Nehru said, "Every modern economic theory today bases itself, unlike the previous ones, on full employment in the country. We cannot produce employment by legislation. Our economic approach must be such that we can reach a stage of full employment within a measurable period of time" (Nehru 1983c: 63).

The role of the State was further underlined in India's Industrial Policy Resolutions of 1948 and 1956 by which the State was expected to intervene in areas where, for various reasons, the private sector could not carry out the task alone (Thakur 1994: 135). However, these resolutions were not opposed to tolerating foreign capital as a means of importing industrial technique and technical knowledge. Within two decades of independence, private foreign capital had come to play a considerable part in the organised sector of the Indian economy. The foreign exchange crisis in the second half of the 1950s further forced the government to change its attitude towards foreign capital. Planning was also envisaged on the assumption that foreign capital would enable the economy to circumvent the problems posed by foreign trade and would lift the economy from low growth rate equilibrium. The attitude towards foreign capital thus became one of enthusiastic welcome (Nehru 1983c: 83). The annual session of the FICCI held in March 1959 also called for substantial foreign investment, which represented an important point of departure for remoulding of India's economic policy (Thakur 1994: 134).

Notwithstanding the strategies employed to sustain the interest of both domestic and foreign capital, India's industrial growth, on the whole, was losing momentum in the 1960s with better performing industrial sectors showing signs of decline. By 1967, the growth of all kinds of industries slowed down and this continued for almost a decade (Swamy 1994: 94–95). The agriculture sector also experienced serious problems, which ultimately resulted in the launching of the Green Revolution that facilitated the penetration of foreign capital in different areas. But the Green Revolution too failed to resolve the contradiction in the Indian agriculture sector (Sharma 2003: 77–102).

Meanwhile, it was argued that the monopoly nature of Indian capitalism led to inefficiency in production. The concentration and centralisation of wealth and means of production increased during the successive plan periods. The policy of import substitution industrialisation amounted to a policy of protecting inefficient and monopolist producers. This was the time when Indian monopoly bourgeoisie began to collaborate with multinational corporations for technology and capital and also to get an edge in the internal and external markets. The intra-capitalist conflicts and differences would soon begin to surface in the aftermath of the crises of the 1960s, of which the India–China war in 1962, the India–Pakistan war in 1965, and the agricultural crisis occasioned by the severe drought of 1965–1967 were the most far-reaching and serious. The impacts of the military and agricultural crises were further compounded by the industrial crisis, though it was clearly more than a mere industrial crisis. This was the retrogression in the rate of growth of the Indian economy, which began from the mid-1960s and reached alarming proportions by the early 1970s (Baru 1983: 39; Patnaik 1981; Patnaik and Rao 1977). Bardhan explained the crisis in terms of the State's inability to reconcile the conflicting objectives of the proprietary classes. He argued that the role of the State had been to mediate between the dominant proprietary classes by evolving a system of subsidies to adjust and accommodate the conflicting pressures of big industrialists, rich farmers and the professionals in the public sector. According to Bardhan, a combination of stagnant aggregate surplus and the growing concessions extracted by the proprietary classes caused the decline of public investment, which adversely affected industrial growth. The bloated bureaucracy intensified this crisis (Bardhan 1998).

Another analysis of the developments over the 1965–74 period depicted the Indian economy as one exhibiting semi-feudal relations of exploitation over a large area and dominated by dependent bureaucratic capital. It said that capital accumulation was constrained by feudal as well as foreign pressures. The State attempted to overcome these constraints within the framework of monopoly capitalism and activated new forces of production. In the process, the prevailing balance of economic forces was drastically altered (KB 1985). Dilip S. Swamy, however, contended that this view underestimated the role of external constraints. According to him, during the mid-1960s, the external constraints in the form of trade and credit became binding and that continued unabated for the next two decades until the economy was completely liberated from State regulations (Swamy 1994: 119).

Thus, the trends in the Indian economy clearly suggested that the slowdown in industrial growth during 1965–75 was mainly due to the slackening of public investment at a time when the demand generated by import substitution under sheltered market was tapering off. The poor performance of agriculture and unchanged income distribution constrained the growth of the home market throughout the period. These constraints and the exhaustion of import substitution possibilities were the necessary conditions for industrial stagnation. The slowdown of public investment proved to be the decisive one. The industrial class, nevertheless, failed to acquire prime quality capital and an autonomous capacity for self-expansion even after 15 years of growth. It continued to be dependent on the State as also on foreign capital and technology for further expansion. Its bureaucratic character and dependence on the State did not change much (Srinivasan and Narayanan 1977).

The 1969 split in the Congress party and the anti-monopoly legislation and bank nationalisation, which followed, were seen by some observers as representing a shift in the balance of power from the monopoly bourgeoisie to smaller capitalists. Addressing the Indian Merchants Chamber in Bombay on 25 October 1969, Prime Minister Indira Gandhi said:

> Exercising a countervailing influence against the concentration of economic power, Government had to step in, whether it is nationalization of banks or the monopolies legislation, which is now on the anvil. All these should be viewed against the realities of our economy in which there is no effective force, except the state, which could mitigate the possible abuses of the concentration of economic power. (India, MIB 1983d: 258)

However, the pressures resulting from the oil crisis of 1973–74 set the background for economic liberalisation in India. When the government decided to borrow from the IMF to cover the external deficit, the IMF seized the opportunity to ensure a decisive change in India's economic policies. The Planning Commission had also adopted a pragmatic approach towards licensing and controls. By 1974, the policy constraints were no longer there. Prime Minister Indira Gandhi was able to enlist mass support and the reins of power had also been tightened. It was an opportune moment for taking the IMF loan, which became the catalyst for resolving the prolonged economic crisis (Swami 1994: 146–47). Thus, by the mid-1970s, the policy of import substitution was relegated to the background and the emphasis shifted to import-led export or export-led growth. Meanwhile, the development of monopoly capitalism created many contradictions in the Indian society. Contradictions between different sections of the dominant classes, and most strikingly between the urban bourgeoisie as a whole and the class of capitalist farmers in the process of formation of certain regions, were becoming increasingly sharp. This intensified the exploitation of the direct producers. In rural areas, the process of capitalist transformation resulted in increased landlessness and often worsened conditions for agricultural labour (Mitra 1977).

The declaration of Emergency in 1975 marked a new phase in the transformation of the Indian State. It served to conceal the contradictions between different sections of the Indian society. The Indira Gandhi government unleashed repression and violence, even disregarding the constitutional obligations. Under the Emergency, the Indian government hoped to activate forces that would break the deadlock between the belligerent proprietary classes and stimulate growth. It wanted the bureaucracy to work efficiently, workers to increase production, state governments to carry out land reforms, etc. Bardhan said that as tensions and frustrations with the old patronage system built up, the legitimacy of the political machine declined, the hegemonic hold of the dominant proprietary classes over the subordinate classes started slipping away even while their economic grip remained strong and some partners in the dominant coalition started looking for more centralised forms of arbitration. Bardhan pointed out that Indira Gandhi was too eager to provide a leadership in this centralised arbitration process. A. G. Frank noted that the institutionalisation of economic, political and military repression under Indira Gandhi's Emergency rule was designed to further favour Indian and foreign monopoly capital without solving the country's structural problems (Frank 1985: 27). Measures introduced during this time such as tax reductions and liberalisation of trade policies were most encouraging for profitable business, both Indian and foreign. The import policy for 1976–77 carried the country towards another giant step in the free market direction and away from planning, as with the industrial licensing it was difficult to say what remained of import control (RBI 1976: 198–201). According to Rajni Kothari

> on the policy front there emerged a highly sophisticated package. In the mid-seventies the World Bank announced the strategy of 'direct attack on poverty' (which neatly coincided with India's call of *garibi hatao*).This gave the bank and foreign aid a strategic role in national development. (Kothari 1990: 119)

During the period of Janata rule (1977–79), economic stagnation was apparently over and public investment in key sectors pushed many industries up and out of stagnation. This was aided by the strict regulation of industrial relations and good harvest during this period. Dilip Swamy noted that the government tried to reorient the economy by allocating more resources to agriculture and rural development and by assigning a special place to small-scale industries (Swami 1994: 171–72). But, according to A. G. Frank, this change was "more rhetorical than real" and the temporary economic fortunes of this period would not alter anything fundamental in India's structural economic crisis (Frank 1985: 37). Nonetheless, the big businesses, whose position had improved considerably during the emergency, began to denounce the Janata policies as amounting to deindustrialisation of the country. When it became unresponsive in terms of new investment, the government attempted to offer concessions but that did not yield desired results (Nayar 1989: 343). However, the Janata government collapsed due to its own internal contradictions and, as Dilip Swamy noted, the coalition–which accorded increasing power to the rich farmers–appeared "incongruent with the relative economic position of the underlying class forces" (Swamy 1994: 172).

The 1980s witnessed major decisions, which greatly changed the political economy of the Indian State, reoriented industrial production, altered class alignments and prepared the ground for a far-reaching transition. The major features of the new policy regime that took shape in the 1980s were deregulation of industries, decontrol of prices, liberalisation of imports, tax reductions, downsizing of welfare funds and increase in deficit spending. These trends, which emerged immediately after the 1974 low conditionality IMF loan, got crystallised into a coherent package in the early 1980s when India had gone in for another IMF loan. This was followed by various initiatives to further liberalise the economy in accordance with the recommendations of various official committees. Throughout the 1980s, the Indian economy experienced a deepening integration with world economy and foreign capital and ever since it became susceptible to international economic fluctuations over which it could exercise no control whatsoever (Bhagwati 1993; Patnaik 1994b: 683–90; 1994a; Sachs et al. 1993).

The Civil Society in Postcolonial India

It is imperative to understand the Indian experiences with liberal democracy before analysing the nature and dynamics of the civil society. The sources of much of the ambiguities and uncertainties surrounding the conceptualisation of civil society and its practices in contemporary India lie with the problem of the construction of Indian modernity (Mohanty 2006).

When India became independent, there already existed a well-developed and relatively mature civil society, which was anti-colonial in nature, but also elitist in character—comprising of mostly Western-educated leaders (Adlakha 2001: 177). In fact, these were the people who led the phase of nation-building process in independent India. The nationalist elite maintained that the objectives of building a modern and prosperous nation guided by the principles of secularism, central planning, and democratic socialism could only be attained under the guidance of a strong democratic State that would be an exemplar and social arbiter, and would play a key role in maintaining political stability and spearheading the nation's strategy of self-reliant economic development.

However, it became quite clear soon that although the nationalist leaders sought to trigger a social change for the better through constitutional democracy, their efforts did not bring forth positive results altogether (Mohanty 2006). Commenting on this social dilemma, Sudipta Kaviraj pointed out that leaders like Nehru expected that the "ordinary Indians would acquire a democratic consciousness, which would ultimately cease to identify themselves through traditional caste categories and demand greater economic equality. Democratic institutions would thus lead, in the long term, to modernist movements for reduction of poverty" (Kaviraj 2003: 158). Kaviraj also delineated how the Nehruvian State was not only negligent about the cultural reproduction of the nation but it performed miserably by failing to create conditions for common sense in Indian politics. What happened in the political history of India was not the melting away of tradition under the powerful light of modernist enlightenment. Those institutions of modernity, like the State, which had to be accepted as part of the modern condition, have been dealt with through a traditionally intelligible grid of social identity and action. The constitutional system in India, therefore, was consistent with the internal principles of liberal constitutionalism, but inconsistent with the self-understanding of social groups. The national State simply assumed that citizens would act as liberal individuals, but failed to set in motion a cultural process, which could provide the great masses of people the means of acquiring such self-understanding (Kaviraj 1995: 311).

Meghnad Desai argued that the Nehru government did not take any meaningful steps to abolish the caste system with its inegalitarian logic of hierarchy and status; rather the society was allowed to reform itself in a rather laissez-faire way, which he called 'social conservatism' (Desai 2005). In the economic sphere, the State-led policies ultimately led to a slow growth output and employment and persistence of poverty and inequality through the first phase of 30 years. With the slow growth of jobs in the private sector, government jobs at all levels became much sought after and democratic electoral system was harnessed to provide this kind of patronage. How this patronage was garnered through the then-existing political–organisational strategy was explained by Myron Weiner. He said that at this point in time, 'party building' involved nothing more than adapting to local power structures. The Congress relied primarily on the support and cooperation of the local landowning interests—in particular, the village landlords and the rich and upper strata of the middle peasantry, to organise the party cadres and mobilise grassroot support for the party. According to Weiner, in its effort to win, the Congress adapted to the local power structure. It recruited from among those who had local power and influence. The result was a political system with considerable tension between a government concerned with modernising the society and economy and a party seeking to adapt itself to the local environment to win elections (Weiner 1967: 15). When these relations of dependence grew stronger, the wider district, state and national party organisations came increasingly to represent a complex pyramid of hierarchical alliances between the dominant rural interests and the Congress party. In effect, from very early on, the party structure, process and policy came to represent the dominant landowning class and castes. Such a political–organisational strategy not only precluded a challenge to the normative and institutional foundations of the traditional social, economic and political hierarchies, but also undermined the pressures from below that could have effectively challenged the hegemony of the powerful groups and classes dominating the Congress system (Mohanty 2006; Sharma 2003: 67).

Moreover, this so-called 'Congress System' not only absorbed the State into its fold of strategic functioning, but also made the State act as the 'Political Leader of Ruling Classes'. The State created the conditions of the reproduction of the ruling classes. First, its law and coercive organisational apparatus ensured the protection of the propertied classes against possible attack by the exploited masses. Second, its fiscal policies fulfilled the material interests of the ruling class fractions such as the big bourgeoisie, regional bourgeoisie landlords and the rich peasantry. Its political programme established their coalition in order to effectively negotiate with struggles by subaltern masses. Third, its dominant ideology engendered the formation of the nation, civil society and 'modern' economic classes by restructuring pre-capitalist social institutions such as caste, tribe, nationality and patriarchy. In these three important realms, the State performed the decisive role—that explains why it must be characterised as the political leader of ruling classes (Mohanty 2006; Patnaik 1990: 29).

This interaction between social conservatism and economic radicalism in the context of political democracy led to non-elite groups getting organised and they did this through their caste or regional identities. Linguistic states had to be created during the 1950s in response to popular pressure from the local capitalists as well as local middle classes who wanted public jobs and public contracts. Next came the 1960s, and the pressure from the rural areas to divert resources to agriculture; this led to the launching of Green Revolution with input subsidies as well as price guarantees for outputs. But even then the discontent due to slow growth rate continued. This broke into floods of protest from tribal, Dalit and lower caste groups in the 1970s, and were brought together under the Lokyan banner (Mohanty 2006; Desai 2005:100).

This was the backdrop which fostered a sense of urgency within all 'dispossessed' (Dalits and other marginalised sections) to launch various modes of dissent from all fronts against the various governmental distributive agencies of 'scarce resources' (Mohanty 2006). During such precarious socio-political situations, "social blocs may form, each with its own panoply of associations, to battle for the control of the State" (as it was the case during the assertion of Naxalite movement); political forces may forge powerful ties with community organizations and civil associations, polarizing society and at times threatening the 'order' that incumbents so cherish (as the Jayaprakash Narayan-led 'Total Revolution' formed ties with students organisation to fight corruption" (Foley and Edwards 1996: 46; Mohanty 2006).

While the protests addressed material needs, they soon became attached to several larger ideological movements, which challenged the Congress-led government. The threat became so potent that Prime Minister Indira Gandhi in June 1975 declared the country to be in a state of Emergency, which remained until the elections in 1977. The experience of Emergency thus, in fact, broke the complacency of the people who took democracy and its benevolence for granted. More than common people, it was a setback to the educated middle class, who realised overnight that the State could also take their rights away. Eventually, the people restored democracy by bringing into power the Janata Party in 1977. The Emergency and the restoration of democracy not only redefined and extended the boundaries of civil society by redefining the relationship of citizens with the State, it also restructured civil society in a significant way, and made it more alert to the transgression of its boundary hereafter by the State. Understandably, the most important consequence of the Emergency for civil society was the question concerning the collapse of State institutions and their inability to protect the rights of the citizens. The civil rights movement had until then remained confined to piecemeal addressing of issues such as the suppression of Naxalites. The Emergency galvanised the movement, as democracy, citizenship and constitutional protection of fundamental rights overnight became important issues for public debate. The People's Union for Civil Liberties (PUCL) and People's Union for Democratic Rights (PUDR) were the two leading organisations formed in reaction to this in the post-Emergency phase (Desai 1986: 91–102).

While the Emergency meant a breach with the Indian democratic practice, and a severe curtailment of civil and political rights (Rudolph and Rudolph 1987: 6–7), it also had a revitalising effect on civil society, which after 1977 witnessed an increase of activities within traditional social movements such as peasants, workers and students, but also amongst the NSMs, including environmental groups and women's organisations (Omvedt 1994; Parajuli 1991; Shah 1990). Mobilising new political identities, these groups challenged the State on local, regional and national levels, as these NGOs were often based in strong grassroots networks. The emphasis on environmentalism and gender issues was also a global phenomenon of this period. The oppression of the State certainly provoked social and political forces to organise against oppression. The image of a democratic and progressive State was also seriously dented. As a consequence, new groups understood the necessity to actively claim their rights and to fight against perceived injustices. State developmentalism as a project was questioned, and from the 1980s onward, the Indian State itself encouraged NGOs to take more responsibility for social development. The number of NGOs in India was growing all the time (Baviskar 2001). The neoliberal reforms of the IMF and the World Bank, which have had such drastic global consequences in the Third World, affected India also where the partial withdrawal of the State resulted in a more active civil society.

It is apparent that the partial failure of the State to address social and economic needs has had effects not only on the levels of development, but also on the quality and character of civil society. In some sense, this failure has spurred groups and individuals to engage in civil society; but the inability to provide basic education and other forms of social services has seriously hampered the development of civil society with low levels of literacy being a case in point. As a consequence, the Indian State and various aid agencies have utilised the competence and infrastructure of civil society in order to encourage social development. NGOs such as women's organisations have been incorporated in the governmental development plans. But this form of cooptation as well as the general trend of State withdrawal also had important consequences for future plans of social development.

While the State is increasingly seen as inefficient and corrupt, the NGOs are defined as committed and accountable. Leaving the negative description of the State aside, the positive image of civil society rests more on an ideological and theoretical definition rather than an accurate appraisal of civil society in India today. Due to the inherent social, religious, ethnic and economic cleavages of Indian society, the civil society is permeated by inequality and various forms of conflict, as noted in the current Indian debate (Mahajan 1999; Saberwal 2001). The expectations of efficiency, commitment and accountability of civil society should be seen in this light also, as various forms of inequality are likely to influence civil society. A more realistic view would be to define Indian civil society as a public arena in which various interests meet and compete, battling against the State, but also against other groups within civil society. This arena would be affected also by the power relations in society at large, reproducing various cleavages and inequalities.

Social Exclusion and Mobilisations

The relative failure of the Indian State created feelings of exclusion amongst large segments of the population, and there were allegations that the State is not neutral, but biased on the basis of class and caste interests (Berglund 2009). These alleged biases, in turn, created sentiments of apathy and also facilitated negative mobilisation and manipulation of various primordial identities such as ethnicity, religion and caste. This segmentation of Indian society has had ambiguous consequences and led to demands and actions that have seriously undermined the democratic system by strengthening exclusivist identities. These are based on religion, caste or ethnicity and are now at the centre of political mobilisation, which involves political parties as well as other parts of Indian civil society. Amir Ali suggests that the colonial experience included the development of a public sphere, but that the private sphere was left not to the individual citizens, but to the native elites. According to Ali, this resulted in the cementing of the community-based identities after independence also, which obstructed democratisation of Indian society, with the current Hindu nationalist challenge as a case in point (Ali 2001). The success of this movement is most evident within party politics, where the main Hindu nationalist party, the BJP, in the 1980s and 1990s developed from a marginal party to be the dominant force of Indian politics. The ideology of the party is a form of cultural nationalism based on the idea of Hindu supremacy and a rejection of the multiculturalism of the Indian nation.

For any long-term analysis of the impact of this Hindu nationalist challenge, it is, however, necessary to include its work within civil society, where it has been continuously working for a redefinition of the established Indian democracy. The movement used civil society to strengthen the Hindu identity and to weaken the position of the minorities, undermining the secular Indian democracy. It is in many senses a struggle of ideology and meaning, reminiscent of the Gramscian definition of the continuous battles in civil society where the outcome cannot be explained solely by class interest and economic power. The Hindu nationalist challenge was also met with resistance from other sectors of civil society, in an attempt to defend the established forms of democracy and minority rights (Berglund 2009). The case of the Hindu nationalist expansion is one example of how the concept of civil society can be applied, without accepting the liberal civil society theory (ibid.). The importance of the sphere 'civil society' is recognised but defined more along the confrontational and ideological lines.

According to Javeed Alam, India has been witnessing "the unhealthy sight of a civil society fighting for self-maximization, which marked absence of inter-community exertions for common good" (Alam 2004: 129). The colonial and postcolonial political practices crystallised the communities and today they act as power blocs in the competitive power politics. Alam notes that

> there was a breakdown of the internal harmony of Indian society. The happy coexistence of numerous small communities, each living with minimal interaction but cordial understandings could no more be taken for granted. Nor was it replaced with competitive coexistence. Rather the breakdown of the old had happened without the emergence and availability of any clear mediating principles. An advantage of one community was more often viewed as the disadvantage of the other. Conflicts between communities become the normal pattern in which first the colonial administration and then the Indian state became the arbiter. (ibid.: 78–79)

The struggle for scarce resources thus reduced the possibility of inter-subjective interactions. The communalising of the civil domain naturally became a major challenge to democratic norms and practices. According to Mustapha Kamal Pasha, religious resurgence is "an inversion of modernisation, from previously state-directed social engineering to a project of social transformation that takes civil society as the instrument and site to reshape political society." He says that the rise of the middle classes and the consolidation of mass media are two major factors linking religious resurgence to civil society. These must be situated within the context of growing cultural divisions and declining State capacity, which bestow civil society a new status (Pasha 2004: 136–37). However, this new status needs to be critically analysed given the nature of representation, articulation and mobilisation that threaten the very social fabric of a country like India. The case of the Hindu Right assertion in the 1980s and 1990s and all its attendant problems are placed for critical scrutiny in the following chapters.

3

The Hindu Right:
History, Ideology and Strategy

The evolution and consolidation of the Hindu Right in India has been a theme of serious academic debates and discussions since 1980s. The ideology and strategy of Hindutva also came in for extensive analysis. The emergence of the Hindu Right in the 1980s and 1990s, however, needs to be understood within a broad framework of the trajectory of Hindutva—starting from the early part of the 20th century, or even earlier in the late 19th century. Significantly, a major running theme of the evolution and consolidation of the Hindutva has been 'how to secure' the Hindu identity and the 'self' against the perceived threats from 'others'. Plausibly, all ideologues of the Hindutva as well as the organisational programmes of the Sangh Parivar underlined the importance of this 'self/other' dichotomy. This is crucially significant in articulating a political doctrine with 'difference' in order to mobilise people and set a track for, eventually, capturing power. This chapter mainly examines the manner in which the Hindu Right organisations tried to articulate Hindutva within a frame of both realist as well as constructivist points of view of 'security/insecurity' through the realm of civil society. It also outlines the nature and functioning of some of the major Sangh Parivar organisations such as the Hindu Mahasabha, Rashtriya Swayamsevak Sangh (RSS), Vishwa Hindu Parishad (VHP) and Jana Sangh.

Locating Hindutva: Tracing the Genealogy

The emergence of the Hindu Right and its implications for India is often understood as a relatively recent phenomenon, starting from the 1980s—perhaps with the decline of 'Congress System'. But while some scholars would argue that the phenomenon in question—Hindutva— could be traced back to the decade of 1920s (Anderson and Danle 1987; Graham 1990; Hansen 1999; Jaffrelot 1996), others would locate the rise of religious politics as a part of modern nationalist identities that were emerging in India in the 19th century (Chatterjee 1993; Lal 1995; Nandy 1983; Raychaudhuri 1995; van der Veer 1994). Scholars of the Euro-American origin, including Lochtefeld (1996), Smith (1989), van der Veer (1994), Daniel Gold (1991), Stanley Wolpert (1993) and Juergensmeyer (1996) and others have dealt with the issue in a variety of ways. However, in India, the debate surrounding the concept of Hindutva was basically a debate over the viability of cultural nationalism. Juergensmeyer (1996: 129) here poses a set of questions: How do we respond to this emergence of religious politics in India? Is it a relatively 'benign' force or a 'demonic' one? Does it have legitimate roots in Indian tradition or is it a 'virus' imported from some sort of worldwide fundamentalist plague? Is it a symptom of social and economic problems or is it purely a religious aberration? Is it a cynical use of religion by politicians or a corruption of politics by religious activists? Juergensmeyer offers an interesting stock-taking of the existing literature on Hindutva in the journal *Religion* (1996), which also carried several related themes.

The debate over Hindutva is itself historically and socially located. Indian scholars often emphasise issues specific to the Indian subcontinent and their own colonial past, whereas non-Indians tend to look at global issues, especially those similar or related to Euro-American concerns. Within the Indian perspective, there is a split between the secularist and non-secularist camps, and within the Euro-American point of view, there are differences between classic liberal and relativist positions (Juergensmeyer 1996). Another question that has given rise to debate is whether the current form of Hindutva in India is native to Indian tradition or an import from outside. Curiously, few scholars seem willing to accept it as indigenously Indian. Those who have held to the notion of a worldwide fundamentalist uprising have seen it as an Indian infection of a near-global plague. But Indian scholars who oppose this view and insist on explaining the rise of religious politics from within an Indian frame of reference also see it as essentially an alien phenomenon (Anderson and Danle 1987; Chatterjee 1993; Graham 1990; Hansen 1999; Jaffrelot 1996;

Lal 1995; Nandy 1983; Raychaudhuri 1995). Raychaudhuri, for instance, has presented an explanation for India's religious revivalism that is at once external and distinctively Indian: the experience of colonialism. In his analysis, the current Hindutva politics of BJP is an extension of what used to be called communalism—the rivalry between Hindu and Muslim communities. And he has asserted what is commonly accepted in Indian academic circles, that communalism was created by the British colonial policy of divide and rule. Even today's communal hatreds, Raychaudhuri averred, are part of India's "damned inheritance"—the "end product" of the "historical contingencies of the colonial era" (Raychaudhuri 1995).

Lal agrees with Raychaudhuri's assessment of the effects of British policy, but stopped short of labelling the current religious politics in India as a product of colonialist-induced communalism. Rather, Lal castigated those who analyse Hindutva and BJP movements as communalist, claiming it is their analysis as much as the movements themselves that have perpetuated a colonialist mentality. In this regard, he shares the perspective of Partha Chatterjee and Ashis Nandy who have also been concerned with how ways of thinking about contemporary politics in India constitute. Chatterjee has called it 'a derivative discourse'—and Nandy has called it an extension of colonialist 'consciousness' and 'psychology' (Chatterjee 1993; Lal 1995; Nandy 1983). Both regarded the recovery of precolonial cultural roots as the unfinished business of the nationalist movement and both longed for a culture-based sense of national identity that is unifying rather than divisive. In that sense they, like Raychaudhuri, have seen the extreme religious movements in contemporary India as perpetuating the colonialist attitude of communalism.

Peter van der Veer, while agreeing with Chatterjee and Nandy, in general, about the effect of British colonial policies, questioned two assumptions of Nandy and other Indian scholars regarding communalism: that there was a unified and syncretic cultural base preceding (or underlying) communal identities, and that current communal hostilities are the direct result of colonial rule. van der Veer called the 'syncretism' thesis, a trope in the discourse of 'multiculturalism' and claimed there was no reason to argue that India lost its tolerance as the result of the colonial construction of communalism. Instead, van der Veer located the rise of religious politics as a part of modern nationalist identities that were emerging in India in the 19th century at about the same time they were emerging in

Europe and other parts of the world. They were parallel histories, albeit interactive ones, and van der Veer asserted that the peculiarities of Indian society and history were indeed peculiarly its own. India's forms of religious nationalism, therefore, could not easily be "reduced to the master narrative of European modernity" (van der Veer 1994).

There are similar contending positions on the nature and dynamics of the phenomenon of Hindutva. Sumit Sarkar viewed Hindutva as 'traditional' and 'religious' (S. Sarkar 1993). By contesting his arguments, Raghuramraju saw it as a 'modern phenomenon' (Raghuramraju 2006: 66–91). However, when political Hinduism is examined in its present variety, one has to look at the movement in its totality. It seems to be very important to look at the transformation that took place in the Hindu society towards more ritualistic patterns of life and how Hindutva has been appropriating these changes in spite of its 'commitment' to the Vedic tradition, which prohibits superstitious rituals. The attempts to invent a unity in spite of rich diversity are the peculiar features of Hindutva. This has been ensured through various organisational networks.

By coming to terms with Western modernity, Hindutva wholeheartedly accepted Western science and technology, its political institutions, military power and, most importantly, their model of nation-state. This constitutes the basic premise of Raghuramaraju's argument that Hindutva is a 'modern phenomenon'. Though at the institutional level it is 'modern', it tends to disrupt the path of development of a modern-secular democracy. Hindutva has been deployed by the Sangh Parivar to crystallise the pluralist Hindu identity in their attempt to formulate a Hindu nation. And, in this process many 'others' are constructed both within and outside the nation. This provides little room for dialogue between the 'self' and the 'non-self' because enmity/threat/insecurity are all essential pre-requisites for Hindutva.

The lineage of Hindutva can be traced back to the period in the 19th century, in the writings and activities of Dayananda Saraswati, Swami Vivekananda, Sri Aurobindo, V. D. Savarkar, M. S. Golwalkar and others. Two streams of thought can be located here, according to Jyotirmaya Sharma—the 'soft version' of Hindutva and the 'hardcore version' (Sharma 2003). Raghuramraju, however, expresses his concern over Sharma's attempts to link Hindutva with the prominent personalities of the 19th-century Indian thought. He viewed that this might provide a fertile ground for Hindutva to appropriate those figures and would theoretically weaken the position of those who oppose Hindutva (Raghuramraju 2006: 87–88). This argument is based upon the premise that Hindutva starts with Savarkar. It is true that the concept of Hindutva was first coined by Savarkar and that he remained its prime ideologue. But it is always contestable whether the very notion of Hindutva was a spontaneous one. Historically, it was the culmination of the process of communal mobilisation in the 19th-century British India. The 19th-century Indian thought itself was a response to the logo-centric view of the Indologists who tend to see India as a "dark, static and superstitious" social formation. Thinkers like Vivekananda and Dayananda Saraswati defended themselves by re-invoking the Indian tradition by which they illustrated an Indian past characterised by its rational order and vehemently criticised the present Indian society for obscuring this 'glorious past' with the present 'superstitious' belief system. Thinkers like Vivekananda were strong supporters of humanism.

Richard G. Fox viewed that communalism is "the hyper enchantment of religion." In his own words, it "is a local instance of how modernity— once it has disenchanted the pre-modern world—built new forms of identity." Given the new means of communication and transportation that travelled along with modernity, these emergent enchanted identities were much more powerful and much more extensive (or 'massive') and therefore potentially much more destructive and violent (Fox 2005: 239). It contradicts with modernity's basic values and functioning within its frame. The British introduced an 'institutional modernity' and legitimated their regime in the colony by comparing the past with the present. Peter van der Veer puts it, "In the eyes of Orientalists, the civilizations of the East were great in the past but are decadent at present" (van der Veer 1996: 56–57). These Orientalist perceptions and criticisms very much influenced the formation of new enchanted identities.

During the 19th century, a new middle class emerged in India. They initiated religious reform movements across the country. As far as the Hindu society was concerned, they found that lack of unity was the root cause of its vulnerability. Comments from Indologists and unequal colonial practices prompted them to rethink about a version of 'modernity' which must have had 'indigenous' (Hindu Brahminical) roots. This amalgamation of the 'tradition' with the 'modern' practices was the core of the Hindu religious movements led by Dayananda Saraswati, Swami Vivekananda and others. Raja Ram Mohan Roy's 'Brahma Samaj' was the first attempt to purify Hinduism and make it competent with monotheistic religions like Christianity and Islam. For instance, Roy questioned idol worship in Hinduism. Like Ram Mohan Roy, Dayananda Saraswati strongly underlined the importance of Hindu unity. They found that the only panacea was the revival of the 'Vedic rituals and institutions' (Majumdar 1981: 110).

Dayananda believed that

> Hinduism in its Vedic formulation possessed the light of truth. The puranas and the rise of a whole constellation of sects had eclipsed that essential truth. For India to regain its glory, it was essential to clear the fog created by the Vama Margis, the Shaivites, the Vaishnavites and several other sects and restore the pristine light of truth that emanated from the Vedas. (Sharma 2003: 14)

He tried to demystify popular Hinduism and restore the Vedic religion. The popular myths and legends were to be discarded, and instead of worshiping idols the Hindus should have worshiped heroes and brave men (ibid.: 33). So what was needed was unity in worship. He also put forward the notion of 'Brahma'. According to Lala Lajpat Rai, Brahman

> may not be god, but he is at all events god like, a subject not only of veneration but of actual worship ... the first great criterion by which a Hindu is determined is that every Hindu must acknowledge the Brahman's superiority and his omnipotence in spiritual and social matters. (Lajpat Rai 1991: 67–68)

Shashi Ahluwalia sums up Dayananda's vision of India as "purged of her superstitions filled with the fruits of science, worshiping one god, fitted for self-rule, having a place in the sisterhood of nations and restored to her ancient glory" (Ahluwalia 1987: 221). It seems to be the inception of the idea of an anticipating 'Hindu nation', which would retain its past glory.

The 'cow protection movement' led by the Arya Samaj and the Sanatana Dharma Sabha were attempts to establish an ideological hegemony among the pluralist Hindu folk. In Hinduism, cow is portrayed as the mother goddess. The Brahminical notion of cow is that a human being from his cradle to grave depends on the cow, just like a child depends on his/her mother. Symbols like 'Kamadhenu' (fulfils every wish of the human being) and 'Lakshmi' (good fortune) are attached to the cow. The ritual of 'Parikrama', 'circumambulation' of cow clockwise and respectfully touching its four feet with one's forehead has great importance in the Brahminical belief system. Milk products are regarded as vegetarian food and labelled as '*Sattvik* food' (pure). The combination of milk, curd, butter, urine and dung (panchagavya, five products from cow) forms an inevitable part of the Brahminical rituals. The mythical life of Lord Krishna, especially his childhood days and his life with Yeshoda (Krishna's mother), and the role of the cow in their relations has great influence in the Indian society (van der Veer 1996: 87–89). Along with the portrayal of the cow as the all-giving mother goddess there is another image of goddess, the image of dangerous Durga on her tiger. When the order of Hindu society was threatened, the goddess assumed her aggressive character. And also Shiva, symbolised by the bull, which produces an image of the independent, self-sufficient male, was always set free by its owners (ibid.: 89–90). Peter Van der Veer observes that

> it is a crucial image, since as a mother the cow signifies the family and the community at large. She depends on the authority at large. She depends on the authority and protection of the male of the family. While mother cow refers to patriarchal authority and to the Hindu state, the rightful kingdom of Rama (ramarajya). It is within the logic of religious discourse that the protection of the cow becomes the foremost symbol of the Hindu-nation state. (ibid.: 90)

The most observable fact in this analysis is the selection of symbols for mobilisation. The symbols have a common appeal among the people, those who are aimed to be mobilised. The symbol has also wide acceptability beyond the cultural divisions. In the present context, Hindutva is also applying the same technique.

In 1882, Dayananda founded the first Gaurakshini Sabha (cow protection organisation) in Punjab. It grew up in many urban centres, in small towns and '*qasbas*' (market centres). The urban and rural centres were linked by the organisational networks of stump orators, especially sadhus. They used to collect money and '*Chutki*' (usually handful of rice) for the establishment of cow shelters. Cow thus became a symbol of unification. But the meaning behind the shared symbol varied from people to people. This ambiguous symbolic representation was the strength of the movement. It enabled them to mobilise the local structures towards ideological pathways. Thus, it had the ability to link the local identities with the broader ideology, which distinguished the cow protection movement from other localised collective action of the period. In the meetings led by the orators, printed posters were distributed, which used to tell stories of the importance of protecting cow. In some areas, Sabha targeted Muslims and in some other areas they targeted the untouchables and the lower caste people (Freitag 2005: 215–16).

In 1888, the High Court of the North Western Provinces decreed that cow was "not a sacred object." This boosted up the cow protection movement. There were many attempts to prevent the Muslims from sacrificing cows on festivals such as Eid. It was argued that the State's hesitation to protect cows had legitimated individuals to take initiatives (ibid.). This movement sought to portray the Hindus as distancing themselves from the colonialists as well as from the Muslims (ibid.: 219) van der Veer observes the following:

> The movement created a rift not only between Hindus and the British but also between Hindus and the Muslims since the latter acted as butchers and also used the cow as a sacrificial victim in their celebration of Bakr-Id, a festival commemorating Abraham's offering of Ishmach. (van der Veer 1996: 86)

Freitag viewed that the cow protection movement was not nationalist but had an impact on the development of nationalism (Freitag 2005: 219–20). He said that its impact was on the nature of the mental and social space carved out for the emerging civil society, on nationalism and the competing community identities that emerged in the early 20th century helped to shape a very differently configured civil society (ibid.: 220).

Indeed, an identity was woven with the logic of 'self/other'. In this sense, the cow protection movement was an attempt to crystallise the Hindu religious identity on a nationalist scale. This resembled more with 'political' than with the 'religious'. This had produced a dichotomy of 'inside–outside' in which the British, Muslims and the Christians were viewed as the 'outsiders' and glorified a native Hindu religious body, which was 'pure' and had originated from the Vedas. Those 'others' were 'polluted'. This was an inception of the religious nationalism in India. The mainstream nationalism that became widespread in the first quarter of the 20th century was more inclusive, especially under the leadership of Mahatma Gandhi. Yet, the religious nationalism had some impact on the mainstream nationalist movement though it was overshadowed by the Gandhian mobilisation tactics which aimed to include broad sections of the masses. However, the militant Hindu nationalism progressed in parallel with the mainstream nationalism and the former, in turn, twisted itself towards a more political one, Hindutva, over years.

Apart from Dayananda Saraswati who propounded a Hindu nationalist revival, Swami Vivekananda was also influenced by the gaze of the Orientalists. But, unlike Dayananda, his attitude towards other religions was ambiguous though he was not antagonistic to them. For example

> Dayananda modelled Christ in the image of the missionaries. Swami Vivekananda had, at least made a distinction between the spirit of Christ and the practice of Christianity as an organised faith. Not so with Dayananda. Christianity was condemned to falsehood because it had not partaken of the light of the Vedas. (Sharma 2003: 38–39)

Vivekananda equated the West with material prosperity and the East with spiritual superiority. His reading of the Indian society was based on the glorification of India's spiritual tradition, especially the 'Advaita Vedanta'. He criticised the Hindu society because of its weak, superstitious and corrupt nature of the priesthood. He recommended that the Hindu race to be dehypnotised with the Advaita. Vivekananda also emphasised the importance of adoption of Western material civilisation by India in its positive terms. And also, the "Occident should learn the lessons of spiritual life" from India. This must be on an equal footing (Raghuramraju: 2006: 40–45). Vivekananda's Chicago Speech was an astonishing representation of this 'politics'. Jyotirmaya Sharma viewed, "In a masterful way, Vivekananda addressed these major concerns of nineteenth century India: Hindu identity, Hindu nationalism and an equal 'dialogue' between Hinduism and other faiths" (Sharma 2003: 76).

On 11 September 1893, Vivekananda delivered his first speech in Chicago. Here he emphasised the high value of 'Hindu tolerance'. He said:

I am proud to belong to a religion which has taught the world both toler-ance and universal acceptance. We believe not only in universal toleration, but we accept all religions as true. I am proud to belong to a nation which has sheltered the persecuted and the refugees of all religions and all nations of the earth.

I am proud to tell you that we have gathered in our bosom the purest remnant of the Israelites, who came to Southern India and took refuge with us in the very year in which their holy temple was shattered to pieces by Roman tyranny. I am proud to belong to the religion which has shel-tered and is still fostering the remnant of the grand Zoroastrian nation. (Vivekananda 2007: 135–37)

Jyotirmaya Sharma asserts that by saying that tolerance is the core value of Hinduism, Vivekananda became the 'prisoner of history'. He had to illustrate that Hinduism had never persecuted. The Hindu violence against the Buddhists was concealed in his statement (Sharma 2003: 84). However, Vivekananda was much more concerned about the Hindu iden-tity because of large-scale conversions and the criticisms from Christian missionaries. He rejected the triumph of any religion with the destruction of the rest. He said:

the seed is put in the ground, and earth and air and water are placed around it. Does the seed become the earth, or the air, or the water? No. It becomes a plant, it develops after the law of its own growth, assimilates the air, the earth and the water, converts them into plant substance, and grows into a plant. Similar is the case with religion. The Christian is not to become a Hindu or a Buddhist, nor a Hindu or Buddhist to become a Christian. But each must assimilate the spirit of the others and yet reserve his individuality and grow according to his own law of growth. (Vivekananda 2007: 137)

The forces of Hindutva appropriated Vivekananda's ideas because of their high assertive potential and also because he was more or less acceptable to everyone. It may be noted that a peculiar feature of Vivekananda's version of nationalism was the celebration of the Hindu spirituality and, in a pragmatic sense, accepting the inevitability of the Western material science for the development of the Indian society. Inculcating spiritual-ity by dismantling the material prosperity or well-being of the people would not make a nation strong, he believed. However, Vivekananda totally discarded the Western political models. Following Vivekananda, Sri Aurobindo also vigorously attacked the very notion of modern state. He viewed that the law of life was diversity not uniformity (Dalton 1982: 180). For Aurobindo, nationalism was a religion, "the passionate aspiration of the religion of the divine unity in the nation" (Aurobindo 1965: 15). Aurobindo viewed that

> Indians were weak and unmanly and therefore required the 'Kshatriya' impulse; they had grown feeble and had to appropriate the 'shakti' of science; to win the 'shakti 'of science they had to re-Aryanise themselves. Re-Aryanising, among other things, meant a rediscovery of Occidental impulses already present in the Indian blood. (Sharma 2003: 59)

His vision of nationalism was the rebirth of the 'Kshatriya' in India. Sharma linked Hindutva with Aurobindo's notion of 'Kshatriyahood'. In his own words

> Aurobindo's contribution to the rise of political Hindutva is second to none. His notion of Kshatriyahood has slided into 'asuratva', his ideals of Sanatana dharma and re-Aryanisation have been turned in to political slogans. Religion, indeed, has become politics, perhaps the only politics we know today. (ibid.: 69)

Bankim Chandra Chattopadhyay, a Bengali novelist and literary theorist had a greater influence on the Hindutva mobilisation. Tanika Sarkar divided Bankim's literary career into two phases. Until the end of 1870, he had given greater importance to the oppression based on caste, class and gender in precolonial India. In the second phase, especially in the last five years of his literary career, Bankim composed three historic novels on Hindu–Muslim antagonism—*Anandamath, Devi Chaudhurani* and *Sitaram*, and also had written two polemical essays *Dharmatattva* and *Krishna Charitra* (T. Sarkar 2005: 162–3). Tanika Sarkar identified the components of Hindu revivalism in this later stage of Bankim's literary career. He viewed it as a link between two transitory periods—one, the 19th-century Hindu revivalism in Bengal, which was not primarily against the Muslim, the other, the assertion of the aggressive Hindutva in the 1920s—which was implicitly anti-Muslim (ibid: 164).

Sumit Sarkar viewed two historic transitions in the genealogy of Hindu communalism

> the first is a transition from a relatively inchoate Hindu world, without firmly defined boundaries, to the late-nineteenth-century construction of ideologies of unified Hinduism, in the context of integrative colonial communication, administrative and economic structures. The second transition, roughly datable to the mid-1920s, is a move in some quarters toward an aggressive Hindutva postulated usually upon an enemy image of a similarly conceived Islam. (S. Sarkar 2005: 273)

The first period was characterised by its religiosity, defensive discourse and less militancy. The second period beginning with 1920 was notable in its politically oriented nationalist aspirations, less religious, more offensive and militant. Bankim's famous hymn "Bande Mataram" is an example of the construction of a new militant Hindu patriotism. He had composed this song in 1875 and later inserted it in *Anandamath*, his influential novel. The hymn became popular in the nationalist struggle and later in communal riots (T. Sarkar: 172–73). The song portrays two images of the mother goddess, Durga, the demon-slaying goddess and Kali, symbol of destruction and revenge (ibid.: 173). The nationalists used the image of Durga against the exploitative regime of the colonialists and the song as an 'abbreviated history' of colonial rule in India and the parallel patriotic struggle for liberation. The RSS employed the image and the song for representing the so-called 'historical' struggle against Muslims. The image of an 'other' was clearly set by the political Hindutva of the 20th century. According to Tanika Sarkar, "Bankim made a distinction between the historical experience of the Muslim rule" and "Islam as an organised religion and Muslim as a personality type." In Bankim's view, the Muslim rule did not bring either material or "spiritual improvement" to India. But the Hindus had much to learn from Islam as an organised religion and also from the Muslims' "supposedly violent commitment to his religion and his desire for power..." Tanika Sarkar quotes Bankim's words, "By imbibing these principles ... the Hindus will be ... as powerful as the Arabs in the days of Mohammad" (ibid.: 177). Those who aspired to reform the Hindu society during the late 19th century were very much influenced by the power of the Semitic religions, especially Islam. They had equated the Hindu plurality with backwardness and the unity of worship with strength.

Savarkar and Hindutva: Ideological Culmination

The Hindu religious revivalism of the 19th century had culminated into an extreme Hindutva posture in the 1920s. V. D. Savarkar was the prime ideologue of this version of politics. Hindutva emerged as a political phenomenon and it had very little to do with the religious practice of the Hindus. Savarkar described that he had coined the word 'Hindudom' when he offered the definition of the word Hindu. Hinduism was concerned with the religious system of the Hindus, their theology and dogma. But this was a matter left entirely to an individual or group conscience and faith (Savarkar 1984: 10). Thus, it seems that he was recognising the plurality of the Hindu religion at one point and, at the same time, trying to invent uniformity by incorporating the Western political model into a rigid cultural frame.

Savarkar distinguished 'Hinduism' from 'Hindutva'. Hindutva was, according to him, not a mere term but a history. He coined the word Hindutva to denote the political history of the Hindu people. Hinduism was only one aspect of Hindutva (ibid.: 11). Hinduism was a derivative of an alien growth. Hindutva, in sharp contrast, was a composite term that embraced "all departments of thought and activity of the whole being of our Hindu race." Here, Savarkar was trying to wrap Hindus with the notion of a 'nation', which he extended to the days of Lord Rama (the central figure of the Indian epic Ramayana). In his *Hindutva: Who is a Hindu*, first published in 1923, Savarkar argued that "we must move away from the label 'Hinduism' and exchange it for the label Hindutva." According to him, "we should not allow ourselves to be confused by this newfangled term." Besides, the term Hinduism was associated only with religious dogma; thus it excluded other religions of the land of *Saptasindhu*, that is, Buddhism, Jainism and Sikhism.

According to Savarkar, the notion of Hindutva adequately addresses three of the main problems with the term 'Hinduism'. First, Hindutva underlines a sacred geography.

The first image that it rouses in the mind is unmistakably of our motherland and by an express appeal to its geographical and physical features it vivifies it into a living Being. Hindustan means the land of Hindus, the first essential of Hindutva must necessarily be this geographic one. (Savarkar 1989)

This sense of motherland is fervently portrayed. Unless one "has come to look upon our land not only as the land of his love but even of his worship, he cannot be incorporated into the Hindu fold."

Second, Hindutva unites all those of the motherland by a common blood. Savarkar puts this categorically when he said that

> the Hindus are not merely the citizens of the Indian state because they are unified not only by the bonds of love they bear to a common motherland, but also by the bonds of a common blood. They are not only a Nation but also a race-jati. The word jati, derived from the root Jan to produce, means a brotherhood, a race determined by a common origin - possessing a common blood. All Hindus claim to have in their veins, the blood of the mighty race incorporated with and descended from the Vedic fathers, the Sindhus. (Savarkar 1989)

Third, Hindutva asserts that as a result of this biological community, all Hindus (must) share a common culture, "the brave and loving defense of the Hindu culture have been incorporated with and bound to us by the dearest of ties—the ties of common blood."

In a longer passage Savarkar expressed this third essential characteristic of Hindutva clearly.

> [W]e Hindus are bound together not only by the ties of love we bear to a common fatherland and by the common blood that courses through our veins and keeps our hearts throbbing and our affections warm, but also by the ties of common homage we pay to our great civilization our Hindu culture, which could not be better rendered than by the word Sanskriti, suggestive as it is of that language Sanskrit, which has been the chosen means of expression and preservation of that culture of all that was best and worth-preserving in the history of our race. We are one because we are a nation, a race and own a common Sanskriti (civilization). (ibid.)

By using the word Hindutva as distinct from Hinduism, as well as exhibiting it as the "triumphant history of a nation," Savarkar tried to respond to the two main comments from the Indologists that Indians had 'no sense of history' and that 'India could never be a nation'. Apparently, the attempts to historicise India's past and reconstruct a new vision of a glorious ancient civilisation was the net result of the overwhelming influence of the Western Enlightenment (Jaffrelot 1993: 517–24). In the aspiration to catch up with the modern West, Savarkar envisaged a 'Hindurashtra' (Hindu nation-State), which seemed to be exclusionary.

In the beginning of *Hindutva: Who is a Hindu*, Savarkar defines a Hindu as a

> ... person who regards this land of BHARTVARSHA, from the Indus to the Seas as his Father-Land as well as his Holy-Land that is the cradle land of his religion. To the converted Christians and Muslims the Hindustan is the Fatherland as to any other Hindu. Yet it is not to them a 'Holy land' too. Their holy land is in Arabia or Palestine. Their mythology and Godmen, ideas and heroes are not the children of this soil. Their names and outlook smack of a foreign origin, so, their love is divided. (Savarkar 1989: 113)

Savarkar asserts

> ye, who by race, by blood, by culture, by nationality posses almost all the essentials of Hindutva and had been forcibly snatched out of our ancestral home by the hand of Violence – ye, have only to render whole-hearted love to our common mother and recognize her not only as Fatherland (*Pitribhu*) but even as a Holy and (*Punyabhu*); and ye would be most welcome to the Hindu fold. (ibid.: 115)

According to him, "Swarajya to the Hindu must mean only that 'Rajya' in which these 'Swatva', their 'Hindutva' can assert itself without being overloaded by any non-Hindu people, whether they be Indian territorial's or extraterritorial" (Savarkar 1984: 81). The Christians and Muslims are outside the boundaries of the 'Hindu nation'. Savarkar notes that the Western historians tainted the Indian history by obscuring the 'greatest resistance' by the Hindu kings against the alien powers. Elsewhere Savarkar describes the resistance of the Maratha kingdom. He equated it with the 'Hindu revival'. Savarkar asserts:

> Although the Hindu revival was ushered in with the rise of the Marathas, it had necessarily to assert itself first in the political and military spheres of Hindu life and create a powerful and national State, which must ever remain the sine qua non of a nation's progress in all other departments of life, yet it did not fail to manifest itself in these as soon as the categorical imperative of national political independence was achieved under the aegis of the Maratha Power. (Savarkar 1971: 225; 1942)

To Savarkar Indian "history is antagonistic." The Hindus and Muslims were "locked in a life and death battle for centuries." There were no possibilities of cooperation between the self and the non-self. The defining and distancing of the 'self' possibility led to the caricaturing of the non-self. As Jyotirmaya Sharma notes: "Desecration of Hindu temples, conversions by 'force or fraud', corrupting of Hindu girls and the overall destruction of Hinduism—these themes were to forever remain Savarkar's short—hand symbols for characterizing Islam" (Sharma 2003: 126–139). By perverting history for political purpose, Savarkar spread hatred and the spirit of revenge. To him the Gandhian notion of non-violence was 'non-self' like Islam (ibid.: 148–49).

In his critique of Mahatma Gandhi, Savarkar said, "Throughout the Palaeolithic and Neolithic periods, the Bronze Age and the Iron Age, man could maintain himself, multiply and master this earth chiefly through his armed strength. In all honesty, the defensive sword was the first saviour of man" (Savarkar 1998: 311). Thus by distancing the 'self' from the 'other' in a rigid frame, Savarkar was trying to militarise the 'Hindu nation' on a Spartan line. Savarkar was a practicing atheist (Chandra 1984: 60) and he had over emphasised the importance of the modern science. He was a fierce critique of the irrational religious practices of the Hindu society; and identified it as the major hurdle on the path of the material progress of the Hindus. At the same time, he underlined the importance of worshiping the achievements of the Hindu forefathers (Navalgundkar n.d.: 180–81). Savarkar also said that

> unity of the people, their modernization and their militarization are the fundamental dimensions of Hindu nationalism: Every nation should be equipped with updated arms and army so as to be ever prepared to face the danger of civil war within the country and aggression from without. (ibid.: 181)

The war-anticipating nation of Savarkar therefore, subjugated an individual to the level of the 'Spartan soldier'.

Regarding the nature of the Hindu nation, Savarkar said, "The Hindus, they being the people, whose past, present and future are most closely bound with the soil of Hindustan as *Pitribhu* (father-land), as *Punyabhu* (holy-land), they constitute the foundation, the bedrock, the reserved forces of the Indian state" (Savarkar 1989). Therefore, he argued that the

Hindus are a nation by themselves because of their religious, cultural, racial and historical affinities and geographical unity and these bind them together to form a homogenous nation (Savarkar 1940: 84). Savarkar sought to build a Hindu nation that would be founded on force, violence, threat of the 'other' and military might. He said, "our State must raise a mighty force exclusively constituted by Hindus alone, must open arms and ammunition factories exclusively manned by the Hindus alone and mobilise everything on a war scale" (Savarkar 1993a: 177). He asked the Hindus to elect only Hindus to represent them in the legislatures as they alone could, according to him, safeguard, defend and promote the interests of the Hindus (Savarkar 1967: 1). Hence he urged the Hindu Sanghatanists to capture political power wherever possible—in municipal boards, legislatures, provincial and central governments—and boycott the Indian National Congress (ibid.: 21–22) and vote only for confirmed Hindu nationalists (Savarkar 1940: 101–03).

But Savarkar knew that this would not happen as long as Gandhi, Nehru and other secular leaders were at the helm of affairs of the national movement. Nehru categorically said, "If you think in terms of any kind of a communal state, a Hindu Rashtra, etc., you are not going to get it, however much you may try" (*Selected Writings of Jawaharlal Nehru*, vol. 7: 404). This led Savarkar to assert that as

neither the Gandhistic ideology nor the pseudo-nationalistic ideology of the Congress can ever cope with this Islamic offensive and as the Hindu Sanghatanist ideology alone can and will be able to fight out this danger successfully, the Government should consist of such Ministers alone who are pledged to the Hindu Sanghatanist ideology alone. (Savarkar 1993a: 177)

Savarkar cherished a nationalism based on Hindu religion and Hindu culture. He said, "To us Hindus, Hindustan and India mean one and the same thing" (Savarkar 1940: 83). The resolution No. 13 passed by Hindu Mahasabha session held from 17 December 1936 to 7 January 1937 spoke of Savarkar as one who was engaged in the cause of Hinduism. It read:

It [Hindu Mahasabha] notes with gratefulness the splendid services which Savarkar has been rendering to the cause of Hinduism and urges the government to remove all restrictions imposed upon him at present so as to enable him to serve more fully and completely his religion, community and country. (File 50 Hindu Mahasabha Resolutions passed at the 18th session, held at Lahore, Kuruvachira 2006)

Savarkar accused Nehru saying that he had been indulging in furious denunciations against the demand for a Hindu nation as if the mere demand for a Hindu nation constituted a danger to his Government (Savarkar 1993a: 170). He said, "Pundit Nehru swaggers on that if the Hindu Sanghatanists persist on in their efforts to establish a Hindu Raj, they would meet with the fate of Hitler and Mussolini" (ibid.: 171). He questioned those who stood for a secular nation saying, "How is it then that the very mention of the name of Hindustan or the Hindu State alone takes your breath out as if you were smitten by a snake bite?" (ibid.: 172).

After he became the chief advocate of the Hindutva ideology, Savarkar gave hints on several occasions concerning the impossibility of a co-existence of Hindus and Muslims. He accused the Indian Muslims of being anti-Hindu, anti-Indian with extra-territorial allegiance (Savarkar 1940: 17, 23). According to him, the entire Muslim community in India is communal (ibid.: 76). In 1939, he said that nationality did not depend so much on a common geographical area as on unity of thought, religion, language and culture. For this reason, the Germans and the Jews could not be regarded as a nation. Later in the same year, he made a statement in the 21st session of the Hindu Mahasabha that the Indian Muslims were, on the whole, more inclined to identify themselves and their interests with Muslims outside India than Hindus who lived next door, like the Jews in Germany. He said, "I warn the Hindus that the Mohammedans are likely to prove dangerous to our Hindu Nation" (ibid.: 31).

Golwalkar and Hindu Rashtra: Aggressive Postures

Like Savarkar, M. S. Golwalkar, the second Sarsanghchalak (supreme chief) of the RSS, also used the same methodological and analytical tools to define the 'Hindu nation'. In an attempt to crystallise a militant Hindu identity, Golwalkar used his own version of 'culture', history' and 'nation' etc. for securitising the majority community, thereby making a sharp distinction between the Hindu civilisations and other cultures and religious systems.

In his *Bunch of Thoughts*, Golwalkar makes an attempt to distinguish the Hindus from others by saying that

> the origin of our people, the date from which we have been living here as a civilized entity, is unknown to the scholars of history. In a way, we are *'anadi'*, without a beginning. To define such a people is impossible, just as we cannot express or define reality because words come into existence after the reality. Similar is the case with the Hindu people. We existed when there was no necessity for any name. We were the good, the enlightened people - the rest of humanity were just bipeds and so no distinctive name was given to us. Sometimes, in trying to distinguish our people from others, we are called the enlightened – the Aryas – and the rest 'Mlecchas'. (Golwalkar 2000: 54–55)

Romila Thapar notes that around 800 BC, the word 'Mleccha' was used in Vedas to denote the people who were unable to speak Sanskrit properly. Later on, the word achieved a social meaning. It was coined to call the people who were living outside the illustrated 'Varna System' of the 'Dharmashastra'. It was a reference to the 'impurity' of the language and customs, used by the upper caste people to characterise a vast chunk of the population including the Muslims. (Thapar 2001: 47–48)

Like Savarkar, Golwalkar also territorialised the Hindu nation. He asserted:

> ... this entire stretch of land from the Himalayas in the north to the oceans in the south inclusive of the numerous major and minor islands alongside its coast, and known to all as Bharath constitute the geographical basis of our national life. (Golwalkar 1968: 6)

In an attempt to historicise the Hindu nation, back to thousands of years, he portrayed the history of the Indian Muslims and Christians as 'short' and called them as 'aggressors' because they came here to build their empire. So they were alien people, 'outsiders'. In his definition of the Hindu nation, Golwalkar viewed the 'Motherland' as 'Dharmabhoomi', 'Karmabhoomi' and 'Punyabhoomi' (Golwalkar 2000: 81–96). He symbolised the emotional attachment of a child towards its mother with the nationalist imaginations (Golwalkar 2008: 55–58). Golwalkar envisaged two types of devotion to the 'Motherland'. One is 'inactive devotion'—religious worshiping of the Motherland, and the other 'active devotion': cent per cent dedication to the protection of the Motherland. In this illustration, the Muslims and Christians were outside the boundaries of the nation who looked to some foreign land as their 'holy places'. Constructing the Hindu 'self' and the Muslim 'other', Golwalkar says:

> (Muslims) have also developed a feeling of identification with the enemies of this land. They call themselves 'Sheikhs' and 'Syeds'. Sheikhs and Syeds are certain clans in Arabia. How then did these people come to feel that they are their descendants? That is because they have cut off their ancestral national moorings of this land and mentally merged themselves with the aggressors. They still think that they have come here only to conquer and establish their kingdoms. So we see that it is not merely a case of change of faith, but a change even in national identity. What else is it, if not treason, to join the camp of the enemy leaving their mother-nation in the lurch? (Golwalkar 2000: 96)

Discouraging any division of devotion to the envisaged nation, he noted that

> for the progress of any country, nation, or society, what is needed foremost is to inculcate intense devotion in every individual towards his country, nation and society, towards its traditions, and an urge to work for its progress and readiness to dedicate everything for its sake without any reservations. (Kurushethra Prakashan 2008: 270)

Golwalkar insisted that other religions in India must subordinate themselves to the Hindu nation. According to him

> ... the foreign races in Hindustan must either adopt the Hindu culture and language, must learn to respect and hold in reverence Hindu religion, must entertain no idea but those of the glorification of the Hindu race and culture, i.e., of the Hindu nation and must lose their separate existence to merge in the Hindu race, or may stay in the country, wholly subordinated to the Hindu nation, claiming nothing, deserving no privileges, far less any preferential treatment not even citizens' rights. There is, at least should be, no other course for them to adopt. We are an old nation: let us deal, as old nations ought to deal, with the foreign races who have chosen to live in our country. (Golwalkar 1939: 47–48)

In Golwalkar's thinking there was no possibility for a composite culture (Golwalkar 2000: 59). Apparently, the mutual antagonism between the 'self' and the 'other' was the strength of the 'nation' propounded by Golwalkar. This antagonistic posture resulting from the process of homogenisation "make friends and enemies." The attempt to distance the 'non-self' was a way to protect 'the self' and make it strong. According to Golwalkar

> (Muslims) had come here as invaders. They were conceiving themselves as conquerors and rulers here for the last twelve hundred years. That complex was still in their mind. History has recorded that their antagonism was not merely political. Had it been so, they could have been won over in a very short time. But it was so deep-rooted that whatever we believed in, the Muslim was wholly hostile to it. If we worship in the temple, he would desecrate it. If we carry on bhajans and car festivals, that would irritate him. If we worship cow, he would like to eat it. If we glorify woman as a symbol of sacred motherhood, he would like to molest her. He was tooth and nail opposed to our way of life in all aspects—religious, cultural, social, etc. He had imbibed that hostility to the very core. His number also was not small. Next to the Hindu's, his was the largest. (Golwalkar 2000)

Golwalkar said that the "exhortation of the leaders" for the Hindu-Muslim unity was too hypocritical. "The Hindu was asked to ignore, even to submit meekly, to the vandalism and atrocities of the Muslims," he alleged. Golwalkar ridiculed that "self-forgetfulness was taught to the Hindus." The Hindus "were taught to forget their glorious history, to forget Rana Pratap, Shivaji, Guru Govind Singh and all such inspiring names and, if at all their memory did intrude, to call them 'misguided patriots'. In fact, history was 'invented' to suit their slogans of Hindu–Muslim unity" (ibid.).

Apparently "influenced by Hitler's ideology of racial purity, Golwalkar wrote in his *We, or Our Nationhood Defined*:

> German national pride has now become the topic of the day. To keep up the purity of the nation and its culture, Germany shocked the world by her purging the country of the Semitic races—the Jews. National pride at its highest has been manifested here. German has also shown how well-nigh impossible it is for races and cultures, having differences going to the root, to be assimilated into one united whole, a good lesson for us in Hindustan to learn and profit by. (Golwalkar 1939: 39)

Writing on the 'Fascism of the Sangh Parivar', Sumit Sarkar said that

> Muslim here becomes the nearest equivalent of the Jew—or the Black (more generally, immigrants felt to be inferior for one or another reason) in contemporary White racism. The Muslim in India, like the Jew in Nazi propaganda, is unduly privileged—a charge even more absurd here than it was in Germany.... (Sumit Sarkar 1993: 165)

However, Golwalkar continued to project the image of Muslims as a community enjoying undue privileges in the country in spite of their 'defiance' and 'rebellion'. This was given a high communal colour too. He says:

> In fact, all over the country wherever there is a masjid or a Muslim mohalla, the Muslims feel that it is their own independent territory. If there is a procession of Hindus with music and singing, they get enraged saying that their religious susceptibilities are wounded. If their religious feelings have become so sensitive as to be irritated by sweet music then why don't they shift their masjids to forests, pray there in silence? Why should they insist on planting a stone on the roadside, whitewash it, call it a prayer spot and then raise a hue and cry that their prayers are disturbed if music is played?....Even today, Muslims, whether in high position of the Government or outside, participate openly in rabidly anti-national conferences. Their speeches carry the ring of open defiance and rebellion. A Muslim Minister at the Center, speaking from the platform of one such conference, warned that unless the Muslim interest was well protected the story of Spain would be repeated here also, meaning thereby that they would rise in armed revolt. (Golwalkar 2000)

The nature of the 'Hindu State' Golwalkar conceptualised was not only of an authoritarian type, but it necessarily possessed aggressive characteristics in views of 'threats' and 'dangers of disruption'. Hence, he sought to "change the present ill-conceived federal structure (of India) to the only correct form of government, the unitary one." His notion of security was therefore increasingly associated with national defence and military capability. For instance, in the wake of the India–China war of 1962, Golwalkar said that the foreign aggression afforded (India) "a golden opportunity" ... "to purge itself of corroding tendencies like selfishness. ... and to recast itself into a single unified and purified entity." The "sense of imminent danger" led the individuals in the nation "to rise above all other petty feelings, to merge their interests in the supreme national good and stand as living limbs of a colossal national personality" (Golwalkar 2000: 313). When China conducted nuclear explosions in 1964, he said that

> the first and foremost sphere where we have to achieve self-dependence is defence. For this we must build up our own war-potential and free ourselves from dependence on foreign aid. The Government should appeal to all the industrialists, scientists and technicians and with their co-operation manufacture, at the earliest, weapons superior to those available to the enemies. The possession of atom bomb by Communist China has made it imperative for us to manufacture the same. That alone will ensure confidence in the minds of the people and the armed forces about our ability to achieve ultimate victory. (Golwalkar 2000)

Thus, by perpetuating and reinforcing an enemy image of the 'other', Golwalkar was trying to politicise and militarise the Hindu identity. However, the selfless devotion of the individual to the service of the society was the core of Hindutva that the Sangh organisations held fast. Here the individual has been subordinated to the nation, and the partaking of the individual with the Sangh (RSS) would bring forth national unity. The non-political character of the Sangh would curb the nation getting divided. In his talk with Saifudin Jeelany, Golwalkar said:

> Hitler's movement centred round politics. We tried to build life without being wedded to politics. It was found that many were gathered for political purpose. But when that purpose failed, unity was lost. We did not want any temporary achievement but an 'abiding oneness'. (ibid.: 519)

Rashtriya Swayamsevak Sangh: Nerves of Sangh Parivar

Among all the Sangh Parivar organisations working in the civil society, the RSS holds sway because it acts as "the main driving force of Hindu Rashtra" (Vanaik 1990). Though Savarkar was instrumental in bestowing Hindu nationalism with an ideology, he did not chalk out any a plan of action by which the Hindus could organise themselves. This mission was taken up by K. B. Hedgewar (1889–1940), who had come into contact with Savarkar in the mid-1920s and then founded the RSS in his home town, Nagpur in 1925 (Deshpande and Ramaswamy 1981; Jaffrelot 2007; Sangh Parivar 2010a). The RSS—which emerged as the largest Hindu organisation in a few years' time—sought to propagate the Hindutva ideology as well as "to infuse new physical strength into the majority community" (Jaffrelot 2007: 16). Since its establishment in 1925, the RSS has been active throughout India and abroad as the Hindu Swayamsevak Sangh (RSS, *Annual Report* 2010b; Sangh Parivar 2010). It is the chief motivator and the core organisation of the Sangh family. The strength of the RSS lies in its ability to develop close bonds among its members and to sustain these links when members join the various RSS affiliate groups (Anderson and Danle 1987; Curran 1951). Each and every organisation of the Sangh Parivar has been inspired by the RSS, which provides an ideological base for their actions (Advani 1990a: 9). The Sangh consists of BJP (its predecessor, Bhartiya Jana Sangha or BJS), Akhil Bharatiya Vidyarthi Parishad (ABVP), Bharatiya Mazdoor Sangh (BMS), VHP, Seva Bharati and Kalyan Ashram. The RSS has also strong influence on various Hindu scholastic centres across the country. The Vivekananda Kendra based in Kanyakumari is an example. In many ways, the RSS has been trying to penetrate into the civil society and maintaining an ideological hegemony through its regular programmes and activities (RSS, *Annual Report* 2010b).

Though RSS became a powerful Hindu movement, it could not have much impact on public life in India as it remained out of politics for long. M. S. Golwalkar, who became the *Sarsanghchalak* (head) in 1940 had made "apoliticism a rule." Savarkar, who revitalised the Hindu Mahasabha after his release from prison in 1937, sought the support of Golwalkar—when the Hindu Mahasabha left the Indian National Congress and became a full-fledged party—but in vain (Anderson and Danle 1987; Jaffrelot 2007).

The general philosophical outlook of the RSS, as it proclaimed, is cultural nationalism manifesting through "integral humanism, aimed at preserving the spiritual and moral traditions of India." The aim of the organisation is, "serving the nation and its people in the form of God—Bharata Mata (Mother India) and protecting the interests of the Hindus in India" (Sangh Parivar 2010). The RSS has been engaged in numerous social service, charity and relief works, as well as actively participated in the political process after 1948. It is well-organised and has a hierarchical structure with the *Sarsanghchalak* being the highest rank. The RSS was banned in India thrice during periods in which the government of the time considered them a threat to the State: in 1948 after Mahatma Gandhi's assassination, during the Emergency in India (1975–1977), and after the 1992 Babri Masjid demolition. The bans were subsequently lifted (Sangh Parivar 2010). RSS's entry into politics, way back in the late 1940s and early 1950s was the result of the negotiations held by a section of its leaders who were favourably inclined towards involving in politics. Though initially reluctant, Golwalkar let them to discuss the issue with Shyama Prasad Mookerjee, who had been President of the Hindu Mahasabha. These negotiations eventually led to the creation of the BJS (the forerunner of BJP) in 1951, on the eve of the first general elections (Anderson and Danle 1987; Jaffrelot 2007).

Over the years, the RSS developed a systematic framework and a very specific modus operandi. Hedgewar called for efforts to work at the grassroots in order to reform Hindu society from below: he set up *shakhas* (local branches) of the movement in towns and villages according to a specified pattern. Young Hindu men were expected to assemble every morning and every evening on a playground for games with martial connotations and ideological training sessions. Golwalkar illustrates below how *shakhas* work every day.

> An open playground. A saffron flag is fluttering in the centre. Groups of youths and boys are absorbed in a variety of Bharatiya games. Resounding shouts of joyous enthusiasm often fill the air. The sight of the daring young men pressing forward with the cry of 'Kabaddi' 'Kabaddi' on their lips thrills the heart. The chief's whistle for order had a magical effect on them; there is instant perfect order and silence. Then exercises follow: wielding the lathi, soorya-namaskar, marching etc. The spirit of collective effort and spontaneous discipline pervades every programme. Then they sit down and sing in chorus a song charged with patriotism. Discussions follow. They delve deep into the problems affecting the national life. And finally, they stand in rows before the flag and recite the prayer 'Namaste Suda Vatsale Matrubhoome' whose echoes fill the air and stir one's soul. 'Bharat-mata-ki-jai' - uttered in utmost earnest furnishes the finishing and inspiring touch to the entire programme. (Golwalkar 2000: 511–12)

The men in charge of the *shakhas*, called *Pracharaks* (preachers), devote themselves to the work of the Sangh; as a part of RSS cadres they could be sent anywhere in India to develop the organisation's network. At the time of India's independence there were about 600,000 *swayamsevaks* (volunteers) (Anderson and Danle 1987; Jaffrelot 2007: 16; Sangh Parivar 2010). The RSS has now over 4.5 million members, according to Sangh organisations (Sangh Parivar 2010).

Shakha is the basic unit of the RSS. By giving a psychologically oriented rigorous training to its cadres, the RSS has been trying to unify the character of different individuals towards a proposed collective entity 'Hindu Rashtra'. One of the many games that played in the *shakha* is *Nau Mat Ka ek* ma (amalgamation of nine into one, in which nine *swayam sevaks* lift one person off the ground by using only one finger each). This is a symbolic expression of the 'power of unity' (Mishra 1980: 54; Sangh Parivar 2010). The Sangh has been functioning through informal networks. As Mishra observes, "The work of the Sangh is through personal contact. These contacts lead to close ties, friendship and personal cooperation, mutuality in personal relations and a desire to work together to solve the problems of a particular area" (Mishra 1980: 55–56). This socialisation process brings forth (bonding) social capital in civil society. The investment in social capital feeds back to the political capital through mobilisation.

RSS is a hierarchical, rigid and patriarchal organisation. Boys are recruited at a very tender age. Girls are prohibited to join the RSS. The leaders of the Sangh prefer not to invest time and energy on the higher age groups, who already have well-formed opinions. They focus on the 'freshets' (Kanungo 2002: 71). The young people are attracted to the Sangh because of their interest in games and sports and, most importantly, its martial arts tradition. The impressive personality of the *pracharaks* (the self-devoted cadres, who indulge in the spreading of the Sangh's message among the people) is important. They always get away from their family and said to follow celibacy. Their physical fitness and performance in martial arts are great inspiration for the youngsters. Their style of narrating stories is another aspect of attraction (Froerer 2007).

The learning system in *shakhas* is 'non-argumentative'. Thus, in the younger stage the individual may not be influenced by any ideology. And the inception of an ideology in a very informal manner through *shakhas* is expected to produce results. This learning system produces cadres, who are subjugated to the Sangh ideology. The Sangh does not tolerate independent individual initiatives. As Golwalkar pointed out, every *swayamsevak* "must be aware of the fact that each one should be for

Sangh and not vice versa." He emphasised the total subordination of the individual for the sake of the Sangh (Golwalkar 2008: 319–25). Golwalkar had given guidelines for the functioning of the *shakhas*. The assembly in each *shakha* should be held every day. It should commence at the exact time. There should be perfect understanding, love and affection among all *swayamsevaks* and ensure a congenial atmosphere. After the completion of *shakha* assembly, the cadres should sit together and make enquiries about who all attended and who all were absent (Kurushethra Prakashan 2008: 281–82). The discussions were portrayed as 'character-building'. But, most often, the theme of the discussion focused on various aspects of 'Hindu Rashtra'. Anti-Muslim propaganda and the glorification of the Hindu warriors were common in *shakhas* (Kanungo 2002: 72). In a pamphlet, the RSS states that

> ... we have to find out a proper ideal which beats in our hearts, throbs in our blood, and which has been with us for generations. It is no use placing before the people a formless spirit as an ideal. It may be all right for the enlightened. But ordinary men like us require an ideal which we can easily see, understand and experience. Then only will everyone develop in himself devotion or ideal, and the ambition to lead a life of pure character will be roused in his heart. Such an ideal is our Nationhood—the great 'Hindu Rashtra'. (RSS 1964: 23–24)

In another pamphlet, the RSS viewed that the ideal of the Sangh "is to carry the nation to the pinnacle of glory, through organizing the entire society and ensuring protection of Hindu Dharma" (Sahitya Sangama 1992: 14). In these pamphlets, an urge for emphasising the importance of a modern 'Hindu Nation State' could be seen. A shift is also discernible here from the spiritually oriented Hindu belief system to a more politically oriented conglomeration, 'Hindu Rashtra'. The glorification of the 'self' is ensured through caricaturing the 'non-self' or the 'other'. Through constant propaganda, the Sangh sought to imagine a nation, 'Hindu Rashtra', by portraying the Muslims and Christians as 'enemies'. This 'enemy' image has been perpetuated through the *shakhas* (Anderson and Danle 1987; Golwalkar 2000; Mishra 1980).

To the RSS, the Muslims, Christians and the communists are 'outsiders' who misinterpret history by denouncing the history of Hindu heroism, which frustrated the invaders. As such, they are portrayed as engaged in protecting their 'imperialist interests' (Goel 1984a: 1–2). The other issue related to this is "the extra-religious and extra territorial aspects of missionary work." The RSS strongly believes that "the evangelisation in India appears to be part of the uniform world policy to revive Christendom for re-establishing Western supremacy and is not prompted by spiritual motives." It argues that as a result of conversions, the convert's sense of unity and solidarity with the rest of the countrymen is affected and this, in the end, undermines his loyalty to his country and the State (Sheshadri 1985: 16). However, in an interview Shripaty Sastry stated:

> RSS is not preaching hatred against any religion ... it just cannot even afford to do so for the simple reason that within the Hindu fold numerous religions flourish. Religion is not the concern of the RSS at all. The attitude of RSS towards any individual or group is based upon: What is your attitude towards this country, towards the people of this country, towards the integrity, towards the welfare and domestic happiness of the millions and millions people of this country? It is on this basis that the attitude of the RSS towards you is determined. (Sastry 1983: 18–19)

This fosters an image that those who believe in 'Hindutva' are the true 'nationalists' and those 'others' are the 'enemies' of the nation. This position necessarily undermines the cultural pluralism and the co-existence of different communities. However, the RSS argued that "the Christians/communists/Islamists had been perverting India's political scene. The only remedy is to revive the Hindu nationalism" (Goel 1984a, 1984b; Sangh Parivar 2010).

The implications of this nationalism are: (i) Bharatvarsha is an indivisible whole and that its present division into Afghanistan, Pakistan, Hindustan and Bangladesh brought about by Islamic imperialism, must go; and (ii) the closed creeds like Islam and Christianity which are not in accord with the spirituality of 'Sanatana Dharma' have no place in India. 'Sanatana Dharma' was explained as "the beginning less and the endless"; and this feature distinguished this religion from the other religions. Bharati Krishna Tirtha writes:

> ... if there be any religion which can hope to remain forever, it can and must be the one and only religion, which was at the very beginning of things and which continues to exist to the present day, our own beloved 'Sanatana Vaidika Dharma'. It, on this account of being 'anadi', (ie beginingless) and

'ananth' (ie endless), in as much as it began with the world, continues to
exist and can only end with the world itself. (Tirtha 1985)

This sort of conceptualisation has been put in place by the Sangh in all
its campaigns.

Another major feature of the RSS campaign was the promotion of the
'Swadeshi' against the systems of capitalism and socialism (Sangh Parivar
2010). And, most importantly, it advocated that "a strong structure of a
central state should emerge in order to preserve the national heritage and
protect the national homeland without inhibiting the multiple expressions of regional, provincial and local autonomies" (Goel 1984a, b; Sangh
Parivar 2010). In sum, establishing a 'Hindu Rashtra' is the leitmotif of
the RSS. With this end in view, the RSS has been appropriating various
cultural spheres across a wide spectrum of the civil society in India making
room for the swayamsevaks to work in those organisations and associations, thereby legitimising the RSS ideology.

The RSS employs a cultural strategy to mobilise people through
festivals. It observes six major festivals in a year. The very nature of these
'utsavs' brings forth an image of politics which transcends the diversity
of religious systems in the Hindu fold without contradicting any of the
worship systems within itself. Some of the festivals are: Varsha Pratipada,
observed on the first day of the new year in memory of those who gave a
new direction to Indian history; 'Hindu Samarajya Dinotsava', observed
on the 13th day of Jyestha (second month of the year) of the Vikrami
calendar to commemorate the Hindu rule in India ; 'Guru pooja', the
festival to worship the teacher, celebrated on the full-moon day in the
month of Ashada (Vikrami Calendar; 'Vijay Dashmi' the festival in com-
memoration of the tradition of victory over evil was the day Lord Rama
defeated Ravana; 'Makar Sankraman', celebration to emphasise the
importance of the 'process of change' and Raksha Bandhan', celebrated
to underline the importance of brotherhood (Mishra 1980: 60). The
RSS has been celebrating these festivals on a nationalist level. The basic
thread that is going through these celebrations is the notion of 'Hindu
Rashtra', its unity and pride beyond the sectarian divisions. Till 20 years
back, festivals like 'Raksha Bandhan' were unknown to South Indians.
Through shakha's intense campaign, now they have become popular in
the southern India. In colleges and schools tying 'Rakhi'—the thread

that is used in the 'Raksha Bandhan'—has become a fashion and this has been popularised by the RSS and ABVP cadres. Curiously, this had been used in north India in a much wider scale. Earlier, both Muslims and the Hindus used to celebrate this festival and it had become a celebration of 'brotherhood' in the true sense of the word. But, over the years, this has been appropriated by the RSS with a more political objective. Naturally, it distances the Muslim identity from the Hindu 'self'.

The RSS *shakhas* are the '*akhadas*' (gymnasia) of the *swayamsevaks*. They get physical as well as mental training to become self-devoted cadres for the Sangh. The purview of Sangh activity is not restricted to the *shakha* alone, but it cuts across all the branches of the Sangh Parivar coordinating the activities of the whole for a particular goal that they described as 'Hindu Rashtra' (Sangh Parivar 2010). Apart from the Sangh family, the RSS also establishes links with the scholastic institutions (for instance, Vivekananda Kendra, Kanyakumari). This centre in the name of Swami Vivekananda was established in 1972. In a pamphlet issued by the centre for branch shows how much its programmes and visions are fit into the RSS frame. This pamphlet offers the guidelines for the branch centres. It emphasises the importance of celebrations. 'Utsava' comes from the root word '*utsarati*' means 'elevating'. The '*utsavas*' are for taking the organisation upward towards its goal and for 'Shaktiparikshan'—testing of the organisational capacity to bring as many persons as possible for the well-organised function, 'Shaktisamvardhan'—to enhance the strength as an organisation by involving as many '*karyakartas*'—in the organisation of the celebration; and 'Shaktipradarshan'—the invitees as well as 'karyakartas' intensely getting the insight into the ideology and functioning of Kendra (Vivekananda Kendra n.d.: 31). The Kendra observes 'Samastha Bharat Parva' during December–January, ending on 12 January, birth the anniversary of Swami Vivekananda. The aims of this celebration are: to bring the focus of the youth to the dynamics of the Motherland, her great present strength and also her destiny to guide the world; to worship 'Bharatmatha'; to spread the message of Swami Vivekananda; focus on the cultural traditions; to pay homage to all those who laid their life for the protection of the Motherland. Schools, colleges, youth organisations and like-minded associations are invited to join the celebrations. The RSS has been very active in all such programmes, thereby penetrating into civil society. The primary duty of the RSS is said to be providing 'selfless service' to the society (Golwalkar 2000: 57). During the time of natural calamities, the RSS provides a helping hand to the victims. Most of the details of its activities are published (RSS, *Annual Report* 2010b) with a view to inspire others. Such civil society activities provide plenty of space for the RSS to come into contact with the public which it gently appropriates.

Hindu Mahasabha and Jana Sangh: Inception to Politics

During the 1920s and 1930s the Provincial Hindu Sabhas, which were formed in the years before the First World War, changed their form from a voluntary character to a somewhat political party. In 1937 V. D. Savarkar became the President of the Hindu Mahasabha. Under the leadership of Savarkar, the Sabha took a direct interest in elections and party politics (Graham 1993: 6). In his Presidential Address on the 19th session of the Hindu Mahasabha in 1937, Savarkar emphasised the importance of Mahasabha becoming political. He observed that

> the independence of India means, therefore, the independence of our people, our race, our nation. Therefore, Indian 'Swarajya' or Indian 'Swatantrya' means, as far as the Hindu nation is concerned, the political independence of the Hindus, the freedom which would enable them to grow to their full height. (Savarkar 2007: 306)

He also called for "vote in defence of Hindutva" (ibid.: 310).

The assassination of Mahatma Gandhi in 1948 was a setback to the Hindu Mahasabha and RSS. The RSS was banned and the Sangh lost its glamour among the people. The ban on RSS was lifted by the Central government on condition that it would write a constitution that was accepted by the Sangh. According to the RSS Constitution

> the Sangh as such has no politics and is devoted to purely cultural work. The individual *Swayamsevaks*, however, may join any political party, except such parties as believe in or resort to violent and secret methods to achieve their ends; persons owing allegiance to such parties or believing in such methods shall have no place in the Sangh. (Graham 1993: 15)

However, the Hindu Mahasabha resumed its political activities soon. The issues concerning the 'national language' and the 'Hindu Code Bill' made the Sabha a central figure in the national political scene (Graham 1993: 18–19; Mookerjee 2007a: 393–96). The insecurity complex generated from the central government's decision to implement the 'Hindu Code Bill' had prompted them the need for strengthening their influence in party politics (Graham 1993: 19). The division between the Hindu traditionalists and the liberal secularists in the ruling party (Congress) widened on the issue of the outbreak of communal violence which occurred in Bengal during the 1949–50. On this issue, Mookerjee and Nehru had differences and Mookerjee resigned from the cabinet in 1950 (ibid.: 21–23). Mookerjee was also against the 'Delhi Pact' signed by Nehru and Liaquat Ali Khan in 1950. Obviously, Nehru's Pakistan policy was not acceptable to Mookerjee. On 21 October 1951 the Bharatiya Jana Sangh was founded in Delhi. Mookerjee was appointed as its first President and also most of its leaders were from the Hindi-speaking belt (ibid.: 28–29).

Hindu Mahasabha, which accentuated the Hindu–Muslim animosity, tended to dismantle the unity of both communities propagated by the Congress (Joshi and Josh 1994: 308). The Jana Sangh also aimed to re-establish itself in a tension-bound society. It followed a party model in the image of RSS. As Jaffrelot notes

> the traversing of social and political space by means of a network largely borrowed from the RSS and the implementation of social welfare act vision were to be the two complementary wings of the Sangathanist strategy. This strategy of penetration of the body of society, according to those who conceived it, would, in the long term, naturally bring the Jana Sangh to power...the Hindu nation would eventually recognize it as it's appointed political representative. (Jaffrelot 2002: 20)

Indeed, its policies and programmes show its natural affiliation with the RSS. Contrary to the Nehruvian idealism on matters of national security, the Jana Sangh stood on the RSS position: 'militarise the nation'. In 1958, at its Bangalore session, the 'Pratinidhi Sabha' of the Jana Sangh had adopted its manifesto and programme, in which it stated clearly on matters of national security: (i) compulsory military training to all young men; (ii) nationalisation of all the wings of the armed forces in their inspiration as well as form; (iii) immediate establishment of defence industries; and (iv) organisation of vast territorial army (BJS 1961). In its Vijayawada session, the party emphasised the importance of manufacturing the nuclear weapons (BJS 1965).

The Jana Sangh stood for a unitary State, contrary to the Indian federal system. Balraj Madhok viewed that the only effective way to curb the fissiparous forces and trends and ensure a stable and strong centre was to have a unitary structure instead of the present federal structure of the Indian government (Madhok 1966: 13–14). Jana Sangh severely criticised the special status granted to Jammu and Kashmir and called for enacting a common civil code for both the Hindus and Muslims (Mookerjee 2007b: 665–675). Indeed, the position of the Jana Sangh was rooted in the RSS methodology. B. D. Graham pointed out that the Jana Sangh lost its glamour because of its tie-up with the RSS (Graham 2002: 154). The increase in the communal riots and the number of people killed during 1967–70 (209 in 1967, 346 in 1968, 519 in 1969 and 521 in 1970) and the allegations against the Hindu nationalists as shown in the reports of the riots of Ranchi, Ahmedabad and Bhiwandi put the Jana Sangh in a defensive position (Jaffrelot 2002: 214–16). The Ranchi riot occurred in August 1967. At that time, a United Front (UF) government was in office in Bihar. In February 1967, a 31-point programme was adopted by the UF government, which included a claim on agrarian reforms. The Jana Sangh was against this cause, but the mass sentiments immediately following the general election were so strong that the Jana Sangh had to agree to it (Jana Sangh had two ministers in the cabinet). Further, Revenue Minister Indradeep Sinha had introduced the Bataidavi Bill, which was against the interests of big landowners. There was strong presence of this lobby in Jana Sangh. This was the background of the Ranchi riot. The Srinagar riot occurred in September 1967. It was worked up on the basis of religious conversion and marriage of a girl of the Pundit community with a Muslim youth. Ashwin K. Roy and Subash Chakravarthy's report on Meerut riots in January 1968 says that

> the responsibility of these riots falls on the local leaders of the majority community. The events show that the plans of the riot were made long ago. This plan was put into execution relentlessly in utter disregard of the loss of lives of human beings. (Vyas 1969: 1–8)

Jaffrelot says that the Jan Sangh

> wavered between two strategies: one, moderate, involved positioning itself
> as a patriotic party on behalf of national unity, as the protector of both the
> poor and of small privately owned businesses, deploying a populist vein.
> The other line, more militant, was based on the promotion of an aggres-
> sive form of 'Hinduness', symbolized by the campaign to raise Hindi to the
> level of India's national language and protecting of cows (by banning cow
> slaughter), the cow being sacred for Hindus but not for Muslims. (Jaffrelot
> 2007: 9; also see Jaffrelot 2005)

The militant faction, in fact, was "the implicit target of an agitation against
slaughtering cows set off in 1966, in the context of the fourth general
elections campaign" (Jaffrelot 2007: 19; 2005).

Vishwa Hindu Parishad: New Religiosity

The failure of the Jana Sangh to promote the RSS ideology in the general
public prompted them to think about a new organisation, which culminated into the formation of the VHP in 1964 (Jaffrelot 2001). Unlike the
RSS the VHP has propounded the 'theistic Hinduism' in a monotheistic
slant (Nandy et al. 1995: 87–88). Ashis Nandy notes that in some northern Indian States the temples at the VHP offices have icons of Ram–Sita–
Laxman–Hanuman, along with the "plaster-of-Paris Bharat Mata spread
eagled across a map of India." "True to the Hindu-nationalist tradition
though, the Bharat Mata dwarfs the icons and the temple is called Bharat
Mata Mandir. And the new greeting, 'Jai Shri Ram', has to accompany
the standard RSS farewell, 'Bharat Mata ki jai (victory to Mother India)."

The decision to form the VHP was taken in the Bombay session, headed
by the RSS leader Golwalkar. According to him, the leitmotif was "to
unite the pluralist Hindu on a single platform for the safeguarding of their
common interest." The prominent religious leaders who participated in the
session included Dalai Lama, Sikh leader, Master Tara Singh and others.
The VHP was formally registered in 1966 with Swami Chinmayananda
as its working president and S. S. Apte as its General Secretary. After the
formation of the VHP, a Marg Darshak Mandal was constituted in order to

direct its activities. It was aimed to 'rejuvenate' the Hindu society, like the 19th-century Hindu reform agenda (Jaffrelot 2001; Nandy 1998: 89–90). Peter van der Veer viewed that the VHP is modern. Instead of rejecting capitalist development, science and technology, the VHP attempted to nationalise these signs of modernity and what it did reject was the secular State, yet, its arguments were based upon the modern democratic principle of 'majority rule'. It argued that "the 'majority community' should rule the country, while the minority communities such as Muslims and Christians, "should accept it as a political reality" (van der Veer 1996: 133). Thus, the VHP and the RSS shared the same views on many issues.

Through its wide networks all over India and abroad, the VHP has been mobilising Hindus on a wide range of issues from the cow protection, Ram temple, jihadi terrorism, to the use of Sanskrit (VHP 2003). It has also networks among the backward castes and Dalits. The VHP has offices and activities in foreign countries too. For better co-ordination of its functions, the VHP divided the world into four regions—USA, Europe, Africa and Middle East, and South Asia. The activities of the VHP in these regions have been growing rapidly (Nandy et al. 1995). The 'Dharma Sansad', a synod of saints and seers of all faiths within the Hindu Society has been helping the VHP. It has also set up two trusts: (i) Bharat Kalyan Pratishthan, which provides education and medical aid to the poor; (ii) VHP Foundation, which has been working for "uplifting the rural poor" (Nandy et al. 1996: 92–93; VHP 2003).

Other Sangh Organisations

As discussed before, the RSS's aim was not merely to penetrate into the civil society through *shakhas*, but it also sought to establish organisations working within specific social categories. Way back in 1948, the RSS cadres based in Delhi founded the ABVP, the students' wing, whose primary objective was to combat the communist influence on university campuses. In 1955, the RSS established its workers' union, the BMS whose major role was also to counter the communist unions in the name of Hindu nationalist ideology. Besides these unions, the RSS created more targeted organisations. In 1952, it founded a tribal movement, the

Vanavasi Kalyan Ashram (VKA) which aimed to counter the influence of Christian movements among the adivasis of India, proselytism and priestly social work having resulted in numerous conversions. The VKA developed a counter strategy by imitating missionary methods and thus accomplished a number of 'reconversions' (Jaffrelot 2007).

VKA has been an integral part of the Sangh conglomerate working among the adivasis. The Kalyan Ashram has been providing infrastructural facilities and financial assistance to the adivasis. It has been running social and educational programmes among the adivasis. The educational activities include single teacher schools, primary, middle and high schools, free hostels, Bal Sanskar Kendra' Balawadi, informal schools, libraries, etc. The Kalyan Ashram is also active in areas of economic development, women empowerment, self-help groups, etc. (VKA 2010a). The Shraddhajagaran is spreading awareness about the Hindu customs and tradition to the adivasis. Through the voluntary activities, the Sangh has been trying to communalise the adivasi space and mobilise them against certain 'threats'. The Sangh is following a different cultural strategy among the adivasis and Dalits. It is not directly imposing one meta-narrative of the past among the various caste groups. Rather it tries to "recreate, reproduce and revise the various forms of pastness" and linking it with an imagined past, which they called—the Ramarajya. Badri Narayan writes:

> In this entire project, history and past have become essential components since the sense of pastness of these communities is being evoked through the process of finding similarities with mythical or historical heroes belonging to these castes who suit the political ideology of the party concerned and with whom the caste members can easily identify themselves. These heroes, picked out from the myths, histories and legends present in the oral culture of these castes, are reinterpreted, recreated and reconstructed to suit the political ideologies of the party concerned, and are then transmitted back to the people as symbols of their caste identities. (Narayan 2009: 5)

Thus, the Sangh has been pursuing a policy by which it started penetrating into the local cultural celebrations of the Dalits and adivasis and gradually bonding those cultural communities on the basis of Brahminical value system. They have been celebrating the mythical characters of those traditional communities in a colourful manner and adding Hindutva flavours to those celebrations. The heroes of these communities are imagined as the chivalrous warriors of the Hindu mythology (VKA 2010b). The Hindutva claimed that the Dalits and the adivasis were the saviours and protectors of the Hindu religion, and they become detached from the Hindu religion because of the Muslim invasion. The leaders of the Sangh are propagating the notion that before the invasion of the Muslims, untouchability did not exist in the Hindu society. The conclusion derived from such stories spread by the Sangh Parivar combine is that the practicing untouchability and the existing pathetic condition of the Dalits are not because of the Brahminical social order but because of the domination by the Muslims (Narayan 2009: 49–51).

The other Sangh organisations that began to make headway in the civil society were 'Vidya Bharati' (Indian Knowledge) established in 1977 to coordinate a network of schools, first developed by the RSS in the 1950s on the basis of local initiatives, and, Seva Bharati (Indian Service) created in 1979 to penetrate India's slums through social activities such as free schools and low-cost medicines (Jaffrelot 2007: 19, 2005). Perhaps the most recent and controversial one emerged in the Sangh family is Bajrang Dal. The VHP was instrumental in the creation of the Bajrang Dal, which is a militant organisation based on the ideology of Hindutva. Established in October 1984 in Uttar Pradesh in the background of the Ayodhya movement, it began to grow in other States in the country. This militant outfit is claimed to have more than a million members of whom nearly a lakh are workers, and is functioning through its *akhadas* (like RSS *shakhas*). The word 'Bajrang' connotes the Hindu deity Hanumān. The Dal's main slogan is "service, safety and culture." The major agenda of the organisation has been protecting India's Hindu identity from the perceived 'dangers of Communism', Muslim 'demographic growth' and' Christian conversion', preventing cow slaughter, building the Ram temple in Ayodhya, the Krishna temple in Mathura and the Kashi Vishwanath temple in Kashi Varanasi. Bajrang Dal, like VHP and RSS, generated fear psychosis about Islamic jihad in India and declared that they were engaged in the campaign across the nation. Bajrang Dal differs from the 60-odd other affiliates of the RSS in that it is not directly controlled by the Sangh. It has no organic all-India structure and is federalised to the point of being anarchic. Loosely put, it is a banner under which gangsters with Hindutva leanings have gathered in state after state. Prevention of both cow slaughter and Hindu–Muslim marriages apart, the Bajrang Dal was at the forefront of anti-beauty contest agitations, anti-Valentine's day celebrations, etc. (Singh and Mahurkar 1999). As an organisation within the fold of the Sangh Parivar, it has come to be handy for channelling the fury of an underclass whose utility as 'foot soldiers' is useful on occasion while allowing BJP to promptly dissociate itself from any outrageous act of violence (Bajrang Dal 2001). However, the reports established that the Bajrang Dal was in the forefront of the demolition of the Babri Masjid and the related riots in the 1990s.

In totality, the Hindu Right in India has been deeply involved in mobilising the masses through extensive network of organisations. The ideology of Hindutva has been propagated by the Sangh organisations through its aggressive interventions in the civil society realm. The focal point of mobilisation is 'self/other' dichotomy and its inevitable cultural logic of securitisation. The process of Hindu Right assertion further gathered momentum in the 1980s and 1990s in the wake of the social dislocations caused by economic liberalisation and neoliberal reforms.

4

Civil Society and the Hindu Right: Hindutva, Militarism and Cultural Mobilisation

State and civil society in India have come under critical challenges since the 1980s. During the last three decades, particularly since the early 1990s, there have been momentous changes within the country and across the world. At the domestic level, there was an unprecedented economic crisis, which affected India's position very badly. The disintegration of the Soviet Union and the socialist bloc, the ascendency of neoliberal/ New Right forces and market economy, the ever-expanding role of global capital, the formation of the World Trade Organisation (WTO), the terrorist attacks on the World Trade Centre in New York on 11 September 2001, and the 'war on terror' were the critical developments during the period.

The economic crisis led India to substantially revise its development paradigm and the economic/industrial policies pursued for more than four decades. When India began to adopt neoliberal policies in the 1990s, many questions emerged with respect to the role of State and civil society, long-held policies of self-reliance, import substitution and others. This was also the period when India experienced new trends and patterns within its political system with communal mobilisation, regionalism, shifting electoral strategies of political parties, governmental instability, etc., having an impact on the State and civil society. Coalition experiments too became an accepted practice during this period with political dispensations transcending traditional ideological moorings began to explore new avenues of political alignment. It is within this backdrop of developments that the new wave of Hindutva and its securitisation of culture and society must be analysed. This chapter begins with a brief analysis of the structural transformation of the Indian State and civil society in the

1980s and 1990s. It then examines how the Hindutva forces cashed in on the emerging situation and deployed new strategies of securitisation through several issues that dominated Indian politics and civil society. The chapter also analyses the perceptions and policies of the BJP-led NDA coalition government during 1998–2004, particularly in relation to issues of security.

State and Civil Society: Structural Transformation

The decades of 1980s and 1990s were marked by major changes in the world economy as well as in the global politico-strategic landscape. The changes in the world economy had their beginning in the early 1970s when it came across unanticipated fall of the 'golden age' (Sweezy 2002: 18–37; UNCTAD 1995: 123–24) of capitalism. The prosperity of the post-war era—sustained throughout the 1950s and 1960s in advanced capitalist countries—had ended up in severe inflation in the early 1970s. Consequently, Keynesianism came under challenge because of the very course of the evolution of the international political economy in the post-war period (Kozlov 1977: 523–27; Pilling 1986: 1–2; Shonfield 1965).

The burgeoning inflation in the 1970s, accompanied by the collapse of industrial production and employment, undermined the very rationale of Keynesianism (Pilling 1986: 6). This mix of inflation and industrial recession was understood as a new trend by a large number of economists (Kaldor 1978: 215) some of whom began to call it as 'stagflation' (Baran and Sweezy 1966; Sweezy 1966: 39–59). The crisis generated other problems too. The Keynesian Welfare State that existed in many countries sought to blend capitalist economic efficiency with social and national cohesion. Samir Amin, however, says that "it was the fear of communism and the radicalisation of the national liberation movements of the peripheries that gave rise to the Keynesian policies and development support of the post-war period" (Amin 1997: 42). Thus, the social consensus on welfarism that prevailed for more than two decades suddenly collapsed in the context of the economic crisis and, inevitably, the Welfare State became no longer suitable, which also called for a rollback of the political and economic advances of the previous years. Seeing the growing public expenditures as the major cause of the crisis, the New Right forces in advanced capitalist countries began to abhor the mounting public spending and praise the virtues of privatisation of social services. Leonard points out that the tensions between the New Right, who rejected all welfare spending and the conservative welfarists, who stood for State intervention, were reconciled in favour of the former (Leonard 1997: 3). According to Foster, the crisis had implications for the mixed economy, Keynesianism, the Welfare State and, above all, the idea of "capitalism with a human face" (Foster 1999: 37).

The fall of the Welfare State in the West, in fact, triggered off a deepening crisis in the developing countries too. The notion of social and economic development as two sides of the same coin was no longer sustainable. The breakdown of Keynesianism thus led to the rollback of social development and welfare initiatives of the UN Development Decade (Berger 2001: 211–34; UN 1970) as these were seen as basically 'nationalistic' and conflicting with the requirements of global capitalist development (Amin 1997: 142). Thus, demands for a free market play were forcefully made by many during this time pointing to the 'bureaucratic inefficiency' and 'fiscal extravaganza' of the Welfare State. Davison Budhoo, who had worked with the World Bank and the IMF for some time and, later, became a critic of these institutions, pointed out that attempts were underway "to replace all development theory" with "Reaganomics and Chicago school monetarism" and to turn "post-war development economics on its head" (Budhoo 1990: 97). A shift of the dominant macroeconomic model could be perceptible at this time—from the Keynesian mode to a monetarist and neoclassical type. The New Right in the West became the proponents of this transition, which later came to be associated with neoliberalism. McChesney says:

> Neoliberalism refers to the policies and processes whereby a relatively handful of private interests are permitted to control as much as possible of social life in order to maximise their personal profit. Associated initially with Reagan and Thatcher, neoliberalism has for the past two decades been the dominant global economic trend adopted by political parties of the centre, much of the traditional left, and the right. These parties and the policies they enact represent the immediate interests of extremely wealthy investors and less than one thousand large corporations. (McChesney 1999: 40)

This period also witnessed a move from the emphasis on national development to globalisation, a heterogeneous and multifaceted process of political, social and cultural change marked by financial deregulation, trade liberalisation and privatisation, in which the State played an increasingly important globalising role rather than its earlier national development role (Kurien 1994: x). Since the early 1980s, the Reagan and Thatcher governments in the United States and Britain, under pressure from transnational companies, took the lead in directing the IMF and the World Bank to encourage financial deregulation, trade liberalisation and privatisation of public sector in the developing countries through SAP, the aim of which was to put them on the track of global capitalist development. Through the strict implementation of structural adjustment policies, the IMF and the World Bank sought to ensure that the developing countries that were seeking loans from the IMF and the World Bank "become faithful adherents to the philosophy of monetarism" (McLeod in Budhoo 1990: vii).

The outcome of the SAP was the worsening debt crisis in developing countries. As a result of recession in the West and the resulting fall in demand, the prices of major commodities exported by the developing countries fell drastically. This caused unfavourable terms of trade and price instability that became very acute for developing countries. Export prospects were considerably restricted due to the protective measures of the advanced capitalist countries. The UNDP estimated that the global market conditions made the developing countries lose economic opportunities worth around $500 billion annually (UNDP 1992: 77–78). The net impact of all this was that the gap between the developed and the developing countries further widened. The South Commission Report (1990) recorded these widening disparities in terms of the expanding power of the advanced capitalist countries. It says that

> the fate of the South is increasingly dictated by the perceptions and policies of governments in the North, of the multilateral institutions which a few of those governments control, and of the network of private institutions that are increasingly prominent. (South Commission 1990: 3–5)

It is in this background that one has to analyse how India began to address such issues within the structural compulsions of the international as well as its own domestic economy in the 1980s. The State and civil society in India began to experience new forms of challenges against the backdrop of a new political economy regime, which was gradually emerging in the 1980s. Its main objective was to ensure a slow but steady rollback of the State, deregulation of industries, decontrol of prices, liberalisation of imports, tax reductions, etc. The new regime began to operate with the IMF loan India borrowed in 1981 and subsequent policy initiatives, which got impetus in 1985 following the recommendations made by several official committees appointed by the government. These were the committees that set the essential framework and background papers for the new economic regime (Ahluwalia 1985; Hussain 1984; Jha 1985; Narasimham 1985; Sengupta 1984). By mid-1980s the public opinion within the country was created against the policy regime of controls and regulations. The three decades of economic policies had already brought the country to an irreversible balance of payment crisis towards the end of 1980s.

Rajiv Gandhi's emergence as Prime Minister in 1984 was a decisive turn. With the proclamation of a new economic policy by the Rajiv government, slogans like 'self-reliance' and 'import-substitution' were substituted by catch words like 'export-orientation', 'technological upgradation', 'efficiency' and 'modernisation' (MIB 1987: 95–98, 98–109 and 147–155). Appropriating the new industrial policy put in place as part of the liberalised economic policy, the corporate sector (both national and international) rushed into the Indian market. The export–import policies announced in 1985 and 1988 under the Rajiv government, and in 1990 under the National Front government led by V. P. Singh, fell in line with the trade liberalisation prescriptions of multilateral financial institutions (Ministry of Finance (MF) 1985, 1986, 1991). To invite foreign firms and get the much-needed foreign exchange for financing the consumer booms, several measures were taken (Ghosh 1999; 295–334; Patnaik 1988: 3–16). In sum, the import-pushed export-oriented development strategy initiated in the 1980s speeded up the integration of the Indian economy with the world economy. The resulting scenario saw acute fiscal and balance of payments crisis, inflationary pressures, deceleration in productive economic activities including employment growth rate, widening of economic inequalities, etc. The economic and industrial policies eventually led to undermining the major public sector industries and indigenous cottage as well as small-scale industries, thereby facilitating the large-scale entry of multinational corporations (CSO 1989; RBI 1988).

Meanwhile, India was pushed into a severe debt trap, which culminated in a major economic crisis in the early 1990s. There was a sharp fall in foreign exchange reserves, soaring inflation, large fiscal and current account deficit, and a heavy and growing burden of debt (Jalan 1991; Nayyar 1996). The Narasimha Rao government which came to power in 1991 embarked on a wave of economic reforms to meet this challenge. These measures initiated under the supervision of the IMF and the World Bank constituted the second phase of a programme designed to restructure the economy with the twin pillars—macroeconomic stabilisation and the structural adjustment policy. It was first initiated as stabilisation policy under the direction of the IMF followed by a structural adjustment policy dictated by the World Bank (Swamy 1994: 245–49; World Bank 1991). They sought to ensure (i) gradual withdrawal of the State from the economic activities as well as from the social sector; (ii) the encouragement of private investment; (iii) increasing reliance on external private capital for economic development; (iv) other gradual privatisation of public enterprises; and (v) the introduction of fiscal and monetary policies that passed on control in all directions of economic policies, from the Indian State to external private finance capital (Patnaik 1994a: 917–21). Thus, the introduction of the reforms constituted a clear departure from the past and the State has been retreating from the socio-economic sphere, perhaps most dramatically since the early 1990s. When the disintegration of the socialist bloc came, it was interpreted as the vindication of the triumph of market ideology and the rejection of the role of the State in the economic sphere (Patnaik 1992: 54).

This was when the World Bank, through its enormous direct and indirect influence, forced its debtors and its member countries to accept 'good governance' as a key component of both developed and developing economies, thereby also assigning importance to the role of the civil society as a facilitator of both democracy and market economy (Berglund 2009). More importantly, the failure of the State to address social and economic needs of the people has had effects not only on the levels of development but also on the structure of the civil society. In a way, this failure impelled groups and individuals to engage in civil society, but the inability to provide basic services hampered the development of civil society. Consequently, the Indian State and various aid agencies utilised the competence and infrastructure of civil society in order to encourage social development. NGOs have been incorporated in the governmental development plans. At the same time, the relative failure of the Indian State created feelings of exclusion amongst large segments of the population, and allegations that the State is not neutral, but biased on the basis of class and caste interests. These allegations created sentiments of apathy and also facilitated negative mobilisation and manipulation of various primordial identities such as religion and caste. This caused many problems that led to demands and actions which seriously undermined the democratic system by the strengthening of exclusivist identities. These are based on religion or caste and are now at the centre of political mobilisation, which involves political parties as well as other parts of Indian civil society. According to Amir Ali, this resulted in the cementing of the community-based identities, which obstructed democratisation of Indian society, with the current Hindu nationalist challenge as a case in point (Ali 2001). The ascendency of this movement was most evident within the party system, where BJP in the 1980s and 1990s grew from a marginal party to a dominant force of Indian politics.

Rise of Hindutva: Securitisation and Mobilisation

Scholars observed that as a result of the extremely personalised rule of Indira Gandhi, especially after the Emergency (1975–77), the 'Congress System' (Kothari 2002b)—a broad consensus within the State and civil society that existed for long—went into decline, creating a political vacuum which was filled by competing regional, caste and linguistic interests (Hardgrave and Kochanek 2000: 151–53). Moreover, as Indira Gandhi's government could not alleviate poverty in the ways that it had promised in the slogan *Garibi Hatao*, the people became disillusioned with the Congress dominance and turned to alternatives. Consequently, the divisions that characterised the Indian politics in the 1980s and 1990s were marked by a more competitive electoral environment in which coalition building and the support of consistent vote banks became the hallmark of a successful political strategy (Nadadur 2006).

It is here that the rise of Hindutva in India needs to be placed within the larger context of the struggle and debate over the secularism of the postcolonial Indian State (Bhargava 1998), on the one hand, and the emerging social issues and tensions following the introduction of liberalisation and privatisation, on the other. This became significant since the 1990s, the decade that saw the end of Congress's dominance and the rise of BJP. Writing on the discourse of violence that the BJP and other Hindu Right organisations carried on during the period, Dibyesh Anand noted that the hate campaign against the minority Muslims was "facilitated and justified in the name of achieving security for the Hindu Self at individual, community, national as well as international levels." He said that the "will to secure the 'self' has as its corollary the will to make insecure the 'other', the desire to control and use violence." The new discourse of security/insecurity that Hindutva set in motion enabled "extreme violence to be normalized, systematized and institutionalized." The 'politics of hate' spawned by the Hindutva was a good example that fed upon, as well as shaped, local societies' conceptions of security/insecurity. The global environment, "with its own dynamic politics of representation of dangers" (Anand 2005), had a direct impact on the civil society.

The decades of 1980s and 1990s were thus marked by the growing fear generated by the Hindu Right that the minority Muslim population was increasing its presence in India, challenging Indian sovereignty and rule of law, and controlling the politics of the country. The 'insecurity' of the Hindus was blown out of proportion, and the BJP, RSS, VHP and other Hindu Right organisations had worked hard within the civil society in the task of securitisation of the Hindu identity. Thus, BJP's emergence as the most dominant Hindu Right force in India in the 1980s was the culmination of a sustained effort on the part of its predecessor, Jan Sangh, VHP and the RSS to bring Hindutva into mainstream politics. According to Nadadur, the BJP and other Hindu Right organisations played on "the fears of the Hindu majority" that the "Muslim population posed a threat to Hindus in India." This was based on the "changing demographics of the Muslim population and the political mobilization in the 1980s and 1990s" such as the growth of Islamic fundamentalism and the changing voting patterns of the Muslim population (Nadadur 2006). This has also been linked with 'terrorism' and 'Islamism'. According to L. K. Advani the ideological basis of terrorism in India has been unmistakably anti-national in its intent and pan-Islamic in its appeal. It is the manifestation of a deeper malaise of the spread of extremism in most parts of the Muslim world, funded as it is by fundamentalist groups based mainly in Saudi Arabia and the Gulf countries.

He wrote that "one of the most virulent forms of terrorism in our times seeks the cover of Islam," which called its "murderous campaign" jihad, and the terrorists

> actually pursue a definite objective: to establish worldwide domination of political Islam, which is also called 'Islamism.' Naturally, India's multi-faith society, the constitutional principle of secularism that has anchored the Indian state, and the cultural-spiritual ethos of Hinduism that have defined the character of both the Indian society and state, are anathema to Islamism. (Advani 2007)

Thus, the Hindu Right organisations and their leaders persistently talked about the 'threats' to the Hindus. A study circulated by the RSS in the aftermath of the 1991 Census read that "the fact remained as prominent as ever that the rate of population growth of Muslims is much higher than that of the Hindus, particularly in some areas where the majority is on the verge of being reduced into minority" (BJP 2006; Nadadur 2006). During this period, VHP leader Praveen Togadia made a strong plea to the Hindus to increase their population. He said that "the Hindus should encourage growth in their population in the light of the demographic changes taking place in the country." Togadia was on a campaign "to make the Hindus take pride in their identity" (*Indian Express* 2005). Similarly, illegal immigration from neighbouring Bangladesh contributed to the perception that the Muslim population in India was growing rapidly. Yet, another campaign that led to the perceived threat from Muslims that Hindus 'experienced' came from "the systematic campaign to drive away Kashmiri Pandits and Hindu families from their natural homeland" (Advani 2007). Mohan Bhagwat, *Sarsanghchalak*, RSS, in a speech said that the

> patriotic forces in the Kashmir valley need to be strengthened ... to restore the demographic balance of the valley. The legitimate demand of the Kashmiri Hindus for permanent and honourable return to their home land

as patriotic citizens of Bharat and followers of Hindutva—well equipped to defend themselves and pledged by the government—needs to be fulfilled immediately. (Bhagwat 2009)

Re-emergence of BJP

The Jana Sangh, which spearheaded the cause of 'Hindu nationalism' for long, ceased to exist in 1977 when it merged with other non-communist parties (such as Congress (O), Socialists and Bharatiya Lok Dal) to form the Janata Party in March 1977 and assumed power at the centre. But the Janata experiment soon fell through when it was caught up in conflicts among its constituent units. The Jana Sangh faction finally left the Janata Party. One of the main causes of the collapse of the Janata experiment was 'the dual membership' (BJP 2010b)—the loyalty of the Jana Sangh faction to the RSS. The question was whether a Janata Party member could simultaneously remain loyal to the RSS (Ghosh 2003: 229). However, it led to the formation of the BJP in April 1980, which, according to Graham, "offered a second chance for Hindu nationalists to bid for majority status in northern India" (Graham 1993: 258). From the very inception, the leaders of the BJP faced two main problems; first, how the new party could be distinguished from the former Jana Sangh, in order to exhibit its 'newness' and to "broaden their electoral reach on both a geographic and demographic basis"; second, how it could be placed as an alternative to the Congress (Malik 1995: 36–38). As a strategy, the BJP declared itself committed to a programme of 'Gandhian Socialism' and introduced a new set of policy documents known as 'Our Five Commitments', intended to produce a national consensus.

The first principle underlined that while "India is one nation and Indians are one people, constituting and mutually accommodating plurality of religious faiths, ideologies, languages and interests," those "who have external or extra-territorial loyalties or are engaged in anti-social activities cannot be by definition expected to contribute to national consensus and therefore will have to be kept out." 'Commitment to democracy and fundamental rights', 'Positive Secularism involving an acceptance of the need to protect fully the life and property of minorities', 'Gandhian Socialism' and 'value-based politics' were other principles the BJP espoused. Graham rightly pointed out that

> in rhetorical terms, this text presented the BJP as a progressive party with liberal and humanitarian concerns, implicitly laying claim to the mantle of the Janata Party and as a furthermore, to the social and political ideal which Nehru's Congress Party had proclaimed in the 1950s. (Graham 2006:160)

Indeed, the BJP had been trying to appropriate the space, which the successive Congress governments had been unable to sustain after Nehru.

Thus, in the 1980s, the BJP was determined to become a counterforce to the Congress. Its leadership criticised the Congress for its 'denial of democracy by imposing emergency in 1975', 'minority appeasement', and distortion of 'secularism', 'corruption', 'unprincipled pursuit of power', 'unbridled consumerism in disregard of India's cultural traditions', etc. (Advani 2007; BJP 2010b; Malik 1995: 38). However, the attempts to broad base its support in the 1984 parliamentary elections failed to attain the expected results. The BJP got only two seats with 7.86 per cent votes in the elections (Ghosh 2003: 230–31). This was a setback to the party. The RSS during this time indicated that the remedy to the crisis lay in the restoration of the leadership's rapport with a sizeable section of its 'selfless cadres' (RSS) still alienated since the Janata rule (Noorani 2000: 61–62; *Organiser* 7 April 1985). It also argued that 'positive secularism' and 'Gandhian socialism' had alienated the party. In the wake of this, the BJP appointed a high power Working Group to study the results of the elections, which later came out with remedial action. The Party streamlined its organisation and "re-pledged itself to 'Integral Humanism'" (BJP 2010b).

Meanwhile, two events in early 1986 provided considerable leeway for BJP's re-emergence, which it skilfully utilised through its mobilisation in the civil society with the help of RSS, VHP and Bajrang Dal. The first one was the order of the Faizabad District Judge on 31 January to unlock the gates of the premises of the Babri Masjid in Ayodhya and the second one was the Rajiv government moving the Muslim Women's Bill in Parliament in February to override the Supreme Court's verdict in the Shah Bano case. The BJP and the Sangh Parivar organisations decided to appropriate these issues, thereby mobilising the majority Hindu community for drawing political mileage. It was during this time that the BJP held its plenary in May 1986 with L. K. Advani assuming the leadership of the party.

The change in leadership had rejuvenated the hardcore members of the Sangh who were motivated by the principles of 'Hindu nationalism' rather than 'Gandhian Socialism' (Malik 1995: 76). As soon as he took charge of the party, Advani said: "if anyone were to ask me which is the most distinctive trait of BJP's personality, I would say that BJP is the voice of unalloyed nationalism. Ours is a 'Nation-First' Party" (Advani 2007; BJP 2010b; Ghosh 2003: 31; Malik 1995: 77). He denounced the cow slaughter and the destruction of Hindu temples in Jammu and Kashmir. During this period, the relationship between the RSS and the BJP got strengthened and leaders like Vajpayee and Advani attended the conclave of prominent *swayamsevaks* (Noorani 2000: 62–63). The Congress was, at this time, on its wane, when Rajiv Gandhi was charged of corruption in the Bofors Scandal. The internal turmoil, compounded by the increasing number of riots after 1980s (in the 1987 Meerut riots alone, about 150 people lost their lives and more than a thousand were injured) also contributed to the strengthening of opposition parties. This clearly paid dividend in the next parliamentary election. BJP's aggressive nationalism and its strategy of electoral alliance brought 86 seats to the party and it became the third largest party in Parliament. The BJP and the left parties gave support to the V. P. Singh-led National Front government. However, this was seen as the victory of a new wave of politics played by L. K. Advani. Thus, the BJP's strategy of gaining popularity needs to be understood in the context of its politics of mobilisation and securitisation since the mid-1980s. Uniform Civil Code (in the context of the Shah Bano case), Article 370 (in the context of the Kashmir question), Ayodhya dispute (in the context of Ram Janmabhoomi-Babri Masjid issue), Mandal Commission Recommendations (reservations for backward classes), and ban on cow slaughter were some of the prominent issues that the BJP, VHP, Bajrang Dal and other Sangh organisations took up for mobilisation in the civil society.

Shah Bano Case and Uniform Civil Code

The Shah Bano Case [AIR 945, 1985, SCC (2) 556, 1985] was one of the most controversial issues in the 1980s, which led to communal mobilisation among both the Muslims and Hindus. It all began when Mohammed Ahmad Khan, a provincial lawyer, refused to pay to his aged, destitute wife, Shah Bano, a small amount awarded by the Madhya Pradesh High Court as monthly maintenance and appealed to the Supreme Court. He pleaded that as a Muslim he was governed by the Muslim Personal Law. The Court held then that Section 125 of the Code of Criminal Procedure (CrPC) applied to all cases, irrespective of the Muslim Personal Law. It also held that if the divorced wife was able to maintain herself, the husband's liability to provide maintenance ceased with the expiration of the period of *iddat* (the span of three months after the divorce). If she is unable to maintain herself, she was entitled to take recourse to Section 125 of CrPC. The judgement went on to make comments on the need to enact a Uniform Civil Code. Some sections of the Muslim religious leadership felt at that time that this judgement was an onslaught on the Muslim Personal Law. Under their pressure, the Rajiv government enacted the Muslim Women (Protection of Rights on Divorce) Act, 1986. While introducing the Bill in the Parliament, the Government declared that it was to provide that

> a muslim divorced woman shall be entitled to a reasonable and fair provi-
> sion and maintenance within the period of *iddat*, by her former husband
> and in case she maintained the children born to her before or after her
> divorce, such reasonable provision and maintenance would be extended to
> a period of two years from the dates of birth of the children. The Muslim
> Women (Protection of Rights on Divorce) Act, 1986

The Bill intended to provide that where a Muslim divorced woman was unable to maintain herself after the *iddat* period, the magistrate was empowered to make her presumptive heirs or the local Wakf Board maintain her. Asghar Ali Engineer viewed that in this case the Muslim elite sections were not motivated by religious concerns or religious fervour, but by "a curious mixture of male chauvinism and political interests" (Engineer 1985). In fact, the Muslim identity was most aggressive during the Shah Bano controversy—the result of 'insecurity' and perceptions that the Muslims had long suffered in India. This "insecurity syndrome" was gently used by the Muslim leadership in the Shah Bano controversy (Engineer 1995). On the other hand, BJP, VHP and the RSS made all efforts to make known that the passing of the Act was a precedent to justify their refusal to accept the jurisdiction of the Supreme Court to adjudicate on matters of faith. According to them, the Act was passed with the perceived intention of making the Supreme Court decision in the Shah Bano case ineffective. The campaign, then, was that Parliament appeased the sentiments of the Muslim community by passing the Act of 1986 and that the Muslim community had therefore 'benefited'. L. K. Advani, who during this time became the President of BJP, observed that Rajiv Gandhi's "capitulation in the Shah Bano case, once again placed a question mark over his maturity as a leader" (Advani 2007). The BJP said that having "done this 'favour' to Muslims" Rajiv Gandhi "proceeded to organise the unlocking of the Ayodhya structure in a bid to please the Hindus" (BJP 2010b). Raising the voice against the 'politics of minorityism', Advani said:

> Since India is not a theocratic state, the religious rights and the identities of the various faith-based communities that constitute the Great Indian Family must indeed be protected. But notions of 'majority' and 'minority' should have no place in the politics and statecraft of our nation much less be manipulated for vote-bank considerations. This divisive mindset jeopardises India as one united, integral and harmonious nation. The Congress party is trying to divide the nation by continuously harping on 'minority protection' in the same way that the British rulers did for their own ulterior motives. (Advani 2010e)

Advani reminded that the "progress, welfare and security of all sections of India's diverse society are inter-related and indivisible." He, therefore, called for Muslims to "come out of the trap of the minority mindset and join the national mainstream with equal rights and responsibilities to build a strong, prosperous and just India" (Advani 2010c). Mobilising the majority community on the issue of the need of a Common Civil Code, Advani remarked:

> A small section of Muslim intellectuals favour Muslim law reform, but are opposed to a uniform civil code. They strongly advocate reform in Muslim laws in India in the matter of polygamy, divorce etc to bring these in line with the laws in Turkey, Pakistan and other Muslim countries. But the anti-uniform civil code campaign that is being systematically built up draws its strength from leaders and sections who are opposed to reform as such and who question the very competence of courts and legislations to deal with the subject. (Advani 1986)

The BJP also understood that the Rajiv Gandhi government was playing both minority and majority cards simultaneously. While appeasing the Muslims in the Shah Bano case, the government also decided to authorise the Hindus to conduct prayers at the site of Babri Masjid by opening the gate of the premises in an attempt to woo the Hindus (BJP 2010b). Encouraged by this, the Hindu Right organisations intensified their struggle for Ram Janmabhoomi.

Babri Masjid–Ram Janmabhoomi Movement

The Ram *Janmabhoomi* movement began to gather momentum when the Hindu Right organisations like RSS, VHP and Bajrang Dal, with the BJP's blessings and participation, launched a series of powerful mobilisations using religious symbols and gestures such as a campaign to collect bricks for the temple, carrying *Ram-Jyotis* (lamps in processions), and holding special *pujas* (worship) in cities and towns. Highly politicised sadhus and upper-caste cadres of the Sangh Parivar constituted the most committed participants in the movement. Very soon, it also began to gather the support of the low and middle-caste Hindus. For them, the movement's main attraction was that it sought to provide a pan-Indian or pan-Hindu and a homogenous, respectable and 'Sanskritised' identity to them, as distinct from the subaltern, marginal and oppressive reality of their (typically rural or semi-urban) existence (Bidwai 2004). When the BJP found the rising popularity and potential of the Ram *Janmabhoomi* movement in the 1980s, most of its leaders also actively participated in it (Engineer 1992; Gopal 1993; Jaffrelot 1996; Sharma 2003).

The Ram Janmabhoomi–Babri Masjid dispute emerged in the 1980s as a socio-political one, not merely as a historical one (MHA 2010, hereafter *Report of the Liberhan Commission:* 58–284). It was the outcome of the competitive assertion of the two identities, the Muslims and the Hindus. The Hindu Right organisations claimed that in the 16th century, the Muslim ruler Babar destroyed a temple at Ram *Janmabhoomi*, the birthplace of the deity Rama, and constructed a mosque at the site. According to the leaders of the BJP, "the Hindus had been trying for centuries to reacquire access to the spot and to reconstruct the magnificent temple." L. K. Advani, in his foreword to the *White Paper* published by the BJP in 1993, said:

> Reconstructing the temple for Sri Rama became the symbol of this rising consciousness ridding the country of the perversities to which it was being subjected in the name of secularism, forging a strong and united country. The object of the movement thus became not just to construct yet another temple, the object became to put our country back on its feet, to purify our public life, our public discourse. (BJP 1993)

According to H. V. Sheshadri, Sarkaryavah of the RSS,

> Ayodhya is not an exclusive incident in the odyssey of the ongoing Hindu Renaissance. But it certainly is the high point of centuries-old struggle, a situation which has been developing and ripening for several decades. (Hindu nationalist) resurgence remained neglected for a long time. The RSS picked up the thread and resuscitated the national spirit through tens and thousands of Shakhas, its multifarious Seva projects, various leading organizations ... This resurgent sprit of national assertion finally found a historic expression in the Ayodhya movement .... (Sheshadri 1998: 3)

The controversy over the Babri Masjid originated in the 19th century (Engineer 1990; Pandey 1993; Shrivastava 1991). Various studies point out that in order to show sympathy to the Hindu majority, it was the British who popularised the idea that the Mughal rulers had demolished Hindu shrines in Ayodhya (Engineer 1990; Shrivastava 1991: 28–29). However, *Babur-Nama* (memoirs of Babar translated by A. S. Beveridge in 1922) stated that the Mughal emperors had visited many temples, but there was no evidence of destroying any temple. Scholars also affirm that there was no evidence of Babur and Aurangzeb ever coming to Ayodhya; nor had they ordered to break the temples in the place (Shrivastava 1991: 67–96). However, the BJP and other Hindu Right organisations continued to argue that "Babur ordered his commander Mir Baqi to erect a mosque at Ayodhya" and that the latter "established the mosque after demolishing the Temple of Sri Rama" (Advani 1992; BJP 1993; Vajpayee 1992; VHP 1991).

However, the issue remained dormant for long. It was in the 1920s, just before the inception of the RSS, that Swami Shradhanand, the leader of the Arya Samaj and a militant nationalist, published a pamphlet *Hindu Sangatham: Saviour of the Dying Race*. Here, he wrote about the first step towards the organisation of the Hindus; the building of one *Hindu Rashtra Mandir* in every city and important towns in India (Pandey 1993: 242–43). Accordingly, each mandir should have a compound capable of holding an audience of 25,000 and a large hall for recitation from the holy texts and epics. Unlike most Hindu temples, associated with a particular tradition or sect and dominated by their own individual duties, these new mandirs were to be devoted to the worship of three mother sprits; *Gau-mata* (Mother Cow), *Saraswati-mata* (the Goddess of learning) and *Bhumi-mata*. The large compounds would provide space for *Akharas* where wrestling and gymnastics would be practiced. All these activities themselves were to be run by the local Hindu *Sabhas* (ibid.). The very notion of *Rashtra Mandir* carried a political meaning, that is, the importance of crystallising the political identity of the Hindus, irrespective of their vivid religious orientations. By rejuvenating the issue of Ram Janmabhoomi, the Sangh was apparently doing the same thing (ibid.).

In 1949, idols of Lord Ram were installed by devotees in the Babri Mosque. Prime Minister Nehru intervened and stopped the Hindus from worshiping there. However, because of the sensitivity of the issue, the idols were not removed. Meanwhile, the Nehru government declared the site 'disputed' and locked the gates to the mosque (*White Paper on Ayodhya* 1993, hereafter Government of India *White Paper on Ayodhya* 1993). Since 1949, the Masjid premises remained locked until it was thrown open in February 1986 by the then Prime Minister Rajiv Gandhi (Government of India *White Paper on Ayodhya* 1993; *Report of the Liberhan Commission* 2009). The process of communalisation was thus facilitated by the Rajiv Gandhi government. BJP said that "the Congress Government told the court through the District Magistrate, Faizabad, that there would be no law and order problem if the temple was unlocked." It took the Government 36 years to acknowledge this. "It is this that had held up the judicial order so long. Thus, it was the threat of direct action by the mass movement, and the deadline that made the Government respond in the manner it did" (BJP 1993. Also see Advani 1992; *Report of the Liberhan Commission* 2009; Vajpayee 1992).

The BJP argued that the Hindus have been "waging unremitting struggle" for centuries "to recapture their holy place." According to the party, the struggle was in three phases. First, by "military expedition and war diplomacy, when barbaric aliens were ruling the country" and there was no rule of law; Secondly, by legal means, when the British established their model of rule of law (from 1885); and thirdly, by mass movement from 1984 (along with legal steps) when rule of law "became insensitive to their legitimate plea even under indigenous dispensation." (BJP 1993)

In 1983, the VHP became the central figure in the Sangh family with its 'sacrifice for unanimity'. It launched three processions (*Ekatmata Yatra*) throughout India with the 'Sacred Water' from the river Ganges. The Ganges water was distributed in towns and villages and, along the way, refilled the pots from local sources of sacred water, especially from the temples. The Ganges became a unifying metaphor, and the VHP stressed the importance of the 'Hindu unity' (Sheshadri 1988: 278–84; VHP 1991). The RSS leader Sheshadri noted that the most striking aspect of *Ekatmata Yatra* was "its exemplification principle of unity in diversity." In his own words, "The countless spots of pilgrimages, temples and Ashrams, which have been till now looked upon mainly as symbols of our *punyabhoomi*, a holy land, have now acquired a new and vital emphasis; they are symbols of a common *Mathrubhoomi* as well" (Sheshadri 1984: 174). However, this symbolic agitation had culminated into a full-fledged mobilisation on the Ram Janmabhoomi issue. Television serials telecast by Doordarshan during this time (such as 'Mahabharata') had also contributed to communal mobilisation. The most striking aspect of these serials was its visualisation of 'war' with the traditional weaponries, and such visualisation was supported by the most sophisticated technologies, which ultimately produced an image equivalent to the modern warfare. The RSS mouthpiece *Organiser* reported that B. R. Chopra's serial 'Mahabharata' ended in July 1990 "reaffirming the age-old cultural unity of India." It has been traditionally described as the 'fifth Veda'—It is the Veda of human life and an epic presentation of the struggle between value-based life and harsh reality (*vastav*). And the overall mobilisation that the Sangh carried on was legitimized on this line, the struggle for a value-based life, that is, *Ramarajya*.

The VHP meanwhile launched another programme named *Ram Puja*. It was a ceremony in which the bricks (*shila*), inscribed with the words 'Shri Ram' were consecrated locally and, then, collected and taken to Ayodhya in special chariots for building the proposed Ram temple. It was reported that the VHP was planning to organise 3.30 lakh programmes, which included door-to-door campaigns, prayers, *kirtans*, discourses, music concerts and symposia in five lakh villages and also the programmes would be organised in about 120 countries (*Organiser* 28 May 1989; VHP 1991). The VHP also announced the *puja* of consecrated bricks in 500,028 villages. The peculiar feature of this campaign was the participation of ordinary devotees through a simple act of consecrating a single brick in the name of Ram, and they were said to be participating in a gigantic programme, which they equated with nation-building (*Organiser* 8 October 1989; VHP 1991).

The role of the 'Soldier Monks' in the Ayodhya agitation was also prominent. Historically, the monastic rivalries were common in the Indian society. Kumbhamela was the major site of resolving monastic rivalries and, most often, it led to sectarian violence. During the colonial period, the British saw it as an unhealthy trend and took measures to prohibit it. The Naga (warrior) Sadhus had great influence among the common people. During the nationalist struggle, they showed their support, but they kept away from the movement because they were unwilling to subordinate their institutional religious loyalties to the Gandhian nonviolent mode of struggle (Pinch 2005: 140–47). However, the Bharat Sadhu Samaj (BSS), an organisation founded in 1956, sought to bring together the sadhus of India for the betterment of the society. The 'hard-line' BSS leaders were fascinated by the aggressive stance of the VHP on the Ayodhya issue and they were invited to the BSS convention. The BJP and the RSS decided to play a behind-the-scene role in the Ayodhya agitation, and the *Sants*, sadhus and *Mahants* led the agitation. Under the auspices of the BJP, various *Dharma Sansads* and *Sant Sammelans* were conducted (Chatterjee 1993: 4; VHP 1991). The VHP and non-VHP sadhus had deep rooted hatred towards the 'aliens' and sought to destroy the reforms and progress made within the Hindu society, thereby re-establishing a fundamentalist Hindu order based on the old Brahminical social order. During this time, the BJP was also able to mobilise them in the name of a proposed *Ramarajya*.

There was another organisation in the forefront of the Ayodhya agitation, Bajrang Dal, the militant youth wing of the VHP. The name of the Bajrang Dal invoked the imagery of the army of monkey warriors in the epic Ramayana. This organisation was primarily seen as an instrument of other organisations. Ashis Nandy notes that

> the VHP had all the essentials to launch a massive agitation of the kind it wanted, a well-planned strategy and financial support to take the issue to the streets. The VHP required, to put it plainly, substantial muscle power under its control to meet the needs of agitation politics. In time, the youth power of the Dal came to fulfill this need of the VHP. (Nandy 1998: 96)

Unlike the RSS cadres, the Bajrang Dal members were known to recruit "untrained, volatile, semi-lumpen elements" (Noorani 2001: 72) and they were mainly from the unemployed educated youths in the urban areas. Nandy specifically pointed out that the cadres of the Bajrang Dal were from poor upper-caste background and from smaller cities and semi-urban town areas. They were also partly educated and jobless (Nandy 1998: 97). The VHP had been gently using these 'frustrated minds' for the mobilisation of the local population. Most often, they were guided by an image of a 'glorious past and a 'perverted present' and the possibility of 'good future'. The VHP sought support by deploying an image of the possibility of a 'glorious future' consistent with the past. However, the organisation was in the forefront of the demolition of the Babri Masjid, which they viewed as the first step towards 'Ramarajya' (Government of India *White Paper on Ayodhya* 1993; *Report of the Liberhan Commission* 2009).

Yet another opportunity for the BJP–RSS–VHP–BD combine to gain further political leverage occurred during 1989–1990 when the National Front government led by V. P. Singh decided to implement the recommendations of the Mandal Commission to provide 27 per cent reservations in public education and employment for the castes officially designated 'Other Backward Classes' (OBCs). The BJP was initially in a dilemma on the issue as it used to get support mostly from the upper caste sections, besides the OBCs, SC/STs and Muslims. The upper caste sections, in turn, started violent agitations against the Government's decision. As a supporter of the Government from outside, the stance of the BJP was crucial. It knew that the party had to appease both the upper caste sections and the OBCs. According to Amrita Basu, "The Government's decision heightened *the salience of caste over religion* and, thus, threatened to fragment the BJP's Constituency" (Basu 2005: 58; Ghosh 2003). The BJP formally supported the Mandal recommendations at the national level and undermined it locally, especially in places where it relied on upper caste support (Basu 2005: 58). However, the BJP sought to deal with it in a clever way. In the background of the emerging crisis, L. K. Advani announced his Ram Rath Yatra with an obvious motive. BJP's basic perception was very clear:

> V. P. Singh suddenly came up with the Mandal report, not because his heart was bleeding for the poor but because he thought that, on this issue, he could dissolve the House to go to the polls, collect some 350 seats and rule the country on his own without the bother of consulting anybody on anything. But it was a gamble that failed, because the BJP had already raised the Ayodhya issue. And it had done so early in 1989, not on the basis of any electoral calculation, but on ideological conviction. Historic wrongs had to be righted, however, symbolically, for a lasting solution of the Hindu-Muslim problem. Advani's Rath Yatra from Somnath to Ayodhya affected a sea change in the political scene. While Mandal had divided the people, Ayodhya united the people. (BJP 2010b)

Although linked to the Ayodhya issue, the aim of Advani's Rath Yatra was

> to raise three fundamental questions that had all along lurked in the collective sub-conscience of the nation but nobody had dared ask them, fearful of retribution from the pseudo-secularists who had ruled India by default since 1947. These questions were: What is secularism? What is communalism? Can national integration be achieved by constantly pandering to minority communalism? Cannot Government reject the cult of minority-ism. (Advani 2010b)

The Rath Yatra began from Somnath on 25 September 1990, the birth anniversary of Pandit Deendayal Upadhyaya and was expected to conclude at Ayodhya on 30 October 1990 after traversing 10,000 km. The importance of Somnath was underlined by the BJP by invoking the historical cases of 'assault' on the Hindu culture. The party and its leaders repeatedly said that it was at Somnath that the assault on Hindu temples and shrines, the living symbols of an ancient nation, by Islamic invaders began (Advani 1990b, 2010b). According to BJP, Advani had to choose

> Somnath as the starting point of his yatra because the reconstruction of the shrine on the rubble of loot and plunder was the first chapter in a journey to preserve the old symbols of unity, communal amity and cultural oneness. The Yatra was scheduled to conclude at Ayodhya because the liberation of Ram Janmabhumi would be the second. (Advani 2010b)

The success of the Sangh combine was its strategic approach to mobilise the pluralistic Hindu folk towards a particular end, the 're-construction' of the Ram temple at Ayodhya. The iconographic choices and expressions throughout the *Rath Yatra* were not simply the representation of the existing 'Hinduism', but a clear-cut attempt to reconstruct Hinduism, towards a new religious and political configuration, called 'Hindu Unity' and *Ramarajya* (Davis 2005: 27–34). However, it cannot be viewed as an imposition of the religious unity, but an attempt to invent a unity by showing emotional symbolic expressions. Like the very definition of the Hindutva, it has nothing to do with the religious belief of the common Hindu, but everything to do with politics. Achin Vanaik observes, "It does not intervene within Hinduism to make choices but posits an opponent for all Hindus regardless of their variant beliefs and practices. This approach is absolutely central to the Sangh combine's task of constructing the desired Hindu unity" (Vanaik 2006: 183).

The other approach was the construction of a loose and more accommodating Brahmanism. But it would cause tension with more popular forms of practice and worship. The first approach was, therefore, found to be more appropriate to frame the Hindutva choices. For example, in the Ayodhya agitation, there was a plurality of meaning, that is a 'community of meanings to Ram'. Through the *Ram Janmabhoomi* movement, the VHP was able to locate the universal 'self' in a particular, originative space. Reintegration with the 'self' then meant a quest to recover one's manifest inheritance. It turned an otherworldly search into an enterprise that was more easily appreciated by a society of private property owners (Datta 1993: 47–50). That means, each and every space must be utilised in this massive process like the role of the priests to '*Hanuman Sena*', or 'Monkey warriors', in the epic, Ramayana. In the Ayodhya agitation, the upper-caste Hindus, Dalits and the Adivasis were mobilised for the realisation of the 'common' cause, the possibility of the '*Ramarajya*'. The Sangh had successfully crystallised the political identity of the Hindus by deploying a common 'threat', the Muslims. The BJP leaders also invoked historical parallels to celebrate the outcome of the Yatra:

> The moral and revolutionary dimension of the Ram Rath Yatra made it comparable to the Salt Satyagraha or 'Dandi march' of Gandhi in 1930. The yatra effectively drove home the point that if Ram represented the ideal of conduct, Ram Rajya represented the ideal of governance. The sheer

magnitude of popular support made it comparable to Tilak's appropriation of Ganesh Chaturthi to mobilise public opinion against colonial rule. The cultural dimension of the yatra made it comparable to the anti-cow slaughter campaign of Gandhi. (Advani 2010b)

The most common feature of Advani's Rath Yatra was the offering of traditional weaponries by local people belonging to different castes (*Organiser* 14 October 1990). Advani was presented with bows and arrows, discs, maces, sword, trishuls and kirpans. This was a symbolic expression of militancy. It was, in fact, not a spontaneous act, but an outcome of a clear-cut conscious strategy by the Sangh. The influence of serials like 'Ramayana' and 'Mahabharata' was apparently significant. 'Ramayana' created a particular version of Rama bhakti, and the Ram Janmabhoomi issue had territorialised it, and this 'politics of space' invented a new version of Rama, who was significantly different from the figure represented in the traditional iconography. The traditional iconography represents Rama in *shanta rasa*. The images then available showed *ugra rasa*, Rama with a bow, pulling the bow string, the arrow poised to annihilate. The background was furnished with Shri Ram Jyoti, and it had a photographic-like image of a temple on it—the temple that was to be built in Ayodhya (Kapur 1993: 74–75). The videocassette produced by J.K. Jain, 'Bhaye Prakat Kripala' showed another image of Rama, 'Infant Ram' who was in the disputed mosque and displaying a variety of 'cute' poses and eventually stringing a bow (Sarkar 1993: 27). As Richard H. Davis pointed out, "If the aggressive young warrior Rama of the posters served as a militant role model for the Hindus taking control of their homeland, the infant Rama called upon maternal devotion from those who would nurture the young reincarnation of Hindu nationhood" (Davis 2005: 41). In order to spread the message of their campaign, the VHP distributed small stickers depicting Rama and the temple. The households were requested to fly saffron flags. The syllable 'Om' was taken as a unifying 'mantra'. The most notable thing was that the VHP did not put its signature in any of these visual products, and exhibited it as the 'spontaneous response' of the Hindu devotes (ibid.). Thus, the Sangh's mobilisational strategy was multidimensional. It addressed almost all sections of the Hindu folk and ensured their presence in the programme (BJP, 1993; Jaffrelot 1996; VHP 1991).

Advani's Rath Yatra was accompanied by massive bloodshed, and several communal riots occurred throughout India (Basu 2005: 71–72; Setalvad 2001). On 24 October 1990, Advani was arrested and the riots grabbed the States of Uttar Pradesh, Gujarat and Rajasthan. The riots were orchestrated by the BJP. The BJP electoral victory in the 1991 elections, particularly in Uttar Pradesh was influenced by these riots (Basu 2005: 72). van der Veer observed that those chief ministers who acted against the Rath Yatra were also influenced by another factor that they were 'low caste' leaders, and were the main beneficiaries of the Mandal recommendations (van der Veer 1996: 5). However, the Sangh generally justified the bloodshed (BJP 1993; Government of India *White Paper on Ayodhya* 1993; *Report of the Liberhan Commission* 2009; VHP 1991). Swami Chinmayananda, founder of the Chinmaya Mission (also the founder of the VHP), in an interview said, "When is it that blood is not there? When you were delivered, when you are a baby was it not in blood? A nation is built in blood. A nation imbrues in blood and a nation disappears in blood" (Pragna Bharati-3). Such statements from the responsible leaders of the Sangh Parivar were a source of legitimation and great inspiration to the Sangh followers. Ashok Singhal, the then Secretary of the VHP, made a statement in an interview.

> I want to appeal to our Muslim brethren once again that there is still time to ponder over it and come to a mutual settlement by handing over the three sacred places to the Hindus, namely Ram Janmabhoomi, Krishna Janmasthan and Gyan Vapi, Varanasi. If they fail to decide on this then we will start our campaign for liberating 3000 sacred places of Hindus desecrated by Muslim vandalism. The choice is now up to them whether 3 or 3000. (Sharma 1990: 14)

According to Balasaheb Deoras, the then *Sarsanghchalak* of the RSS, "The determination for reconstruction of *Ram Mandir* does not emanate from any feeling of ill-will or hatred towards any religion or creed. On the contrary, it is a step in the direction of creating the feeling of *Sarvadharma Sambhava* in them." It means equal respect for all religions. It is based upon the question of tolerance (Deoras 1990: 13–14).

The long years of communal mobilisation through more than 84 organisations controlled by the RSS culminated in the destruction of the 460-year-old Babri Masjid on 6 December 1992 (Government of India

White Paper on Ayodhya 1993; *Report of the Liberhan Commission* 2009). In July 1992, the then Prime Minister P. V. Narasimha Rao had assured the Parliament that he would try to find a solution to the Ayodhya issue within four months. By early November 1992, the Sangh combine announced, "the Rao Government failed to find out a solution to the issue and it would go ahead with the proposed 'Karseva' with effect from 6 December 1992" (BJP 1993; VHP 1991). When the mobilisation of the *Karsevaks* progressed, the Supreme Court actively intervened in the issue. The BJP-led State government in Uttar Pradesh had assured the Supreme Court that it would allow the *Karsevaks* to perform only the symbolic ceremony of '*bhajans*' and '*kirtans*' (Esteves 1996: 230; Government of India *White Paper on Ayodhya* 1993; *Report of the Liberhan Commission* 2009).

Similarly, the leader of the opposition in the Lok Sabha, L. K. Advani and the then Chief Minister of Uttar Pradesh, Kalyan Singh also assured the protection of law and order situation through various press meetings and public conferences. Meanwhile, Advani and M. M. Joshi started a new round of Yatras from two places in Uttar Pradesh, Varanasi and Allahabad, asking the people to join for '*Karseva*'. Thousands of others had indulged in seeking public support and mobilising the public. Lakhs of people were thus mobilised. Much before the time fixed for '*Karseva*' Uma Bharati and Sadhvi Rithambara, with around 2 lakh *Karsevaks* had taken their positions at the disputed site (*Report of the Liberhan Commission* 2009). An hour before the so-called symbolic '*Karseva*' was planned, at 11:40 AM, the first batch of '*Karsevaks*' reached the top of one of the domes of the Masjid. The forces were apparently frozen by the Uttar Pradesh Chief Minister. The Central Reserve Police was also inactive. Within five hours, the three domes of the Babri Masjid were pulled down with pickaxes, hammers, crow bars, roper shovels and iron rods. Indeed, this assault was "systematic" and "pre-planned." The BJP called it as a 'spontaneous' act and was beyond control (BJP 1993; VHP 1991). Two points mainly counter the very notion of 'spontaneity'. First, without a pre-planned effort, no one could bring down such a mighty monument within a short time of five hours; and second, the picture showing Uma Bharati embracing and hugging M. M. Joshi, when the third dome was collapsing, was the finest evidence of the BJP's role (Esteves 1996: 235–36; Government of India *White Paper on Ayodhya* 1993). The Liberhan Commission, which inquired into the demolition of the Babri Masjid brought out vast evidences it gathered during its tenure that spread over 17 years, including statements of witnesses and official records. One of the key conclusions of the one-man commission is that the "entire build-up to the demolition of the structure was meticulously planned" and that there is "nothing to show that the top leaders of the BJP were either unaware of what was going on or were innocent of any wrongdoing." The Liberhan Commission's task was to investigate the sequence of events leading, and all facts and circumstances relating to the occurrences at *Ram Janmabhoomi–*Babri Masjid complex on 6 December 1992 (MHA 2009). The *White Paper* issued by the Government of India also brought out concrete evidences of the role of the BJP and other Sangh organisations (Government of India *White Paper on Ayodhya* 1993). The BJP, in reply to the Government's White Paper, brought out another White Paper to counter the Government's position where it argued that

> the Ayodhya movement appears to have taken the lid off the Muslim community in India and set-off a debate which that community was consistently held incapable of. It has not stopped, at that. The Ayodhya movement has made all secular parties less allergic to Hindutva and the Marxists now find even Swami Vivekananda agreeable. (BJP 1993: Chapter VII)

The provocations for the demolition were outlined by the BJP: The general and growing Hindu resentment against pseudo-secularism and minority appeasement; the allergy of most political parties to Hinduism and the consequent loss of national identity; the political effect implicit in the Babri structure, which is an invader's victory monument; the deliberate pseudo-secular attempt to ignore the truth and clothe it with religious sanctity; the identifying of a mosque structure in Sri Rama's birthplace as a symbol of minority rights and secularism; the insulting interpretation of Sri Rama and the Ramayana by Marxists under the cover of secularism; the characterisation of Babar as secular and the Ayodhya movement as communal; and ignoring the fact that for 37 years till 1986 the idol of Rama was behind bars and under lock at Ayodhya—the most provocative sign for any Hindu, forcing the Hindus to fight for everything on Ayodhya. BJP says that "the cumulative effect of all this produced a volcanic explosion at Ayodhya which could not have been controlled except by an understanding system—the Government, the courts and the political parties." It also said that "the demolition of the disputed structure was an uncontrolled and, in fact, uncontrollable upsurge of a spontaneous nature, which was provoked only by the callousness of the Government in dealing with the Ayodhya issue without understanding the sensitive nature of the issue" (BJP, 1993: Chapter VI). The Liberhan Commission, on the other hand, came to the conclusion that "the mobilisation of the *Karsevaks* and their convergence to Ayodhya and Faizabad was neither spontaneous nor voluntary. It was well-orchestrated and planned" (*Report of the Liberhan Commission* 2009: 917, Para 158.9).

The BJP came down heavily on the Liberhan Commission Report and said that it

> has failed to come up to the expectations of the people. It has failed to dig out facts and serve the purpose for which it was constituted. The report appears to be the handiwork of a prejudiced mind was pre-determined to give the report on a particular persons and or institutions. (BJP 2009: 7)

Criticising the Liberhan Commission Report, L. K. Advani said:

> I am proud of my association with the Ayodhya movement. I was grieved over the demolition of that structure but the establishment of a huge Ram Temple on that spot in keeping with people's aspiration is my aim in life and until it happens, I will keep pursuing it. (Advani 2009: 18)

An editorial that appeared in the RSS mouthpiece *Organiser* later commented that what happened in Ayodhya on 6 December 1992 was "a spontaneous manifestation of the collective Hindu angst and faith." It reads:

> if the demolition of one structure, which the Muslims and their cohort pseudo-secularists believed was an insignia of an invader's victory to be preserved for future generations, pushed the nation to 'the brink of communal discord', how many times should the nation have been pushed to the brink and beyond when temples were destroyed in hundreds in independent secular India? .... December 6 is etched in the memories of Hindus as a day of bravery, to be celebrated and sung in folk narratives for centuries to come—as the day when the Hindu unleashed his power and demonstrated what he can do when pushed against the wall. (BJP 2009: 25–26)

After demolition of the alleged structure on 6 December 1992, three organisations namely RSS, VHP and Bajrang Dal were banned through

Government notifications under the Unlawful Activities (Prevention) Act, 1967 on 10 December 1992 (Government of India *White Paper on Ayodhya* 1993). However, the Sangh Parivar celebrated the demolition across the country and it was followed by an outburst of communal violence in Mumbai, Surat, Ahmedabad, Kanpur, Bhopal, Delhi and several other places. In Mumbai, more than thousand people were killed and many Muslim women were mass raped (Engineer *2001*). The demolition of the Masjid and the accompanying communal violence helped the BJP to securitise the whole issue, thereby polarising the population into groups. The party very skilfully utilised the issue for electoral gains. From 1989 onwards, the BJP had made considerable progress in terms of the number of seats that it won in various elections as well as the percentage of votes that they secured. In the southern states too, there was progress in the percentage of votes that the BJP had gained (Election Commission of India 2010).

BJP, Hindutva and the NDA Rule

The demolition of the Babri Masjid had invited widespread criticisms against the BJP and its support organisations from all over the world (Engineer 1992; Gopal 1993; Jaffrelot 1996; Sharma 2003). The BJP was, therefore, in a defensive posture for some time. Yet, the increase in the voting percentage of the BJP (also of its predecessor Jana Sangh) was amazing. It had risen from 3.06 per cent in 1951 to 7.74 per cent in 1984, 11.36 per cent in 1989, 20.11 per cent in 1991, 20.29 per cent in 1996, 25.4 per cent in 1998 and 23.75 per cent in 1999. In the 1999 Lok Sabha elections, the BJP had secured 298 seats and became the ruling party at the centre with a clear-cut majority in Parliament (Election Commission of India 2010). Apparently, the common factor in the increase in the popularity of the Jana Sangh and the BJP was their indebtedness to Hindutva and cultural nationalism (Advani 1990a; Vajpayee 1992). L. K. Advani, later, acknowledged that the "BJP's subsequent trajectory of meteoric growth was due to the Ayodhya movement." He also admitted that the movement had "changed my profile in Indian politics" (Advani 2007).

The ascendency of the BJP as the ruling party of India during 1998–2004 represented the revival of Hindutva. Communal sentiments continued to echo in the writings and campaigns of the BJP, which tended to see Hindutva as a unifying force that would create a national identity and ensure social cohesion for India. A manifestation of this ideological prejudice in the nation-building process could be discernible in the Election Manifesto of BJP in 1996. In the introduction entitled "vision, faith, and commitment" of the BJP, the Manifesto declared, "The present millennium begun with the subjugation of our ancient land. Let a re-invigorated, proud, and prosperous India herald the next millennium" (BJP 1996). It concluded with an appeal to all patriotic Indians to assist the BJP in the task of reconstructing a nationalist Hindu Rashtra. The section in the 1996 Manifesto entitled "Indian Immigration: A Democratic Invasion," construed the Muslim immigrant refugees of Bangladesh as democratic threats to India unlike the Buddhist immigrant refugees (Chakmas) to India from the CHT of Bangladesh. In the same manner, BJP's slogan "justice for all and appeasement for none" was motivated by the communal goal to restore a sense of 'Indianness' within the Hindu Rashtra, perceived to have been undermined by the 'pseudo secularism' of the Nehruvian legacy. According to the BJP President, L. K. Advani, democracy and liberalism as preached by Nehru were denuded of their Indianness. He believed that "India is what it is because of its ancient heritage—call it Hindu, or call it Bharatiya (India). If nationalism is stripped off its Hinduism, it would lose its dynamism" (Advani 2007, 2010e). However, the BJP specified that the concept of Hindutva as the underlying basis of a Hindu Rashtra did not mean religion. Rather, "it means a pan-Indian identity." Yet, the success of the BJP in establishing the discourse of Hindutva as the nationalist identity of India might help to use the terms Hindutva, Hinduism and the Indian national identity synonymously. According to the BJP

> Hindutva awakened the Hindus to the new world order where nations represented the aspirations of people united in history, culture, philosophy, and heroes. Hindutva successfully perpetuated an image of India in concomitant with their 'ideal' state of Israel. (BJP 2010b)

There were several instances in which the BJP–VHP–RSS combine had indulged in the constructions of 'self' and 'other' on the basis of religious identity. A VHP leader, Sadhvi Rithambara, supported the Hindus in the Ram Janmabhoomi–Babri Masjid movement in 1992 as "a fight for the preservation of a civilization, for Indianness, for national consciousness" and the BJP spokeswoman, Sushma Swaraj, suspected alleged treachery on the part of the Muslims against India because the former "rooted for Pakistan during the two Indo-Pakistan wars." The BJP claimed that its nationalism has been based on "one nation, one people, one culture." Thus the concept of Hindu Rashtra "becomes virtually essential to Hinduism as the dominant religion in India." Muslims were constructed as "invaders and foreign transplants" (Das 2002: 80–82). It openly said:

> Muslims, led by the Islamic clergy and Islamic society have innate unwill-ingness to change, did not notice the scars that Hindus felt from the Indian past. It is admirable that Hindus never took advantage of the debt Muslims owed Hindus for their tolerance and non-vengefulness. (Ibid.)

Referring to the concessions Muslims always enjoyed, the party said

> India even gave the Muslim minority gifts such as separate personal laws, special status to the only Muslim majority state—Kashmir, and other rights that are even unheard of in the bastion of democracy and freedom, the United States of America. Islamic law was given precedence over the national law in instances that came under Muslim personal law. The Constitution was changed when the courts, in the Shah Bano case, ruled that a secular nation must have one law, not separate religious laws. Islamic religious and educational institutions were given a policy of non-interference. The list goes on. (BJP 2010b)

While Hindutva sought to carve out a cultural space during this period, the BJP as a ruling party began to face a serious dilemma in the realm of economy. In the 1990s, the BJP's economic policy was caught between two contradictory tendencies: 'pragmatism and ideological purity'. The moderates in the party tended to be more 'pragmatic' than 'nationalistic' on economic matters. For them, cultural nationalism was more important than economic nationalism. For the right-wing of the party, cultural and economic nationalism constituted two sides of the same coin. The right-wing apparently took a backseat in the actual functioning of the party. Hence nobody expected serious departures from the reform process initiated by the Congress party in 1991 (Arulanantham 2004). The BJP's

1998 election manifesto had expressed a strong swadeshi (self-reliance) component, causing speculation that the party would end the programme of external economic liberalisation initiated by the Congress government of Narasimha Rao in 1991, and move to protectionism. It said:

> The economy of India has come under tremendous pressure because of misguided tariff reductions and an uneven playing field for the Indian industry .... It is clear that foreign capital will be only of little value to the national economy, though crucial to some sectors like infrastructure.... While the declared agenda [of every nation] is free trade, the undeclared, but actual agenda is economic nationalism. India too must follow its own national agenda. This spirit is swadeshi. (BJP 1998: 2)

The BJP's slogan was "vote for BJP is vote for nationalism" (*Organiser* 15 February 1998). The document, however, spoke of 'calibrated globalisation'. It suggested that although internal liberalisation would continue, the state would intervene to protect Indian industry from foreign competition and regulate external influence in the economy (BJP 1998). Yet, despite the pre-election rhetoric of swadeshi, external economic liberalisation continued during the BJP's tenure from 1998 to 2004. Not only did the BJP fail to modify the policies of its predecessors, but it systematically accelerated globalisation. Thus, the notion of swadeshi was deployed to appeal to intra-party elements and find an electoral space in response to the liberalising agenda of the opposition. However, after assuming office, the leadership switched positions to appeal to the middle class, which embraced globalisation.

It may be noted that while in opposition, the BJP opposed the Insurance Regulatory Authority (IRA) bill in 1997, which sought to privatise the State-run insurance industry and invite foreign investment. Later, the BJP government passed a bill privatising the insurance industry, allowing up to 40 per cent foreign equity in the newly deregulated market. In 1995, the BJP undertook a campaign against the Dunkel Draft, which sought to widen the General Agreement for Trade and Tariffs (GATT) and create the WTO. The party also opposed the introduction of product patents in compliance with the WTO's subsequent Agreement on Trade Related Aspects of Intellectual Property Rights (TRIPS), and argued that reduction of customs duties should be conducted on a "case by case basis." In Parliament, the BJP blocked the Patents Amendment Act allowing for product rather than process patents. Yet in 1998, the BJP passed the Patents Bill (with support from the opposition Congress party), ushering in the product patents they had opposed and aggressively moved to phase out customs duties. The party also aggressively sought to phase out customs duties according to WTO schedules (Arulanantham 2004; Ghosh 2001; see Hansen 2001a; 2001b; Nayar 2001).

The BJP leadership defused tensions within the Sangh Parivar by relying on the politics of compromise and coalition politics. Strict party discipline silenced the BJP's own swadeshi contingent. According to Achin Vanaik

> tensions undeniably exist between the virulent cultural nationalism of the RSS, traditionally associated with protectionism, and the BJP's current pursuit of neo-liberal objectives. But they are containable, as the two wings of the Sangh operate a tactical division of labour: the BJP does not compromise too much on Hindutva; the RSS restrains itself on the NEP. (Vanaik 2001)

The BJP's decision to test nuclear weapons in May 1998—signalling India's arrival as a nuclear power—strengthened the hand of the reform faction. The nuclear explosions were greeted with euphoria within the Sangh Parivar for having displayed Indian power and assured its status in the world. This gave the pragmatists a certain political space to continue reforms. Arulanantham notes that

> the rhetoric of Swadeshi was a ploy to energise 'the base' while differentiating itself from and obstructing the ruling governments. Once in power, the pragmatists exerted their influence to continue liberalisation and to satisfy the urban middle class. This group harboured a sense of "India's greatness" and found the BJP's articulation of power appealing. As this case suggests, nationalism and globalisation are not necessarily opposing forces but sometimes self-reinforcing—in other words nationalism can facilitate movements that give rise to globalisation and in turn feed back onto itself to create stronger national identities. (Arulanantham 2004)

Hindutva and Education

The BJP's education policy also sought to legitimise the cultural logic of Hindutva (Kumar 2001). An assessment made by the National Council of Educational Research and Training (NCERT) in 1996 noted that the textbooks used by Vidya Bharati—the educational wing of the RSS—were "designed to promote bigotry and religious fanaticism in the name of inculcating knowledge of culture in the young generation." Children in these schools were "indoctrinated in religious intolerance, the inferiority of non-Hindus, and the collective blame of Muslims and Christians for wrongs against Hindus at various points in Indian history, as interpreted by Hindu nationalists" (Narula 2003). The West and its culture were projected as "enemies of Hindu culture." Religions such as Islam and Christianity were depicted as "alien to India," as they were the religions of foreign invaders—the Mughals and the British. The historical reconstruction of "Muslim and Christian atrocities" and their projection onto the present as a 'threat' to the integrity and security of India were powerful weapons in legitimizing the violence against Christians and Muslims (Elst 1997). Tanika Sarkar writes that

> if the motif of infinite, elastic revenge unifies past, present and future, then the production of an appropriate historical memory is crucial for the generation of the new political culture. History teaching, textbooks and historical scholarship have been special targets of Sangh attacks. They need to assert their monopoly over historical truth, for there is a strange symmetry between their historical allegations and their present violence. They assert that Muslims broke temples, and then they demolish mosques. They allege forced conversion, and then they command victims to utter the name of Ram or to convert. Legends of rapes of Hindu women abound, and Muslim women are then raped freely. (Sarkar 2002)

Leaflets depicting Muslims as 'terrorists' intent on destroying the Hindu community were also in circulation years before the 2002 attacks. RSS and VHP leaflets circulated in August 1998 proclaimed: "India is a country of Hindus.... Our religion of Rama and Krishna is pious. To convert [or] leave it is a sin." Another leaflet by the VHP in Bardoli, Gujarat, warned, "Caution Hindus! Beware of inhuman deeds of Muslims.... Muslims are destroying Hindu Community by slaughter houses, slaughtering cows and making Hindu girls elope. Crime, drugs, terrorism are Muslim's empire" (Narula 2003).

Sangh Parivar's strategy was to assert its cultural-educational goals across a wide spectrum of education (Elst 1997). There was a conscious attempt to Hinduise the educational system, root out liberal and leftist influences, and to re-write history in order to justify its anti-minority out-look. This was evident not only from the much publicised agenda sought to be implemented at the State Education Ministers' Conference held in October 1998 but also from the massive textbook revision undertaken by the Sangh Parivar in keeping with this design (Taneja 2002).

The basic agenda was incorporated through moral education and general knowledge texts that concentrated on inculcating a Hindu consciousness and 'pride in being a Hindu'. In the Government schools, in the BJP-ruled States and in the 20,000-odd Vidya Bharti schools and the *shishu mandirs* all over the country, the prescribed syllabus presented Indian culture as Hindu culture, totally denying its pluralistic character and the contribution of the minorities to the creation of the Indian identity. Everything Indian was shown to be of Hindu origin and the minorities were characterised as 'foreigners' owing their first allegiance to political forces outside this country. The communal and sectarian interpretation of history also extended to the study of the national movement, where the Muslims were painted as the enemies of the nation responsible for partition, and the Hindu communal forces as the greatest patriots and nationalists. In the name of 'Indianised nationalised and spiritualised' education, there was an attempt to polarise and divide people along religious lines by communalising their consciousness. Through a distortion of facts, there was an effort to reconstruct history and tradition along communal and sectarian lines. In fact, it was quite clear what the agenda paper at the Conference meant by the abrogation of the Articles 29 and 30 of the Constitution. Uma Bharti, the Union Minister of State in the Ministry of Human Resources went to the extent of saying that the "Kashmir problem finds its roots in the teaching pattern in the Madrasas and that there is a need to closely monitor them."

In BJP's agenda, science was to be necessarily combined with spirituality, thereby obscurantism and chauvinism were freely allowed to masquerade as national pride. Vedic Mathematics was introduced in the Uttar Pradesh schools but had to be withdrawn (Jayaraman 1993: 100). The implementation of the compulsory Saraswati Vandana and Vande Mataram mandate in the Government schools in the BJP-ruled States, the renaming of towns and streets, *bhajan mandalis*, 'social service' festivals, even sporting events, particularly cricket matches between India and

Pakistan, were transformed into lessons of popular education outside the formal classroom. The BJP also filled the top positions in the Indian Council of Historical Research (ICHR) with historians known for their association with the VHP campaign on Ayodhya and without any credibility in the field of history writing. The Indian Council of Social Science Research (ICSSR), The Indian Institute of Advanced Studies (IIAS), Nehru Museum and Memorial Library, All India Council for Technical Education (AICTE), University Grants Commission (UGC), etc., saw the induction of RSS–VHP supporters and followers in high positions.

In 2002, the NDA government spearheaded by the BJP made an attempt to change the NCERT school textbooks through a new National Curriculum Framework. The changes made were deemed to be of the Hindutva ideological leanings of the party, which were regarded as a narrow sectarian and Hindu chauvinist ideology (some media referred to it as 'saffronisation' of textbooks). The NDA government's term prompted criticism when it attempted to 'saffronise' public education by raising the profile of Hindu cultural norms, views and historical personalities in school textbooks and portraying other religions in a negative light. The BJP justified that their only goal was to overhaul the stagnant and saturated institutions like NCERT and free them from the dynastic control and hegemony of the Indian National Congress and the Communists. Party members also pointed out that their goal was not to promote sectarianism, but present a more accurate picture of Indian history and Indian culture (such as Vedic Science), which was being downplayed by the left-wing ideologues (Kumar 2002; 2001; Yadav 2002). *The Vision Document 2004* issued by the BJP on the eve of 2004 elections continued to reflect this approach. It sought to rectify "the biases in history education, increasing the moral and cultural content in syllabi, and restoring the neglected focus on character-building" (Advani 2010a).

Hindutva and the Gujarat Carnage

In 2002, the state of Gujarat experienced a traumatising episode of communal violence in which the Muslims were aggressively targeted. Gujarat was even called "Hindutva Laboratory" (*Asian Age* 25 March 2002).

The State government ruled by the BJP has been held responsible for accentuating the violence. Although the extent of its logistical involvement has been debated (for instance, Advani 2007; Brass 2003; Engineer 2002; see Government of Gujarat 2008 [hereafter *Nanavati Commission Report 2008*]; *Gujarat Carnage 2002*), the rhetoric of many Hindu Right organisations created and demonised a religious 'other'. The protagonists of Hindutva used a language that created pervasive religious binaries, which were instrumental in the recurrence of violence.

Between 28 February and 2 March 2002, hundreds of people—mostly Muslims—were killed in Gujarat, apparently aided and abetted by the BJP-ruled state government headed by Narendra Modi. Intermittent violence against Muslims continued in the months that followed. In the aftermath, thousands of people were rendered homeless and internally displaced. Numerous inquiries and commissions—such as the National Human Rights Commission (NHRC) of India—held that Narendra Modi, as the Chief Minister of the State, had complete command over the police and other law enforcement machinery during the period. They all condemned the role of the government in providing leadership and material support in the politically motivated attacks on minorities in Gujarat. Commenting on the carnage in Gujarat, the NHRC in its proceedings of 6 March 2002 noted that a large number of reports have

> appeared which are distressing and appear to suggest that the needful has not yet been done completely by the Administration. There are also media reports attributing certain statements to the Police Commissioner and even the Chief Minister which, if true, raise serious questions relating to discrimination and other aspects of governance affecting human rights. (NHRC 2002: 21)

The Commission pointed out that "there was a comprehensive failure on the part of the State Government to control the persistent violation of the rights to life, liberty, equality and dignity of the people of the State" (NHRC 2003). It also took serious note of the inadequate response from the Government of Gujarat to address the human rights violations in Gujarat. The Commission said that the "initial failure to protect human rights was compounded by the failure—at least thus far—to provide justice to those whose rights had been violated" (NHRC 2004: 28). Every major Indian and international human rights organisations such as

Amnesty International, Human Rights Watch, Commonwealth Initiative for Human Rights, Citizen's Initiative, PUCLs, PUDR condemned the Gujarat violence, and pointed to the complicity of the Government of Gujarat in the execution of the event. K. R. Narayanan, former President of India, said that there was a 'conspiracy' between the BJP governments at the Centre and in Gujarat behind the riots of 2002 in Gujarat. Narayanan said, "There has been government participation in Gujarat riots. I had sent several letters to the then Prime Minister Vajpayee, and also talked to him. But he did not do anything effective" (*Hindu* 2 March 2005).

The chain of events started on 27 February 2002 when the Sabarmati Express carrying the Sangh volunteers, who were travelling to aid in the construction of the Ram temple at Ayodhya, caught fire in the town of Godhra, killing about 59 pilgrims inside one coach (*Nanavati Commission Report 2008*). Although various reasons have been cited, including arson by a Muslim mob, the cause of the fire has been still debated. Communal riots soon erupted in the city of Ahmedabad and in some villages around the state. Estimates say that within a few days, nearly 2,000 people were killed and 100,000 were displaced and moved to relief camps. Humanitarian organisations claimed that up to 2,500 were killed and 140,000 were displaced (Parker 2008). The BJP-led NDA government's Ministry of Home Affairs' *Annual Report 2003-04* recorded that 722 communal incidents took place in the country in 2002 claiming 1130 lives and resulting in injuries to 4,375 persons (MHA 2004). However, these riots were called 'pogroms' by professionals from various fields, including scholars such as Stephen Wilkinson (2005: 3) and Paul Brass (2003: 390) because of the highly disproportionate number of Muslim casualties.

Chief Minister Narendra Modi and other leaders belonging to the Hindu Right organisations alleged that the Godhra tragedy had been a pre-planned Muslim conspiracy to attack Hindus, subvert the State, and damage the economy. In addition, Modi further sought to stoke religious passions of the majority Hindu community by taking the decision to bring the charred remains of the victims of the tragedy to Ahmedabad in a public ceremony intended to arouse passions. On 1 March 2002, at the height of the violence in the state, Narendra Modi declared that he would control the "riots resulting from the natural and justified anger of the people" (*Asian Age* 25 March 2002).

Investigations found that many Muslim-owned businesses were destroyed. Inventories of Muslim businesses, including hotels with Muslim partners, and Muslim residences were made available to the mobs by BJP, VHP and Bajrang Dal leaders and cadres, and the Gujarat State Police, as were voter registration lists/electoral rolls that aided in the targeting of Muslims in mixed or dominant Hindu neighbourhoods. Witnesses described how Sangh Parivar mobs were armed with liquid gas cylinders, tridents, knives and sticks. People from rural areas were trucked into neighbouring villages and towns to participate in the violence, sporting the uniform of the Sangh, saffron scarves and khaki shorts. Mob leaders used cell phones to coordinate the movement of thousands of armed men through densely populated areas. Many of the mobs descended upon Muslim neighbourhoods, homes and businesses, hacking and burning people and property. Women and girls were beaten, thrown into wells, targeted for rape, gang rape and collective rape, sexually mutilated and burnt. Instead of intervening and taking decisive action against the State government, the Central government ruled by BJP-led NDA chose to minimise the seriousness of what happened, with senior Central government leaders alleging without proof, Pakistan's ISI involvement in Godhra.

Referring to the communal violence in Gujarat, L. K. Advani, who was then the Union Minister for Home under the NDA Government, said that the "events were 'indefensible' and 'a blot on my government'." Advani was all "the more distressed" because "they blemished the Vajpayee government's widely appreciated record, until then." Later, in April, in the parliamentary debate, Advani said:

> I am a sad man as I participate in this debate. Our government's clean and proud record of riot-free governance for the past four years has been sullied. When I look at what has happened in Gujarat in its totality, I cannot but say that both Godhra and post-Godhra violence is condemnable and shameful. (Advani 2010d)

Yet, Advani defended the role of Narendra Modi in the whole episode saying that "Gujarat made spectacular progress" under him. He said that "people of all castes and communities in Gujarat have benefitted" from his "commitment to security, development and clean administration." He went a step further and said that "Modi's re-election has highlighted several lessons which are relevant not only for Gujarat but for the whole country. I have no doubt that my party's spectacular victory in Gujarat would indeed become a turning point because it signals the BJP's resurgence" (Advani 2007). Dibyesh Anand writes:

The BJP state leadership, which was clearly identified as complicit with the Gujarat 2002 killing machinery, was confident of gaining electorally after the riot and the fact that this confidence paid off is an indictment of the silent majority. The electoral victory in the State Assembly elections of December 2002—the best performance ever by BJP on its own in any state in India—challenged most factors that are seen as important in India's electoral democracy (e.g., anti-incumbency factor, lack of development and strength of the opposition) and showed that violence against Muslims had paid off. This cannot be explained by the instrumental interests of the Hindu majority alone but by the lack of compassion for the Muslim victims. There was a curious reversal of responsibility as many Hindus blamed Muslims for the violence and saw themselves as the victims whose security was threatened by 'the Muslim'. (Anand 2005: 210–15)

Similarly Smita Narula offers an insightful observation said:

To demand equal protection of the law for all or to protest when the government kills its own citizens is deemed a threat to the integrity of the nation and an attempt to defile India in the eyes of the international community. Conversely, outright murder or rape in the name of avenging past and present attacks on Hindus (whether fact or fiction), or constructing a Hindu temple where a Muslim mosque once stood, are all patriotic acts in the service of one's country. In the governmental arena, patriotism cloaks itself in the garb of national security. In an age in which even extrajudicial state action is condoned in the name of fighting terror and in which ter-rorism has become the involuntary monopoly of the non-state (and often Islamic) actor, political opponents and religious minorities become easy targets. (Narula 2003: 57)

Thus, the anti-Muslim violence in Gujarat in 2002 was cloaked by the Hindutva organisations as 'inevitable' and 'understandable' acts to secure the Hindu 'self'. The discourse of security thus offered the Hindu Right organisations "a tool to legitimize violence as nonviolence, killers as defenders, rape as understandable lust, and death as non-death" (Anand 2005: 203–15). The NDA government continued to exploit the rhetoric surrounding the global 'war against terrorism' in order to target religious minorities and political opponents. Most notably, the long debated anti-terrorism legislation, the Prevention of Terrorism Act (POTA), was pushed through parliament in March 2002. Its close resemblance to the much misused and then lapsed Terrorists and Disruptive Activities (Prevention) Act (TADA) of 1985 (amended 1987) foreshadowed a return to the widespread and systematic curtailment of civil liberties.

Securitisation: Pokhran-II and Kargil War

In critical IR literature, security has been conceptualised as a 'productive discourse' that produces insecurities to be operated upon, as well as defines the identity of the object to be secured (Campbell 1998; Krause and Williams 1997; Lipschutz 1995; Weldes et al. 1999). This questions the dominant conceptual framework of security that considers insecurities as unavoidable facts, while focusing attention on the acquisition of security by given entities. It foregrounds the processes through which something or someone (the 'other') is discursively produced as a source of 'insecurity' against which the 'self' needs to be secured (Anand 2005: 203–15). As such the discourses of insecurity are about 'representations of danger' (Campbell 1998; Dillon 1996). Dibyesh Anand says that insecurities, in such conditions, are "social constructions rather than givens— threats do not just exist out there, but have to be created." All insecurities are "culturally produced in the sense that they are produced in and out of the context within which people give meanings to their actions and experiences and make sense of their lives" (cited in Anand 2005; Weldes et al. 1999). Insecurities and the objects that suffer from insecurities are therefore mutually constituted. That is, in contrast to the received view, which treats objects of security/insecurity themselves as pre-given and natural and as separate things, we treat them as mutually constituted cultural and social constructions and thus products of processes of identity construction of self–other. Anand further says that the argument that security is about representations of danger and social construction of the 'self' and the 'other' does not imply that there are no 'real' effects. What it means is that there is nothing inherent in any act or being or object that makes it a source of insecurity and danger (Anand 2005).

Security is therefore inextricably interlinked with identity politics. How we define ourselves depends on how we represent 'others'. This representation is integrally linked with how we 'secure' ourselves against the 'other'. Representations of the 'other' as a source of danger to the security of the 'self' in conventional understandings of security are followed by abstraction, dehumanisation, depersonalisation and stereotyping of the 'other'. The 'other' gets reduced to being a 'danger' and hence an object that is fit for surveillance, control, policing and possibly extermination (Anand 2005; Foucault 1979, 1988). This logic of the discourse of security dictates that the security of the 'self' facilitates and even demands the use of policing and violence against the 'other'. This can be exemplified in the case of Hindutva's politics of representation, which legitimises anti-Muslim/anti-Pakistan stance in the name of 'securing' the Hindu body politic at various levels. 'The Muslim' is seen as a 'threat' to national, state and international security. These representations of 'the Muslim' as a danger to the 'security' of the Hindu body politic facilitate the politics of hate against the Muslims in India (and inevitably against Pakistan too). While the Gujarat carnage (2002) is an example of this campaign of Hindutva in the realm of domestic politics, Pokhran-II (1998) and Kargil War (1999) represent two other major instances in the realm of national security/defence whereby representations do matter for legitimising the logic of cultural nationalism. Pratap Bhanu Mehta writes:

> The installation of a BJP-led government at the centre was supposed to have a profound impact on at least one area of governance, defence. Here was a government committed to more self-confident and aggressive foreign policy posture, unencumbered by idealistic pieties in international relations, openly confrontational in its approach to Pakistan, and given to a shrill rhetoric of militarism. When India conducted its nuclear tests, many feared that it would be engulfed by a rising tide of militarism, a security obsession that would adversely affect its development priorities. The rhetorical postures of the government, its open commitment to 'coercive' diplomacy, and loose and wild talk threatening war, all seemed to signal the onset of a new militaristic state. (Mehta 2003)

The NDA government's decision to test nuclear weapons in May 1998—signalling India's arrival as a nuclear power—strengthened the hands of the pro-reform elements within the party. The nuclear weapons tests were welcomed with euphoria by the Hindu Right organisations for having displayed 'Indian power' and assured India's status in the world. This gave the pragmatists within the BJP considerable leverage to proceed with neoliberal reforms. The VHP projected nuclear weapons as a "symbol of militarised Hindu revivalism" and celebrated the blasts with the cry of "Jai Shri Ram" (Manchanda 2002: 366). According to Runa Das, the BJP's nationalist agenda constructed an 'internal' Othering vis-à-vis Islam/Pakistan, thereby justifying India's nuclearisation policies (Das 2002: 76–89).

The BJP's project of gaining for India 'global recognition' and a rightful place among the leading powers called for substituting the Gandhi–Nehru traditions with "images of Hindu masculinity and martial-endowments." For K. N. Govindacharya, the ideologue of BJP, forging a Hindu India "embracing Kshatriya/Shakti [warrior] tradition of revolutionaries instead of the timorous Brahminical Bhakti [devotional] tradition" was the main psychological makeover for BJP foreign policy (Chaulia 2002). 'Operation Shakti' (Pokhran-II) was rightfully regarded within BJP ranks as their moment in history. "Synthesising the tenets of political realism and the moral mission of the party," the BJP marked the anniversary of the explosions as "resurgent India day." The BJP's historical connection between the bomb and national vitality is well known (Ghosh 1999). The party (as well as its predecessor Jana Sangh) and the other Sangh Parivar organisations never tried to conceal their nuclear posture (Seethi 2005). In the 1998 General Elections, the BJP campaigned with an ideology of Hindutva that envisaged a 'great' India as a militarily powerful India. Its election manifesto stated that the "frenetic pace of military expansion and modernization by some of our neighbours" had not been addressed by previous administrations: "Since 1991, the country's defence budget has been declining in real terms ... from 3.4 per cent of the GDP in 1989–90 to a mere 2.2 per cent this year," and it listed numerous defence projects that had been delayed for the lack of adequate funds. The manifesto committed the party to a specific list of strategic, organisation and deployment options, including: the establishment of a National Security Council to "constantly analyze security, political and economic threats and render continuous advice to the Government (as well as to) undertake India's first-ever Strategic Defence Review." The manifesto also indicated the re-evaluation of India's nuclear policy with a view to exercising the "option to induct nuclear weapons" and "expediting the development of the Agni series of ballistic missiles" (BJP 1998).

Strength has always been visualised by the BJP primarily in terms of 'hard strength' (military might). Jana Krishnamurthy, the then President of BJP, believed that nuclear weapons would "give us prestige, power, standing" and foreclosed India from being "blackmailed and treated as oriental blackies" by the Western world (Chaulia 2002: 220–21). The publication of RSS named *Organiser* wrote:

> In this world ambience India has stirred the nuclear club with its reverberations echoing all over the world. The BJP-led Government has finally decided to prepare the nation to enter the *dharmakshetra*. India, like the Pandavas, has collected the sack of weapons from the Shami tree. The Pandavas, too, were denied their due share, their very right to existence. But then dharma was on their side: And the rest is history. (*Organiser* 24 May 1998)

In a congratulatory letter, the RSS leader H. V. Sheshadri appreciated the Prime Minister of India for the nuclear explosions. He said, "all the world has got a loud and clear message that India can no more be treated as a second or third rate nation now" (Sheshadri 1998: 3). The VHP leader Ashok Singhal said, "Hindu Sadhus and religious leaders, in a bid to 'immortalise' the recent nuclear tests at Pokhran, are planning to set up a *shakti peeth* (seat of divine power) near the blasts' site." "India intends to be powerful in the interest of world peace, in keeping with the preachings of Lord Buddha," he quipped, adding that there could be no peace without power. "Look at the Hindu deities, they all bear weapons in their hands," Singhal remarked (*The Pioneer* 18 May 1998). In a letter to the Prime Minister, Rashtra Sevika Samiti Pramukh Sanchalika Usha Tai Chati said that "this singular historic feat has aroused the dormant self-respect of the nation" (*Organiser* 24 May 1998). Aijaz Ahamad said that the 'consensus' behind the BJP's dangerous nuclear adventure was "an attempted consensus behind Hindutva". The "Security adventurism had satisfied the hard-core elements in the Sangh" (Ahamad 1998: 21)

Generally, India's nuclear explosions were viewed as the advancement of the country in the realm of science and technology. Referring to the technical details of the tests, R. Chidambaram, Chairman of the Atomic Energy Commission said, "Five explosions in less than 48 hours is some kind of a world record ... it becomes even more significant when one notes that all these devices were of different types" (Chidambaram 1998: 11). Justifying the Pokhran-II, Prime Minister Vajpayee and Foreign Minister Jaswant Singh said that the decision to conduct the tests was taken after due consideration of all factors relevant to India's national security. These tests sought to "address the security concerns of the Indian people and provide them with necessary assurance" (MD 1999; MEA 1998, 1999). However, on 28 May 1998 Pakistan exploded five nuclear devices and one more on 30 May in Chagai. In a post-Chagai statement, Pakistani Prime Minister Nawaz Sharif said, "Our hand was forced by the present Indian leadership's reckless actions" (Ram 1998). As a response to the Pakistani nuclear explosions, Vajpayee said:

> A new situation has been created by Pakistan's tests but India is prepared to meet any eventuality. We are committed to maintain deterrence. (The Pakistani action) has vindicated our policy and stand .... In fact, Pakistani's clandestine preparations forced us on the path of a nuclear deterrent. We had our concerns. (MEA 1998, 1999)

Vajpayee established a National Security Council in April 1999 "to analyse the military, economic and political threats to the nation and render continuous advise to the government." Two new offices have been created—Chief of Defence Staff and Defence Intelligence Agency (DIA) to integrate weapon acquisition, logistics and strategy, hitherto performed compartmentally by the Chiefs of Army, Navy and Air Force (Ministry of Defence (MD) 2000). Pursuant to the BJP mantra of "security first and the rest will follow," a massive military modernization drive was under-way with party claims of "the largest ever increase in defence budget." In Advani's words, a "comprehensive systemic overhaul to meet security challenges of the 21st century" was being carried out for the first time in independent India's history (*The Hindu* 23 May 1998). On 17 August 1999, the NDA government released India's draft nuclear doctrine pre-pared by the 27-member National Security Council and Advisory Board, which called for "development of a credible, minimum deterrent" (Joshy 2010; Kargil Review Committee 2000: 205; MD 2000). The BJP sought to justify its policy of "defence diplomacy, coupled with adequate prepared-ness of our armed forces," "reviewing the security environment to cover all aspects of defence requirement and organisation," and "institutionalisation of forward planning" (BJP 1999: 27, 62, 70).

The war that broke out in Kargil (in Jammu and Kashmir) between India and Pakistan in May–July 1999 was the first direct ground war between the two countries after they had developed nuclear weapons. The war took place when Pakistani forces and Kashmiri militants were detected atop the Kargil ridges and 14 July when both sides had essentially ceased their military operations. It was believed that the planning for the operation, by Pakistan, might have occurred in early 1998. The incursion of Pakistan-backed armed forces into territory on the Indian side of the Line of Control (LoC) in Kashmir and the Indian military campaign to repel the intrusion left hundreds of Indian soldiers dead and several hundreds wounded (Kargil Review Committee 2000). The Kargil war provided a huge boost to the campaign of Hindutva forces and thereby the electoral future of the BJP. The war generated a "unifying response of binding a nation together as never before" claimed by the NDA government. The public saw for themselves that Indian military personnel, assigned to winkle out the infiltrators entrenched in commanding heights lines in line of fire "performed heroically" (MD 2000).

According to Rita Manchanda, the way in which the mass media—a major realm of civil society—participated "in shaping and even driving the changing terms of the discourse of Indian nationalism—that is militarized Hindu nationalism—was particularly evident during the Kargil conflict." She characterised it as India's "first war in a media society" (with satellite news channels brought the images and sounds of war in real time to the drawing rooms of viewers). It was also "first experience of war as spectacle and war as infotainment." Manchanda said that

> the media not only reported the Kargil war, but endowed militarism with a nobility of purpose and defined nationalism as patriotic flag waving, dangerously intolerant and demonising of the 'other'—in this case, all Pakistanis. Pakistan and the people of Pakistan became the enemy, fused in the media shaped popular imagination with rogue states and Talibanised terrorists. (Manchanda 2002: 23–30)

Amitabh Mattoo and Kanti Bajpai observed that

> it was a discourse that closed off any discussion on the political "why and wherefore" of the Kargil conflict as an event, glamourised war and martyrdom and spurred a jingoistic hysteria of militarised patriotism. Calls for ceasefire and peace were derided and worse denounced as anti-national.

Security became exclusively military security, at whose territorial altar was sacrificed the notion of human security. (Mattoo and Bajpai 2001)

During the war, two media images dominated. The first, the "representation of the jawan, unyielding, etched against the silhouette of dangerous mountains, the markers of the boundaries of the other land, the nation. It was a statement of aggressive territorial nationalism." The second one, "the endless televised spectacle of ceremonially draped coffins, ritualistic public mourning of heroic martyrs while dry eyed families waited for the privacy to weep and maybe question why their sons were dying?" A martyrdom was constructed around "the media hyped shradhanjali kitch, that defined a patriotic nationalist discourse of self-sacrificing macho heroes who died valiantly asserting … fresh from one victory and raring to go on to another" (Manchanda 2002: 23–30).

Following the outbreak of the war, the BJP and other Sangh organisations unleashed a violent campaign across the nation. Political leaders, strategic analysts and sections of the media in India called for a more aggressive war and the opening of new fronts (Mattoo and Bajpai 2001). There were also calls in India for the bombardment of Pakistani supply routes to Kargil. Some went even further. Kushabhau Thakre, then national president of BJP, suggested that the ultimate aim, after evicting infiltrators from the Kargil region, should be to take back the part of Kashmir held by Pakistan. According to the BJP leaders, unilateral ceasefires against militants and 'Pakistani mercenaries' would be signs of weakness and softness before 'a duplicitous adversary' and difficult for (the BJP) cadre to swallow (*The Hindu* 24 November 2000). Narendra Modi said that "defensive steps will neither protect innocent people nor bring about a change of heart among terrorists and that the time has come to pay Pakistan back in its own language" (Chaulia 2002: 224–25). Home Minister L. K. Advani later on wrote that

India had been a victim of Pak-sponsored terrorism since the beginning of the 1980s. But it is only the determined and concerted efforts of the NDA government that made western democracies accept that Pakistan was, indeed, the sponsor of cross-border terrorism against India. As a matter of fact, our diplomatic offensive succeeded in another related objective: in making them realise that Pakistan's abetment of terrorism was a threat not only to India but to the entire world. (Advani 2007)

Having won the Kargil conflict, the NDA predictably played heavily on its national security credentials during the 1999 general elections. Its 1999 manifesto expounded the war leadership shown by the caretaker administration, which "rose to the challenge and acted decisively... [and the] last of the Pakistani intruders were cleared from the Kargil Sector on 27th July." The manifesto also was very specific in noting the high ratio of national security pledges made in 1998 and their achievements in just thirteen months of government, including exercising the nuclear option, successfully testing a second-generation Agni ballistic missile, increasing the defence budget, and creating an NSC to advise the government on all matters of national security. In October 1999, the NDA headed by BJP came back to power, which won a comfortable majority in the 13th Lok Sabha. In contrast, the Congress suffered its worst defeat ever.

The December 2001 terrorist attacks on the Indian Parliament further widened the rift between the kernel of the party and moderate elements within the NDA government. The BJP rank-and-file felt that their past appeals to the Prime Minister not to negotiate with Pakistan had been vindicated with "yet another betrayal." Calls for a declaration of war on Pakistan for complicity in the Parliament, drawing parallels with America's war on the Taliban after September 11, were made regularly from the RSS, while Vajpayee adopted a more mellow tone while warning that India's "patience is running out." His position was that India would "go more than half the way to meet Pakistan" if there were credible reductions in infiltrations into Kashmir and an end to jihad (Chaulia 2002: 215–34).

Thus, the mobilisation of the Hindu Right organisations since the 1980s saw aggressive campaigns and violent incidences—from the demolition of the Babri Masjid to Gujarat carnage, from Pokhran nuclear explosions to Kargil war. Using the vast spectrum of the civil society in the country, the Sangh Parivar unleashed security-centred assertions and identity-based mobilisations almost simultaneously. The revivalism of Hindutva was, in fact, propelled by the structural transformation of the Indian State and civil society since the 1980s. The BJP's rise to power in the 1990s can, thus, be explained in terms of the crisis of the Indian polity and economy caused by social dislocations following the introduction of liberalisation and neoliberal reforms.

5

Hindutva Politics:
Post-9/11, Post-Gujarat India

A decade-long strategy of BJP, since the electoral debacle in the 2004 General Elections, culminating in the stunning victory in 2014, has to be understood in the context of critical engagements carried on by the Hindu Right forces through the civil domain. The neoliberal policies obviously generated insecurity complex in the social psyche of the masses and the Hindutva forces have been employing a grand strategy of 'securitisation' by dividing the society into 'friends' and 'foes' through cultural mobilisations and crystallising the political identity of the majority Hindu community. The ideology of Hindutva depicted the religious minorities as a threat to the Hindu/Indian nation and called for the political integration of the pluralist Hindu folks to counter the threat posed by the Muslims and Christians who have 'external loyalties'.

The demonisation of Muslims reached its peak with the terrorist attack on the twin towers of World Trade Center (WTC) and Pentagon on 11 September 2001 and the subsequent attack on the Indian Parliament on 13 December 2001. These incidents provided the Sangh Parivar a much-needed impetus to legitimise its anti-Muslim stand, and State machinery was increasingly used to depict Muslim/Pakistan as the threat to the Hindu/Indian nation. In tune with George W. Bush's classification of 'good Muslims and bad Muslims', L. K. Advani commented that: 'not all Muslims are terrorists but all terrorists are Muslims'. In this context, it would be interesting to analyse how "Hindutva has also served to integrate India into the current cultural logic of US imperialism premised on a permanent conflict with 'Islamic' terrorism" (see Lankala 2006). At this critical juncture of social history, the caricaturing of the other/Muslim was dreadful at the local, national and international levels. There was, however, a concerted effort from the Hindu Right to characterise the Indian experience (as 'victim' of Islamic terrorism) in terms and conditions of the United States and extended support to the US celebrated 'war on terror' campaign. Advani said, "Had the terrorists managed to enter Parliament House, the magnitude of the devastation would have eclipsed the September 11 incidents" (*Pioneer News* 2001). In a similar vein, Prime Minister A. B. Vajpayee said, "We saw it on September 11 and we have seen it again on December 13" (Lankala 2006: 96). According to Home Minister L. K. Advani, India "had already set up Joint Working Groups (JWGs) against terrorism with the USA, Canada, the UK, Germany and Israel" and has been "making systematic efforts to forge ties with other democratic countries in the past few years." He said that the US had "experienced terrorism now, only in the 21st century. But India had witnessed a trailer (of the coordinated terror strikes) in March 1993 in Mumbai when serial blasts took a toll of 253 innocent lives." While only one person was named as responsible (for the attacks on USA), there is one country (Afghanistan) which has been providing him shelter. Since the 1993 Mumbai blasts, India had also held one person responsible and told the world that there was one country, which was providing him refuge. Advani said that the target of terrorism was the civil society and democracy and the realisation that India was not the only target would go a long way in wiping out terrorism (Advani 14 September 2001).

It was very often perceived that the attack on the Indian Parliament was an attack on Indian democracy and secularism. L. K. Advani also used a secular tone to caricature Pakistan, by portraying it as the 'irrational' political formation in the Indian secular nationalist narratives. He said:

> Pakistan—itself a product of the indefensible Two-Nation Theory, itself a theocratic State with an extremely tenuous tradition of democracy—is unable to reconcile itself with the reality of a secular, democratic, self-confident and steadily progressing India, whose standing in the international community is getting inexorably higher with the passage of time. (MEA 2001)

Concerted efforts were underway to portray Muslims as 'terrorists' and 'pro-Pakistanis', as they were against the steady progress of India. This was also a reflection of the images produced by the global media networks and statist propaganda to the extent that there was an enduring conflict between the forces of democracy and the 'irrational' Muslim world. An impression was also put in place, through media and other intelligence reports, regarding the terrorist attacks, which were always against the Muslims even though there were Hindu militant attacks too reported from many parts. Thousands of Muslims were massacred in the post-Godhra terror in Gujarat where state machinery was used to handle the targeted minority community. The attacks on the Muslims were justified at various levels. Consequently, an ordinary Muslim gets marginalised in the public domain and his commitment to the nation can be questionable based on the assumption that 'all Muslims are terrorists'.

In the emerging scenario, the hate speeches by the Sangh leaders, especially in the post-Godhra period had blown out of all proportion inviting criticisms from various quarters. The Godhra incident was even termed as a terrorist attack, just as Modi said: "a pre-planned, violent act of terrorism" (*The Times of India* 28 February 2002). He further said that Godhra was a "mass murder, a terrorist act aimed at long-term damage" (*The Times of India* 7 March 2002). During his 'Gaurav Yatra', which came after the Gujarat carnage, Modi took the Muslim community to task saying that "relief camps are actually child-making factories. Those who keep on multiplying the population should be taught a lesson" (*The Hindu* 10 September 2002; also see *Asian Age* 15 September 2002). Harish Bhatt, a VHP leader said, "Now it is the end of tolerance. If the Muslims do not learn, it will be very harmful for them" (*New York Times* 6 March 2002). VHP international working president Ashok Singhal termed Gujarat as a 'successful experiment' and warned that it would be repeated all over India. He said, "Godhra happened on February 27 and the next day, 50 lakh Hindus were on the streets. We were successful in our experiment of raising Hindu consciousness, which will be repeated all over the country now" (*The Indian Express* 4 September 2002). The VHP international working secretary, Praveen Togadia, warned that "the reply to Godhra will be given today in Gandhinagar, tomorrow in Delhi and the day after in Pakistan" (*The Times of India* 15 September 2002). The RSS resolution at its Bangalore meeting on 18 March 2002 reads, "Let Muslims under-stand that their real safety lies in the goodwill of the majority." The hate speeches threatened the secular fabric of Indian democracy, shrunk the liberal space and thereby highlighted the exclusionary narrative of the Hindutva politics. Amidst the enduring conflicts and turbulent social relations, between some sections of the Hindus and the Muslims, the Hindu Right organisations actively intervened in the civil society with a view to perpetuating the project of 'securitisation' in the context of the perceived threat posed by the 'Muslim World'.

On the other side, the BJP-led NDA government pursued a full-scale liberalisation/privatisation policy notwithstanding criticisms from the 'swadeshi' factions of the Sangh Parivar. The Muslims were even portrayed as a 'threat' to the rapidly progressing Indian economy and thereby sought to legitimise the reforms and bypassing all opposition to the privatisation process.

The Vajpayee government showed its commitment to the WTO regime by eliminating quantitative restrictions (QRs) on imports by 2002 and to please the Swadeshi factions, provided tariff protection to Indian products. It allowed 26 per cent Foreign Direct Investment (FDI) in the insurance sector and print industry. Other sectors including civil aviation, pharmaceuticals, real estate, mass rapid transport system (MRTS), hotels and tourism, banking and telecom were also opened to FDI. Hotel, tourism, courier services, drugs and MRTS were earmarked for 100 per cent FDI through an 'automatic' route. More importantly, the NDA government set up a separate ministry for disinvestment to speed up decisions on privatisation of public sector undertakings. Arun Shourie, a committed advocate of economic reforms, was appointed Minister for Disinvestment, with responsibility for negotiations relating to the sale of publically owned enterprises. By July 2001, 27 firms had been cleared for disinvestment including Videsh Sanchar Nigam Ltd. (VSNL) (Frankel 2008: 733–34). However, the Vajpayee government was not a success in achieving a grand consensus on privatisation; it invited mass criticism from the Sangh as well as others including the trade unions. Francine R. Frankel notes:

The Privatisation provoked intense controversy—from labour unions; state governments in which a unit was located; administrative ministries whose power and sometimes very existence was endangered by privatisation, e.g., civil aviation, telecommunications, power, steel and shipping. Beyond this tangle of interests, the tentacles of corporate India began to penetrate the decision-making process with the largest enterprises manipulating politicians, legislators, bureaucrats and journalists, not only to advance their own projects but to prevent another company from succeeding. (2008: 734)

Meanwhile Vajpayee's influence on the BJP and Sangh Parivar apparently declined due to his stand on liberalisation and Ayodhya. In the Ayodhya issue, both Vajpayee and Advani rejected the demand of VHP to give out space for the Ram Temple. The pro-liberalisation faction in the Sangh Parivar faced severe criticism from RSS Sarsanghchalak K. S. Sudarshan who returned to New Delhi from Nagpur after an absence of two years. By appropriating Mahatma Gandhi's ideal of rural-based swadeshi economic model, he denounced the Western model or the ongoing liberalisation of the economy and called the pro-reforms officials as "sons of Macaulay and Marx", and he called for the 'saffronisation' of education policy to restore self-respect and confidence among the people. Asserting that "no one converts voluntarily" he declared that "India is a Hindu rashtra," and Hinduism a way of life, asking "if the people of Islamic Indonesia can accept Rama and Krishna as their ancestors, why cannot Indian Muslim do so?" (ibid.: 734–35).

The reassertion of the hardliners in the Sangh Parivar appeared to be an attempt to overcome the legitimacy crisis faced by the Vajpayee government due to rapid liberalisation of the economy in which common people experienced exclusion as well as alienation. It was also an attempt to equip the party for the next parliament election on the eve of the defeat in the Uttar Pradesh assembly election. The Gujarat 'experiment' was an electoral victory and Narendra Modi came to power for the second term. In Gujarat, the BJP contested 182 seats and won 138 seats with 49.12 per cent votes. It was an increase of 10 seats as compared with the 1998 elections in which BJP secured 117 seats with 44.81 per cent votes. However, in Uttar Pradesh the BJP came down from 174 seats in the 1996 election to 88 seats with 25.31 per cent votes. Bharatiya Samajvadi Party, which was in the third position in the 1996 elections got 98 seats with 23.19 per cent votes and became the single largest party. In Gujarat, the Sangh Parivar was able to consolidate the 'Hindu' votes beyond caste/class divisions, but in Uttar Pradesh the strategy did not work properly and caste politics overshadowed Hindu communal consolidation. In this background, the Sangh Parivar sought to radicalise Hindutva politics in order to consolidate the Hindu votes.

Electoral Debacle and the Hindutva Politics

The strategy of the BJP in the 2004 parliament elections was mainly based on its 'India shining' campaign, on the one hand, and politicising Sonia Gandhi's 'foreign birth', on the other. The 'India shining' campaign emphasised India's achievements under the Vajpayee regime, which included the Pokhran II nuclear tests, its victory in the Kargil conflict and 'good governance'. By caricaturing Sonia Gandhi as a foreign national, the BJP sought to generate a campaign that if the Congress would come to power India would be led by a foreign/Christian national. It tried to make up its campaign to communalise society by initiating a campaign against Sonia Gandhi. This was led by Gujarat Chief Minister Narendra Modi and Madhya Pradesh Chief Minister Uma Bharati (*The Hindu* 8 May 2004). At the national political scene, the BJP made an attempt to manipulate the election trend as a "fight between the patriotic Indian national and a foreign national." The 'Vision Document' the manifesto of the BJP read:

> The Congress era in Indian politics is now over. And the BJP's era—the era of nationalist, democratic and development-oriented politics—has begun. The BJP is proud that it has given India and the world a leader of the calibre of Shri Vajpayee. As Prime Minister, he has harnessed the national energy and transformed the national mood. With his fierce integrity, long tapasya, commitment to the ideals of democracy, indomitable patriotism and statesmanship, he has shown that he is an embodiment of India's best political traditions. (BJP 2004a)

However, the Congress countered the BJP campaign by introducing new icons in Indian politics. Rahul Gandhi became the Congress candidate in Amethi constituency in Uttar Pradesh, where the late Rajiv Gandhi had contested and won previously, and Priyanka Vadra also publicly appeared for election campaigns. The Congress also employed a strategy of making ambiguity regarding its prime ministerial candidate. It was even argued that the people might expect the young Rahul to become the next Prime Minister. It was the re-invoking of the images of late Rajiv Gandhi (as well as by introducing Rahul Gandhi in Indian politics) that the Congress was able to mobilise the masses for an electoral victory.

In the 14th Lok Sabha election, the BJP faced an unexpected defeat. Though it contested in 364 constituencies, it won only 138 seats with a voting percentage of 22.16, an immense decrease (44 seats) from the number of seats it secured in the last election and 1.6 per cent decrease in the voting percentage. In the 1999 election, the BJP contested 339 constituencies and bagged 182 seats with a voting percentage of 23.75. The performance of the Congress in 2004 was much better compared to previous elections. Congress contested 417 constituencies and secured 145 seats with a percentage of 26.53. However, compared to the BJP, the Congress had a margin of only seven more seats. In this context the per-formance of NDA was also very important. The NDA lost 112 seats falling from 298 to 186, and the allies of the BJP contributed only 51 seats and 13.8 per cent votes in the 2004 elections as compared to 118 seats and 17 per cent votes in the 1999 election (*Election Commission Report* 1999, 2004). The poor electoral performance of the allies was the reason behind the electoral debacle of NDA in 2004. The biggest setback to the NDA occurred in the states of Tamil Nadu, Maharashtra and Andhra Pradesh. Chandrababu Naidu's Telugu Desam Party signalled a major setback in the parliamentary election alongside its defeat in the Assembly polls where the Congress alliance won 226 seats out of 394. The BJP allies also faced minor losses in several other states, including Delhi, West Bengal, Haryana and Himachal Pradesh (*Election Commission Report* 2004).

Studies explaining the electoral debacle of the BJP in 2004 vary in their interpretation. According to some, the poor performance of the NDA made a change in the alliance arithmetic (Sridharan 2004; Yadav 2004). The BJP failed to understand the political situation in the states and that very much reflected in the selection of the allies. The anti-incumbency factor in the states influenced the electoral outcome. Though the majority of the states were ruled by the BJP or its allies, the states ruled by non-NDA parties too faced a similar verdict. As Suhas Palshikar and Centre for the Study of Developing Societies (CSDS) Team concluded

> in most cases, the people were dissatisfied with the performance of their state government. The combination of disapproval of the state governments and protest against the economic conditions may have worked against the NDA. Perhaps, a closer look at the people's response to the questions related to economy can tell us more about these elections. (*The Hindu* 20 May 2004)

The BJP's 'India shining' campaign was not sufficient to catch voters because unlike in the 1998/1999 elections, the masses were much aware that the reforms were elite-based and elite-serving. More so, no mass consensus on reforms had developed at that time (Suri 2004). There was an enduring conflict between the social concerns of the masses and the legitimisation of reforms. In India, the reforms were introduced and implemented by distracting the attention of the common man through emotive issues. However, the report on the farmers' suicide and its connections with economic reforms generated debates in the media. During the 1999–2004 period, the rate of farmers' suicide was reported to be very high (National Crime Records Bureau 2004). It was in this background that the ultra-reformist governments of Chandrababu Naidu in Andhra Pradesh and S. M. Krishna in Karnataka lost power. The BJP's 'India Shining' campaign under Vajpayee's leadership was a soft Hindutva politics and, unlike in the previous election campaign, they did not make much use of emotive issues except the campaign on Sonia Gandhi's 'foreign birth'. However, both these campaigns did not contribute much leverage to BJP in 2004 elections. Because of the relative insignificance of national issues, the people reflected on the performance of the concerned state governments. The national election was more regionalised; however, the election results from various states showed that there was a strong resistance to the economic policies of the central and state governments (Suri 2004).

The general sentiment among the Sangh Parivar with regard to the electoral defeat was on a central point that the 'dilution of the Hindutva ideology' detached the people from the party and called for strengthening the Hindu nationalist ideology. The BJP was in a dilemma that there was strong resistance from its allies against sticking back on the Hindutva agenda (Ramakrishnan 2004). The following response from L. K. Advani makes it clear.

> In the last 25 weeks the party has gone through a bad patch But that should not make us forget the ground we have created during the last 25 years and our capability to forge ahead to greater heights ... One simple lesson to learn is, united we stand, divided we fall. Human life is largely wasted in the hang-over of the past or anxieties of the future. But the art of happiness is in confronting the present. The 2004 Lok Sabha election result was neither a conclusive rejection of the BJP ideology nor a convincing mandate for the Congress-brand of communal politics. (*Organizer* 8 January 2006)

There were various reports in the *Organizer* reinstating the importance of Hindutva ideology in politics. Rajnath Singh viewed that "dilution of ideology leads to indiscipline" (*Organizer* 8 January 2006). He emphasised that ideology was "no hindrance in coalition politics" (*Organizer* 29 January 2006). Arun Jaitley opined that "nationalism is our basic inspiration" (ibid.). Pramod Mahajan, the general secretary of BJP, stated that "ideology is like the banks of river. As long as a political party flows within its banks, it is a boon to the nation and the moment it crosses its banks, it becomes a curse to the society" (ibid.). These statements were made in response to the bourgeoning questions, comments and doubts about the 'relevance' of the Hindutva ideology in the background of the electoral debacle of 2004. Consequently, there was an attempt to calibrate the Hindutva agenda to reconcile with the setback in the general election and to invigorate the BJP cadres. As part of the agenda, the Sangh Parivar radicalised its campaign on various issues. Regarding the issue of singing *Vande Mataram*, the Sarsanghchalak of the RSS said, "*Vande Mataram* should be compulsory in all schools and academic institutions and Indians irrespective of their religion or faith should have no objection to reciting the national song." Replying to a question about the protest from some people to the recitation of the national song, he said, "Those who do not have faith in Bharatmata have no right to live in the country." Terming the whole controversy as a dangerous sign, he said that "such controversies led to the partition of the country in 1947 and cannot be allowed again." (*Organizer* 3 September 2006)

Many times since independence, the Sangh Parivar used the issue of 'Vande Mataram' to question the 'loyalty' of the Muslims to the Indian nation. However, there was hardly any citation about Vande Mataram in the prominent Sangh literature before independence. During the independence struggle, the rhyme played an important role in uniting/mobilising the people against the British but the Muslims showed their ill-feeling about the song because of its extreme Hindu religious contents. In the post-independence period, the Sangh Parivar has been using this nationalist rhyme to sideline the Muslims and during election times, probably, this was an important issue used by the Parivar to bracket the Muslims and to secure the Hindu vote bank. In the 2004 election, this was an issue. The minority cell of the BJP in the city of Agra organised a meeting of the Muslims in order to mobilise the community in the coming parliament election and ended up with the singing of Vande Mataram by 50 Muslims. The singing of Vande Mataram in BJP meeting was not customary. The controversy started when a local Muslim cleric came out with a 'fatwa' decreeing that "all the Muslim singers of the Vande Mataram by singing it indulged in polytheism and as a consequence ceased to be Muslim." The mufti also decreed that their marriages stood annulled and they should re-solemnise their marriage (Islam 2004). This made a voyage of comments from the Sangh Parivar pointing that those who are "hesitant of singing Vande Mataram are anti-nationals." Like many other issues such as the uniform civil code, Article 370, Ram Janmabhoomi, Islamic fundamentalism, the issue of Vande Mataram also became an improvised expression of the thread of Hindutva politics, "Muslims, Christians and Communists are not loyal to the Indian nation."

After 9/11 terrorist attack and the attack on the Indian parliament, the issue of Islamic terrorism got wider currency in the Parivar circle. Beyond its campaign against Islamic terrorism, some sections of the Sangh Parivar started the Hindu version of terrorist attacks. Bal Thackeray, an associate of the RSS, gave the call for the formation of the suicide squads, in the editorial of Saamna, the mouthpiece of the Shiv Sena. "Islamic terrorism is on the rise in India and in order to counter Islamic terrorism, we should match it with Hindu terrorism," the unsigned editorial said in Marathi. It continues, "Just like Islamic extremism, to safeguard the country and Hindus we must create Hindu suicide squads if Hindu society is to be saved." The editorial also urged that Hindus should "create terror" in Bangladeshi settlements on the outskirts of Mumbai and elsewhere in Maharashtra state (Reuters, Bombay). Evidently, there were incidents of bomb attacks on the Muslim concentrated areas like mosques and other places. The bomb blasts in Parbhani, Aurangabad, Jalana and Malegaon revealed the involvement of some of the Sangh conglomerates. Around this time in April 2006, two Bajrang Dal workers were killed while making bombs in Nanded. In the Malegaon bomb blasts, concrete evidence against RSS became explicated. An important culprit in this incident was Pragya Singh Thakur, a member of ABVP, the student's wing of the RSS. It was her motorcycle, which was used for explosion (*Times of India* 25 October 2008). A serving military officer, Lt Col Prasad Shrikant Purohit, Swami Dayanand Pandey, and retired Major Upadhyay's role in the blasts was pursued by Hemant Karkare, the Chief of the Maharashtra Anti-Terrorism

Squad (ATS), before the 26 November 2008 terrorist attack took place on Mumbai (see Puniyani 2012: 19–20, 2013: 245–46).

The Sangh Parivar's involvement in the terrorist activities were torched with confessions by Swami Aseemanand, leader of Abhinav Bharat, a Hindutva extremist organisation, who suggested that with the help of many mainstream leaders in the Hindutva organisations, over the past few years the Hindutva terrorist groups have been engaged in advanced extremist activities. His confession on 18 December 2010 pointed to his involvement in many terrorist attacks, which included the bomb blasts in the Samjhauta Express (February 2007), Hyderabad Mecca Masjid (May 2007) and Ajmer Dargah (October 2007) (Ramakrishnan 2011). However, during this period the investigations by various State agencies targeted the Muslims. Many Muslims were taken into custody without any proper evidence and they spent almost four years in jail (Katakam 2011). This unlawful detention, criticised by various human rights organisations, was based on a prevalent assumption that 'all terrorists are Muslims'.

The Kandhamal violence in Orissa against the Christian minority was another incident, which was an onslaught on the democratic/secular tradition of India. The reported atrocities against the Dalits, adivasis and Christians on 24 August 2008 were a continuation of the communal tensions that erupted out of a march, organised by Hindu communalist groups on 23 December 2007 relaying "Stop Christianity. Kill Christians." Between July and December, Hindutva forces organised rallies across Kandhamal raising sentiments against Christians in the district. In December 2007, massive attacks against the minorities were unleashed causing several deaths, looting, damage and destruction of several hundred houses, churches, shops, educational and health institutions. The violence that commenced in August 2008 was the continuation of the attacks on Christians by the Hindutva forces. The violence set off with the murder of Swami Laxmananda Saraswathi at his Ashram in Jalaspata in Kandhamal along with four fellow leaders of the VHP. There were media reports quoting police sources that Maoist involvement in the killing was suspected; however, the Sangh Parivar in Orissa alleged that "extremist Christian groups" were responsible for the violence. *Organizer* reported that

> it is a well-known fact that the Naxals generally attack such rich people who possess much money, property or ammunition. In order to snatch them

away from them, Naxals make them target. But Swami Laxmanananda who dedicated his entire life for the poor, downtrodden, Harijans and Vanvasis did possess nothing so valuable, then why would the Naxals attack him? Naxals have no business with religious matters. All the previous 10 attacks were made by the Christians, not by Naxals. It will not be out of place to mention here that in 2006, in an interview with this correspondent Swamiji had narrated about some true incidents how Naxals used to come to his reformation programmes and attend his religious, cultural programmes. Swamiji had no rivalry with Naxals. Hence the government's Naxal attack plea is not at all believable. (*Organizer* 7 September 2008)

However, Harihar Nanda, the central convener of Hindu Jagaran Manch said, "Communist ultras are hand in glove with Christians to eliminate Hindus from Orissa. The Maoists are adequately funded by the Christian NGOs." Indresh Kumar, Member, RSS National Executive, said that "conversion is a sin and a crime against God and it must come to an end in order to maintain peace and tranquillity in the world." VKA's national president Jagdev Ram Oraon said, "Kandha Vanvasis are the integral part of the Hindu society. They cannot be separated from the mainstream of the nation. Every attempt of the Christian missionaries to convert them should be answered properly" (*Organizer* 30 November 2008). And it was a message for massive attack on the religious minorities. The Sangh Parivar opened up physical and psychological violence against the Dalits, adivasis and Christians, and more than 25,000 people were directly affected by it (Report by National People's Tribunal on Kandhamal 2010).

Pralay Kanungo viewed that the Kandhamal violence was the result of the ethnic conflict between Kandhas, the original inhabitants of Kandhamal and the Panas, Dalit Christians, which was conveniently converted into a Hindu–Christian communal confrontation orchestrated by the Sangh Parivar. The socio-economic progress of the Panas was a matter of great concern for the upper-caste Hindus. With the support from the State and Church, the Panas got education and a minority of this community entered into bureaucracy and politics. Kanungo writes:

The emergence of the Panas as an assertive community has become an eyesore to the upper caste Hindus, not only in Kandhamal but also in other parts of Orissa. Thus, stereotypes of the pana as "betrayer", "cunning", "deceitful", "exploiter", etc, have entered into the caste discourses in Orissa. (2008: 17).

The Parivar was able to divide the society along communal lines even though the issue was basically ethnic. This was the net result of the ground work in the society, initiated by the Sangh Parivar. The civil society in Orissa was almost silent, and it was the reflection of the ideological expansion of Sangh Parivar in all walks of life. The RSS runs 25,000 *shakhas* in the state and has about 25 very active affiliates like VHP, VKA, etc., which are very active in the civil society. Through these organisational networks in the civil society, the Sangh made inroads into the society and started disseminating communal propaganda (Kanungo 2008: 17). The *'Ghar Vaapsi'* programmes (re-converting Christian tribals to Hinduism) engineered by the Sangh Parivar have been generating communal tensions in the tribal areas. Through various organisations like Akhil Bharateeya Varanasi Kalyan Ashram, the Sangh Parivar has been incorporating the Dalits and adivasis into Hinduism—a part of its grand strategy of consolidating the Hindu votes by crystallising the political identity of those historically marginalised sections by using them against the Christians and the Muslims.

On the eve of the 2009 parliament elections, the Sangh Parivar used certain new issues like Ram Sethu to communally mobilise the people against the Central government. The Sethusamudram Project, which was to make a waterway through the Palk Strait between India and Sri Lanka, launched by the Central government opened up a new debate, and, according to the Sangh, the project was an onslaught on the Hindu tradition and culture (*Organizer* 4 November 2007). The VHP said the Sethusamudram shipping canal project would cause the demolition of the Ram Sethu, which was mentioned in the epic Ramayana. The history of Sethusamudram Project goes back to the British period. It was in 1838 that efforts were made to dredge this channel in order to enable big ships to navigate along the Indian coast, but it did not succeed. In 1955, the Indian government constituted the Sethusamudram Project committee to examine the feasibility of dredging. The committee recommended that the canal project be linked with the Tuticorin Harbour Project and that both projects be undertaken simultaneously. In 1963, the Government of India sanctioned the Tuticorin Harbour Project, but Sethusamudram Project was not taken further. The Tuticorin Harbour was not able to compete with Colombo, which was developed into a big container terminal. Tuticorin Harbour could not be approached by big ships and the smaller ones, which reached it from East Coast of India had to go around Sri Lanka, travelling 500 extra kilometres. The project was revived in 1994, and in 1999 the NDA government led by A. B. Vajpayee under pressure from its ally AIADMK took it up and in the 2000–2001 budget allotted ₹4.8 crores for a feasibility study of the Sethusamudram Project. In 2004, under the NDA regime, the government approved a budget of ₹3,500 crore to create a shipping channel. The NDA lost in the 2004 elections and the Congress-led United Progressive Alliance (UPA) government headed by Prime Minister Manmohan Singh inaugurated the Project on 2 June 2005. Dredging started in July 2006 (Jaffrelot 2008). BJP leader Subramanian Swami filed a petition in the Supreme Court, and as a response, the Central government submitted an affidavit, which reads:

> Contents of the Valmiki Ramayana, the Ramcharitmanas by Tulsidas and other mythological texts, which admittedly formed an important part of ancient Indian literature [...] cannot be said to be historical record to incontrovertibly prove the existence of the characters, or the occurrence of events depicted therein. (*The Indian Express* 2008)

This argument evoked strong reactions from the Parivar. The VHP general secretary Pravin Togadia said:

> This government has the most dangerous anti-Hindu virus in its head. It is not just the Rameshwaram Ram Sethu this government wants to break, but all Hindu places and to finish Hindu dharma. They snatched Shri Amarnath land, they ordered Jyotirlingam Tryambakeshwar to stop puja, they have been giving self-contradictory statements about Sri Ram not just in media and in public but also in the highest court. This is the dirtiest and cruellest game of the government to finish Hindus. (*Organizer* 3 August 2008)

L. K. Advani said, "Sethusamudram project is a ridiculous idea." Narendra Modi made a violent attack on the Congress saying that "what will Sonia Gandhi know about the faith of Hindus? She is an Italian after all." Union Minister Kapil Sibal reinstated the Congress position, "there is no scientific evidence to prove that Ram existed" (CNN-IBN Report 23 September 2007). All India Anti-Terrorism Front chairman M. S. Bitta said:

> I will sacrifice my life to save Ram Sethu.
> [He continues]
> India is identified with Lord Ram. It is a blasphemy to question His existence. If it is Ram today, tomorrow it could be Lord Krishna and

Guru Gobind Singh. Today, they want to build a canal by destroying Ram
Sethu. Tomorrow, they may want to build an air strip by demolishing
Harmandar Sahib. There should be a strong law which would deal with
any politician insulting any religion as a terrorist. (interview with Bitta,
Organizer 14 October 2007)

The VHP leaders launched a mobilisation campaign under the
leadership of Sadhvi Rithambara and Satyamitranand Giri. The RSS
created a new organisation devoted to the defence of the Ram Sethu,
"The Rameshwaram Rama Sethu Raksha Manch" (The Rameshwaram
Association for the Defence of the Ram Sethu). The agitation reached its
culmination point in late December 2007 when the Manch organised a
huge rally in Delhi. It was attended by VHP leaders, including Ashok
Singhal and Pravin Togadia, BJP leaders including the Chief Ministers of
Madhya Pradesh, Rajasthan, Chhattisgarh, Uttarakhand and Himachal
Pradesh, and RSS leaders, including K. Sudarshan, the Sarsanghchalak
(Jaffrelot 2008). In the Ram Lila festival, BJP mobilised troupes from
Cambodia, Bali, Sri Lanka, Java, Thailand and Singapore and according
to Madhya Pradesh Chief Minister Shivaraj Singh Chouhan

> Lord Rama is India. Without him India is nothing. Not just India, Ram
> Lila is staged in other parts of the world too. Therefore, we have organised
> this festival to tell the reality to those people who, through an affidavit,
> questioned the existence of Lord Rama. (CNN-IBN Report on Ram Sethu
> 8 June 2008)

However, the Sethusamudram project remained a 'hard nut to crack', and
it was in this background that the 2009 elections were held.

One of the central issues projected by the BJP in the 15th Lok Sabha
election campaign was the lack of a strong leadership—the root behind
the pitfall of Indian development. As in the 2004 elections, there were
attempts to highlight the foreign identity of Sonia Gandhi. The BJP
election Manifesto reads:

> The nation was thus burdened with a Prime Minister who was in office but
> not in power; and, a Government that was in power but not in authority.
> This was supposed to be a Government that would work for the welfare
> of the 'aam admi'—the common man. As it prepares to exit office after
> five years, the Government has nothing to show by way of extending a

'hand' to the 'aam admi'. (*Manifesto of the Bharathiya Janatha Party 2009 Lok Sabha Election*)

The BJP projected L. K. Advani as its Prime Ministerial candidate and generated an image of a stronger leader against the weaker one (*BJP Manifesto 2009*). Advani said, "If some parties in India wish to be guided by foreign-born ideologies and foreign-born leadership, they will certainly realize the limitations of doing so" (*Organizer* 10 February 2009). The manifesto mainly highlighted three goals, 'good governance', 'development' and 'security'. However, the BJP was not able to achieve the expected electoral mileage in the 2009 election. BJP contested 433 constituencies and won 116 seats with a voting percentage of 18.8, while the Congress won 206 seats out of 440 seats contested, with a voting percentage of 28.55 and achieved a splendid victory. There were studies conducted on the 2009 Election and the victory of the Congress. Suhas Palshikar viewed that a series of vital decisions by the UPA government from 2004 to 2009, a series of pro-people legislations and policy initiatives such as the National Rural Employment Guarantee Act (NRGEA), the Right to Information Act, the Forest Act, etc., very much influenced the electoral outcome (Palshikar 2009). The hate speeches by the BJP leaders especially by L. K. Advani, recounting of the Prime Ministerial qualities of Narendra Modi by the prominent leaders of BJP like Arun Shourie, Arun Jaitley and Yashwant Sinha also caused a negative impact on the performance of BJP in the election (Vyas 2009). The electoral debacle of the BJP in the 2009 elections raised many questions within the Party. However, the performance of the Party in 2007 Gujarat Assembly elections (117 seats out of 182 contested and 15 seats in Parliament election where the Congress got only 11) (Election Commission Report 2007/2009) facilitated the entry of Narendra Modi into national politics.

The 'Silent Movement': Hindutva and the Indian Civil Society

The pitfalls of the Hindu Right in electoral politics did not mean that it was a setback to the ideology of Hindutva as many accentuated it soon after the defeat of the BJP in 2009 elections. The Hindu Right forces have been very active in the society in various forms through various organisational networks, ranging from adivasi groupings to big trade unions. Through copious organisational networks in every corner of life, the Hindutva forces were making inroads into the society. By appropriating the civil domain with a wide array of organisations the Hindu Right has been 'silently' penetrating into the society and ultimately capturing the mobilisational space of various cultural groups. Indeed, the neoliberal reforms heightened the insecurity complex in the society and, by culturally appropriating the currents, the Sangh Parivar was able to fragment the society communally. However, there is no one word answer to the question about the electoral debacle of BJP in 2004 and 2009. It was the net result of a combination of factors, including the absence of a 'national issue' capable of consolidating the Hindu vote bank nationally, the lack of a charismatic leader, and even though L. K. Advani was projected as the prime ministerial candidate in the 2009 election, the BJP was not able to ensure trust among the right-wing Hindus regarding issues like construction of the Ram temple at the disputed site in Ayodhya. L. K. Advani became an icon in the national political scene by mobilising the Hindus on the issue of Rama Janmabhoomi–Babri Masjid. However, the debates on temple construction were abrupt after getting power at the centre and became circled among the organisations like VHP. The 'trust deficit' among the masses with respect to the BJP was an important factor that influenced the electoral outcome. However, amidst the electoral setback, through various organisational networks in the civil society, the Sangh Parivar was widening and strengthening their influence among the social groups, which were outside the cultural base of Hindutva. The structural changes under the neoliberal regime made a favourable condition for the assertion of the Hindu Right forces.

The neoliberal economic reforms, in accordance with the dictum of the world financial institutions, had very badly affected the poor sections. The economic disparity at the national and global levels increased (Peet 2010). The economic reforms negatively affected the primary sectors and small-scale industrial sectors. In the aftermath of the Gujarat violence, there were studies conducted on how the "reforms" generated social tensions and community conflicts (Chatterjee 2010). The insecurity complex which emanated out of the globalised environment forced many identities to come out to the centre stage against the neo-colonial exploitation of the resources and environment. In India, historically marginalised sections like the adivasis, Dalits and other deprived sections were on their struggle against the ruthless exploitation of modern capitalist system and several extremist organisations too were gaining momentum. The 'right assertion' of these deprived sections has invigorated the civil and political domains. This critical process expanded the democratic arena and also changed many political equations both locally and nationally. The privileged position of the upper class/caste combines was threatened by these developments in the society. It was in this background that the Hindu Right forces started asserting in India. The Sangh has since then been attempting to appropriate the mobilisational space of the excluded sections and to assimilate them to the broader framework of the Hindutva. The incorporation of the Dalits and the adivasis into the Hindu cultural system was the outcome of the recognition that the support from these sections was so decisive for attaining political power. Pralay Kanungo notes:

> To counter 'Mandal' politics, which had checkmated Hindutva's growing influence among the backward castes in north India, the RSS initiated 'social engineering'. This was a major shift from Golwalkar's traditionalist perspective which preferred 'Sanskritisation' as the ideal instrument of social change. Besides approaching the backward castes, the RSS also speeded up its work among Adivasis and Dalits through its affiliates like the Vanavasi Kalyan Ashram and Seva Bharati. (2010: 91)

Through social engineering by various organisational networks within the Dalit/adivasi spaces, the Sangh Parivar has been expanding its area of influence across the rigid caste hierarchies. The RSS strategies such as 'Samajik Samarasta' (social harmony) and 'Samarasya Sangama' (confluence for harmony) directed the Sangh cadres to contribute to the development of the villages. However, these strategies sought to attract the marginalised sections towards its political project rather than offering them any substantive economic alternative. They gave a lot of emphasis on 'compassion, fellow feeling and social harmony' rather than on a concrete developmental alternative (Kanungo 2010). Through various strategies, Hindutva has been trying to make new '*bandutvas*' (relationships) with the marginalised sections and ultimately incorporating them into the broader framework of the historical *varna* system of the Hindu social system.

Virginius Xaxa viewed that the acculturation of the tribes, the 'absorption' or 'assimilation' into the Hindu society was natural and a slow process. Unlike conversion into Christianity, the transition is more of a process than an event. However, the Hindutva categorisation of tribes as 'Hindus' was misleading. The protagonists of Hindutva overlooked the differences and stick on to the 'similarities'. But as a natural religion the tribal religion shared as many attributes in common with the religious practices of the tribes in America or Africa as with Hinduism in India (Xaxa 2009: 19–36).

The Hindutva agenda was used to homogenise the pluralist Hindu folk through various mobilisations in the civil society. In this process, the Hindu Right appropriated the mobilisational space of the marginalised by manipulating history and mobilising them against certain highlighted "threats" like the Christians and the Muslims. However, in a 'globalised' environment, the self-assertions of the deprived sections like Dalits/ adivasis in the society have been recasting the socio-political arena by making it more inclusive. On the contrary, the mobilisations under the banner of Hindutva were an attempt to keep the system more exclusion- ary by strengthening the old social hierarchies and distorting the age-old 'composite culture' in the society. Images like friends/foes, insider/outsider and civilised/uncivilised were the core of the Hindutva thinking. Through the organisational networks in the civil society, the Hindu Right produced/ reproduced security issues, which were moulded into an antagonistic cultural frame. The Sangh Parivar thus tried to transcend the cultural contradictions prevailing in the Hindu social systems and thereby gradu- ally assimilated the Dalit/adivasis into the cultural logic of the Hindutva.

The Hindutva approach towards the marginalised sections like the Dalits and adivasis was 'strategic'. In their discussions, they gently avoided the oppressive caste system and the bitter experiences of those commu- nities by portraying Muslims and Christians as the 'other' of the Hindu 'self'. They depicted Muslims and Christians as the root cause of their pathetic conditions, diverting the frustrated minds against those religious minorities. It was well documented that the Sangh organisations like the VKA, Vanavasi Seva Sangh and others were at the forefront of the violence against the minorities elsewhere in India (Awaaz 2004; Human Rights Watch 2002; South Asia HRDC 2000). Without understanding the exact politics of such organisations in the civil society, DFID and USAID argued that "given the strong tradition within faiths and/or religions towards a service orientation, faith-based organisations can be used to disburse development aid" (Patel 2010).

The Hindu Right outfits have been following a different cultural strategy among the adivasis and Dalits. It is not directly imposing one meta-narrative of the past among the various caste and tribal groups, rather than "recreating, reproducing and revising the various forms of pastness" and linking it with an imagined past, which they called the *Rama rajya*. According to Badri Narayan, the sense of collective past is a major tool for identity assertion. The sense of pastness helped the communities to fight the anxieties and insecurities that emanated out of their increasing feeling of temporariness. The sense of pastness, especially among the Dalits, represented the forms of folklore, popular histories, myths, rituals, commemorative ceremonies, etc., which tell the stories about not only their glorious past but also their constant struggles for survival. From 1980s onwards, some of the political parties have been mobilising these communities by re-invoking their sense of pastness and, ultimately, politically appropriating them (Narayan 2009: 9–12). The Sangh Parivar has been trying to occupy the mobilisational space of the marginalised through manipulating the historical facts and dividing the society into friends and foes.

However, the VKA resisted the terminology of 'indigenous people'; instead they preferred to called them '*vanavasis*' (forest dwellers) as against '*gaonvasis*' (village dwellers) or '*shaharvasis*' (city dwellers). This was an attempt to use the tribals at the bottom of the Hindu social hierarchy and culturally appropriate them for implementing the political agenda of the Sangh Parivar, the Hindutva. The Hindu Right was pursuing a policy by which it took part in the local cultural celebrations of the Dalits and adivasis, and gradually bonding those cultural communities within the broader framework of the Hindu social system, which highlighted the Brahminical system as the true value system. They have been celebrating the mythical characters of those traditional communities in a colourful manner, adding Hindutva flavours to those celebrations. The heroes of these communities were imagined as the chivalrous warriors of the Hindu mythology. Hindutva claimed that the Dalits and the adivasis were the saviours and protectors of the Hindu religion, and they became detached from the Hindu religion because of the Muslim invasion. The Hindu Right has been propagating the notion that before the invasion of the Muslims, untouchability did not exist in the Hindu society. The conclusion derived from such fake stories spread by the Sangh Parivar combine is that the practice of untouchability and the pathetic condition of the Dalits were not because of the Brahminical order but because of the domination by the Muslims (Narayan 2009: 49–51). However, the very essence of the caste system, its ordering tendencies, its code of conduct—Manu samhita—was totally discarded from the Hindutva discussions. Historically, the tribals were outside the social ladder of the Hindu social system. As part of their political project, the Hindu Right has been trying to incorporate them specifically for two purposes: one, to strengthen their organisational and political base, and second, to use the frustrated adivasi youths for implementing the Sangh agenda in the streets, to handle the Christians and Muslims in India. The ideology and the overall mobilisational tactics revealed the fact that the Hindu Right forces have been trying to crystallise the old social hierarchies and mobilise the Dalits and adivasis against other minority communities such as Muslims and Christians (Joshy 2011).

Hindutva has been expanding its base in different regional contexts in multiple ways. Taking inspiration from Michael Billig's 'banal nationalism', an expression used by the author to understand how informal national feelings were constantly reproduced in daily life through routine symbols and speech habits, Daniela Berti et al. used the concept of 'entrenchment' to address a multiplicity of processes, mechanisms and even paradoxical dynamics of assimilation by which Hindutva has been making inroads into the society in different regional contexts (Berti et al. 2011: 2). Through various organisational networks, it was very active in the civil society; however, most probably its affiliation with the RSS was always hidden. In Kerala, in order to counter the Marxist influence in the fields of art and culture, the RSS set up various organisations and the first of them was 'Tapasya'—an art and literary forum specialising in organising music and dance performances and literature festivals. Balagokulam was another organisation (also known as children's cultural movement), which promoted the collective teaching of music, dance and poetry for children with the aim of spreading the Hindu cultural tradition (Guillebaud 2011: 29–30). A Rakshadhikari teacher of Balagokulam said that

> children have to develop, not merely through formal teaching. We want to bring out what they know. It has to be informal. Thus, awareness grows

and children can take a part. Balagokulam has been created to develop their interests and knowledge. This is very important. Informal teaching is best. It establishes ideas, the prestige of the nation in the minds of children. (quoted in Guillebaud 2011: 44)

More importantly, Balagokulam in Kerala became popular because of its *Janmashtami* celebrations, commemorating the birth of Lord Sree Krishna. As part of the celebrations— where RSS cadres play a leading role—, Balagokulam arranges processions in each and every city, town and village centre. In these processions, children are dressed as *Krishna* and *Radha*. It is worth noting that the participants are not mere children from the Sangh family. Even ordinary believers participate in the processions without knowing that it is orchestrated by the Hindu nationalists.

Pralay Kanungo notes, "Hindutva, in terms of strategy, shows admirable powers of adaptability—swinging from volatile and violent, to soft and silent—depending on the specificity of the context" (2011: 91). In his analysis on Hindutva's entrenchment in Arunachal Pradesh, Kanungo viewed that the north eastern part of India had a history of strong resistance against the hegemony of Indian nationalism and the states like Mizoram and Nagaland with an overwhelming majority of Christian population had been fiercely hostile to the ideology and politics of Hindutva. However, in the course of time the Sangh Parivar has made inroads to these states in the northeast and Arunachal Pradesh has turned out to be a Hindutva stronghold. Over the last three decades, the Sangh Parivar has been silently mediating with different tribal communities in Arunachal Pradesh through its various cultural organisations and consolidating its support base (ibid.). The Hindutva adherents in Arunachal Pradesh started working through the educational sector. Vivekananda Kendra, Kanyakumari, opened schools in the region and the RSS entered through the Vivekananda Kendra. Some key features of the school are the following: admission is only be given to children in the age group of 5–6 years; these are residential schools, giving importance to tradition in curriculum—emphasis on "respecting, preserving and nurturing the traditional culture, values and customs of the people of Arunachal Pradesh." During the last three decades, Vivekananda Kendra Vidyalay (VKV) alumni have come to occupy the top-most positions of bureaucracy and other fields of social service, and these former VKV students are the torchbearers of Hindu nationalism in the state. The VKV has two major affiliates—Arun Jyoti, a cadre-based organisation working in the cultural arena indulged in integrating Hinduism with indigenous tradition, and Vivekananda Kendra Institute of Culture (VKIC), whose fundamental aim is to 'defend' indigenous culture from the influence of 'alien' culture. In this mission, the VKIC has built a strong alliance with the intellectuals of the local communities and coordinates the activities of different indigenous organisations. Arunachal Vikas Parishad (AVP) is an affiliate of the RSS working among the tribal sections. Instead of starting a branch of VKA, the Sangh organisation working among the adivasis, started this new organisation to deal with the indigenous communities living in different cultural backgrounds and making it more inclusive in the general background of northeast India. AVP is an umbrella organisation that coordinates the activities of different indigenous organisations (Pralay Kanungo 2011: 103–17). The financial globalisation amplified the historical struggles by the Dalits/adivasis and it triggered a new wave of democratic upsurge in many parts of India. It was in this background that the Hindu Right ascends and, in many ways, they have been appropriating the mobilisational space of the historically oppressed sections with the politics of fragmentation and integration. The civil society is an important area of action for the Sangh Parivar and it was through this space that they have been spreading hate politics in the society.

Politics of Anti-Graft Movements

The anti-corruption movements led by Anna Hazare and Baba Ramdev opened up a new debate in Indian political landscape especially in the background of the civil society surges in many parts of the world. However, in India the 24-hours-news-media-celebrated-movements in the civil society were structured around the theme 'corruption', and ironically those who led these movements gently disregarded the exact reasons behind the heightening of corruption. Arguably, it is worth mentioning that the 'SAPs' with instructions from the IMF and World Bank intensified corruption at all levels of life. In parallel, it should be noted that in the modern capitalist system, money making has become a socially reputed/accepted activity and, naturally, corruption has become 'habitualised'/'normalised'. The political personnel who set the boundaries of the game (the key decision-making power regarding Liberalisation, Privatisation and Globalisation vested in the hands of the representatives of the people) have become the protagonists of corruption scandals. In this scenario, the ruling class has been facing 'legitimacy crises' and overall developments have generated 'frustration' and an 'insecurity complex' in the common psyche. As in many other societies, the people in India too were expecting a 'Messiah' or 'saviour' to rescue them from their miserable situation. It was in this background that Anna Hazare and Ramdev emerged in the Indian political scene with a couple of far-reaching slogans without addressing the root cause of the problem, without any concern about the movements progressing in the Indian civil society by the Dalits, adivasis and other deprived sections (Joshy 2012).

The Hazare Movement and Ramdev Episode

In her writings, Arundhati Roy expresses her concern about the corporate media-celebrated anti-graft movement by Anna Hazare as follows:

> Among the millions of understandably furious people who thronged to Jantar Mantar to support Anna Hazare and his team, corruption *was presented as a moral issue, not a political one, or a systemic one*—not as a symptom of the disease but the disease itself. (*Indian Express* 30 August)

The movement itself could be seen as a 'tension-absorbing mechanism', which was capable of diverting people's anxiety, unrest, frustration and insecurity complex towards a particular piece of legislation and ultimately 'silencing' the people. By not questioning the ongoing process of neoliberalism, the root cause of intensified corruption, the movement led by Hazare and Ramdev was, in many ways, a system-supporting one for preserving it without any alteration.

In the emerging neoliberal scenario, the civil society is playing multiple roles in multiple contexts. In many societies the organisations and movements in the civil society upheld the human values and standing for the protection of human rights as is ideal. At the same time, the realm has also been appropriated by the neoliberal agencies for the implementation of their economic programmes. It is important to note how the neoliberal institutions appropriate the civil domain. It was well investigated in many studies how the neoliberal mindset is constructed and, according to David Harvey, it is constructed through myriad institutions in the civil society, which encompasses universities, NGOs, media, corporations, schools, churches, professional associations, political parties, statist institutions like bureaucracy and judiciary and international financial institutions like WTO, IMF, World Bank, etc. The corporate backing and funding of civil society provides sufficient impetus to the process. The 'ground works' in the civil society later helped facilitate the capturing of political parties and, ultimately, State power (Harvey 2005: 40, 2007). Neoliberalism has thus transformed itself into a 'common sense' of the time. This 'common sense' is constructed through 'cultural socialisation' by various agencies and the institutions in the civil society that play a decisive role in moulding social behaviour. In the emerging scenario, this process gently obscures the ground realities/problems faced by the multitude and perpetuates constructed fears to divert the frustrated minds from the real issues. To a greater extent, the civil society in India is also used as a space for celebrating traditional values, and in many movements, especially of the Rightist orientation, there is a conscious effort to re-invoke traditions to counter the 'crisis of the present' without questioning the fundamentals of the prevailing exploitative system.

At the global level, the neoliberal regime has been legitimised on the ground that it provided 'liberty and freedom' to the people. According to this perspective, these positive values are threatened not only by fascism, communism and totalitarianism but also with the intervention of the modern State. It calls for a regime change across the world to suit the neoliberal agenda. According to Harvey

> an open project around the restoration of economic power to the small elite would probably not gain much popular support. But a programmatic attempt to advance the cause of individual freedom could appeal to a mass base and so disguise the drive to restore class power. Furthermore, once the State apparatus made the neoliberal turn it could use its powers of persuasion, co-optation, bribery, and threat to maintain the climate of consent necessary to perpetuate its power. (ibid.: 40)

The advocates of neoliberalism are sceptical about the majority rule. They believe that it will adversely affect constitutional liberties and rights of the individual. They call for the presence of a strong middle class to ensure political stability and favour governance by 'experts' and 'elites'. It denounces the importance of parliament in a democratic system and gives emphasis to 'executive orders' and 'judicial decisions' (Harvey 2005: 66–67). Thus neoliberalism accentuates the importance of a technocratic rule, the rule by the 'able', the elites, instead of the people's parliament. By demanding for legislation on the 'Lokpal' the Anna team appeared to have envisaged an apex body of technocrats.

With the advancement of neoliberalism in India, the propensity, intensity and the amount of corruption has tremendously increased. The political corruption too became acute. The 2G spectrum scam is obviously the biggest (1.76 lakh crore) in India. The former telecom minister A. Raja who, according to the Comptroller and Auditor General of India (CAG), evaded norms at every level in order to award 2G licences in 2008 at a throw-away price, which were pegged at 2001 prices. In the Commonwealth Games scam, it was estimated that of the ₹70,000 crore spent on the games, only half was spent on Indian sportspersons. The Fodder Scam was worth ₹900 crores, wherein an unholy nexus was involved in the fabrication of "vast herds of fictitious livestock" for which fodder, medicine and animal husbandry equipment was supposedly procured. The Hawala Case ($18 million bribery scandal), which came in the open in 1996, involved payments allegedly received by country's leading politicians through hawala brokers. The Bofors case, IPL scam, mining scam, etc., are some of the nationally debated corruption scandals in India. Most importantly, nationally reputed politicians were the prime accused in these scams.

As Harvey pointed out, neoliberalism is 're-distributive rather than generative'. It takes wealth from poor to the rich, both nationally and internationally. As an alternative to the Marxian notion of 'primitive accumulation', Harvey used the term 'accumulation by dispossession'. The accumulation by dispossession comprises the characteristic feature of *privatisation and commodification*—its aim is to open up new horizons for capital accumulation (the privatisation of public utilities like water, telecom, transport; social welfare schemes like public housing, education, health care, pensions; public institutions like universities, research labs, prisons, etc.) and commodification of everything, including nature, cultural forms, histories and intellectual creativity. Indeed, in a capitalist system, there is a natural tendency for commoditisation. The commoditisation presumes the existence of property rights over process, things and social relations that can be traded subject to legal contract (Harvey 2005: 160–66). The legal boundary between the free exchange of commodities and the sphere outside of it are always set by the political personnel of the State. The capitalist tendency towards push outward of the temporary legal boundaries generates 'corruption'. The proponents of neoliberal reforms claimed that the pre-fixing of the legal boundary was the root cause of corruption under the 'licence-quota-permit raj' and created the impression that the 'reforms' would push out the legal boundaries and, consequently, the corruption would disappear or get minimised. But in a society, no matter how far the boundary can push outward, a legal boundary will remain. Then the inherent tendency of the capitalist system to push it outward would generate corruption. At the same time, the very process of capitalist penetration explores the pervasiveness of the capitalist values, and those who are responsible for fixing the boundaries, the politicians representing the ruling class, become the most significant practitioners of corruption. The logic of modern capitalism makes them 'corrupt' (Patnaik 2011).

In her critique on Anna's 'media-celebrated' anti-graft campaign, Arundhati Roy in an interview to the CNN-IBN, and also in her writings in *The Hindu* pointed out various issues, which basically questioned the very credibility of the movement. According to Roy, the civil society's Jan Lokpal Bill was a "dangerous piece of legislation." The Jan Lokpal bill was draconian, in which a panel of carefully chosen people would administer a giant bureaucracy with the power to police everybody from top to the bottom—it would function as an independent administration. This can also be an unaccountable corrupt institution—"Two oligarchies instead of just one" (Patnaik 2011; Roy 2011a). Roy pinpointed various reasons for such scepticism about the campaign. "The movement is a copy-book World Bank agenda," an NGO-driven movement by Kiran Bedi, Arvind Kejriwal and Manish Sisodia (all the three core members run NGOs and are Magsaysay Award winners; and the World Bank and Ford Foundation are funding the anti-corruption campaigns). The writer said, "Anna Hazare was picked up and propped up as the saint for the masses. He was not the brain behind the movement." However, for around 10 days the media, including the 24-hour news channels celebrated the campaign. Such media enthusiasm was not seen when thousands of farmers committed suicide elsewhere in India (Roy 2011a, 2011b).

Anna's anti-graft movement constructed an image of the re-incarnation of Gandhi. This was an attempt to appropriate an image, which had wide appeal among the common people and to absorb their anti-systemic feelings with a piece of legislation. According to Prabhat Patnaik:

> But as against this disengaged participation by many is the intensely engaged activism of the one man who is undertaking an indefinite fast. The movement revolves around him. He is the messiah who draws the crowds and brings hope to those whom he draws. His intense activism is the dialectical counterpoint of the non-activism of the thousands around him. They condition one another. He is intensely active because the others are happily inactive; on the other hand, because he is active, the others can be happily inactive. (Patnaik 2011)

There is a clear-cut distance between the celebrated Anna movement and the ongoing struggles of the adivasis, Dalits and other deprived sections elsewhere in India. These people were struggling for their survival, which was threatened by the profit-thirsty industrialists and the neoliberal State. The leaders of these minority groups were critical or indifferent about Anna's campaign. The civil liberties movements like PUDR and PUCL were kept out of the Anna movement. It may also be noted, Irom Sharmila's protest, in defence of right to life and civil liberties for the people of Manipur and for the withdrawal of the Armed forces Special Powers Act, had completed a decade and, ironically, Anna had kept mum regarding the struggles for rights. The symbolic expression of "having a Dalit and Muslim girl to offer coconut water and honey to Anna to break his fast did not conceal the gap between the campaign and the people's movements elsewhere in India" (Mohanty 2011: 16–19). Mohanty called for the importance of 'bridging' Anna's anti-graft campaign and the people's movements. However, the symbolic expression of this movement resembled that of a 'new age spiritualism'. Anna was apparently trying to reduce the people's unrest, frustration and anti-systemic feelings to a particular piece of 'legislation'.

To a greater extent, Anna's movement created an image that he was the only one who could save the nation. Kanti Bajpai pointed out that in Anna's movement "there is a combustible mix here of hero worship, cult propagation, populist absolutism and irrational exuberance, mass hysteria, de-politicization, militarization, and, increasingly, signs that religion and agitation politics are being intermeshed" (Bajpai 2011). However, the overall image and rhetoric resembled that of the New Right movements in India. These movements were set in a rigid framework, which did not allow multiple voices/choices but had to stick on a 'Yes' or 'No' (Joshy and Seethi 2010). Roy notes:

> Meanwhile the props and the choreography, the aggressive nationalism and flag waving of Anna's Revolution are all borrowed, from the anti-reservation protests, the world-cup victory parade, and the celebration of the nuclear tests. They signal to us that if we do not support the Fast, we are not 'true Indians'. (Roy 2011a)

Indeed, Anna was nurturing an 'apolitical space' in the Indian society and it was easily vulnerable to the New Right political appropriation.

The Ramdev episode was the finest example of the 'illiberal' developments in the Indian civil society, which threatened democracy, its institutions and secular credential. Some of his demands were similar to the position of the BJP, broadly the Sangh Parivar. His demands were unrealistic, which included 'tough Lokpal Bill, with a provision for death sentence for the corrupt', 'abolishing ₹1000 and ₹500 currency notes', 'replacing the British-inherited system of governance, administration, taxation, education, law and order with a swadeshi alternative', 'reforming the electoral system to ensure that the Prime Minister is directly elected by people', 'promoting Hindi at the expense of English', etc. (*The Hindu* 2 June 2011). Ramdev stood for a radical alteration of the Indian constitution, as he believed that it would curb corruption. His demands resonated with the broad agenda of the Hindu Right, and like those organisations his campaign also spread chauvinistic cultural nationalism. The most important thing was that if these types of self-styled "gurus" or "babas" come to the public space and start mobilising the people with their cultural capital towards certain ends like this, in a multicultural society like India, it would only strengthen social polarisations. Thus, the Hindu

Right politics in India has been progressing by fragmenting the society as friends and foes.

Gujarat Model: Laboratory for Hindutva

The 'Gujarat Model' under Chief Minister Narendra Modi got national and international attention due to its ultra-capitalist/neoliberal position. The Gujarat model exhibited a true neoliberal scheme of 'developments', orchestrated by a strong military state capable of implementing a neoliberal agenda by suppressing opposition and speeding up reforms by providing infrastructural facilities and financial support to the big industrialists. It was the capacity of Modi to implement the neoliberal agenda, first orchestrated in the Latin American State of Chile during 1970s under the dictatorship of General Pinochet, which made him a media figure and the most trusted friend of the industrialists. In Gujarat, Modi executed social engineering policies for the better implementation of the neoliberal scheme of things. The ethnic cleansing of the minority communities in the post-Godhra riots with the support of the statist machineries showed the images of the overwhelming power of the state to handle opposition and in such a way Modi set the platform for reforms. Not surprisingly, in the post-Godhra Gujarat Assembly elections (2002), even though the vote share of the BJP was reduced, it won five more seats in comparison with the 1998 elections. This showed the consolidation of the Hindu votes and the miserable political condition of the Muslim sects because of the lack of an alternative.

However, in 2014, the big industrialists in India were more influenced by the anti-minority stand of Modi in Gujarat rather than his pro-business atmosphere and leadership. In fact, in 2002, many prominent industrialists like Tata, Azim Premji and Godrej condemned the post-Godhra violence in Gujarat and the role of the state government in the incident. At a meeting of the Confederation of Indian Industries (CII), these industrialists criticised Modi to his face. Modi responded harshly at their 'pseudo-secular' stand and for maligning Gujarat. He used a strategy of Gujarati *Asmita*, or Gujarati pride or sense of self, for consolidating the Gujarati interest in the CII. After the CII meeting, businessmen close to him set up a rival organisation, the Resurgent Group of Gujarat (RGG) and threatened to leave the CII for insulting Gujaratis. Tarun Das, President of the CII was in a miserable condition that more than 100 companies from Gujarat were threatening to leave the CII, which would cripple the organisation's presence in western India. In the emerging scenario, the Vajpayee government also supported Modi (Desai 2014). Radhika Desai notes, "tough love having achieved its purpose, Modi turned on the charm, and the freebies. Now capitalists began receiving unstinting regulatory cooperation and extravagant giveaways from the Gujarat government. This was the alleged 'development' of the 'Gujarat Model', the other prong in Modi's post-2002 strategy" (ibid.: 55). The continuous electoral victory of Hindutva in Gujarat, its nationwide 'acceptance' or celebration as a 'model' seemed to be the result of multi-pronged strategies of the Sangh Parivar. Indeed, the neoliberal model of capitalist development and the consolidation of the capitalist interests in Gujarat made Modi a national figure.

The capitalist development in Gujarat, especially after the reforms, enabled the agrarian propertied class to penetrate into the urban sectors of the economy and the assimilation of this class into the urban economy further advanced the State's ruling bloc. This resulted in the blurring of the agrarian industrial propertied class division and all propertied class groups having fairly uniform interests. The absorption of the Gujarati middle caste groups into the status of the Gujarati elite also smoothened the emergence of a new political bloc of the propertied. In this development, the Hindutva forces did a tireless job in consolidating the class interest and also absorbing the anti-systemic feelings. It sustained a strategy of ideological penetration into the labour as well as the subaltern groups. The ideology of Hindutva provided services to the Hindu propertied class in multiple ways: (i) through various organisational networks, Hindutva has been assimilating the subaltern and other deprived sections into the Hindu social system. They are so fascinated by the social status that they may get with the upper caste groups by religious re/conversion into Hinduism. By assimilating these sections to the Hindu social system, the Sangh Parivar used the frustrated minds against religious minorities. (ii) Hindutva provided a sense of identity to the Hindu propertied class and their purpose in political power. In this process, they have distanced the 'other'/Muslim propertied class. In various communal riots, especially in the post-Godhra violence, Muslim shops were targeted, looted and destroyed. (iii) Hindutva has been uniting the Gujarati Hindu NRI community elsewhere in the world through their organisational networks and they occupy key positions in many of the Sangh organisations abroad (Desai 2011: 364–65). In this progression, the consolidation and 'securitisation' of the 'self' necessitated distancing and handling of the 'other'. Interestingly, the very Hindutva logic of fragmenting the society into friends and foes was effectively applied in Gujarat. The Sangh was also able to consolidate the pluralist Hindu folk, both in terms of economic and cultural interests, which provided a somewhat Gujarati identity to the propertied class. The propertied class in Gujarat became an influential section in national politics and its influence in the Parivar became crucial.

Narendra Modi, the champion of the Gujarat model, became so acceptable to the Indian capitalist class because of two reasons (i) the inability of the UPA government to pursue reforms without generating legitimacy crisis; (ii) the investment-friendly atmosphere created by the Modi government in Gujarat at any cost. The Gujarat model was therefore interpreted as part of the agenda of selling the economy to big corporate houses and thereby protecting the interests of industrialists by privatising key sectors like ports, roads, railways, electricity, etc. In the name of development, primary sectors were neglected by not providing sufficient water and electricity and the resources were diverted to the industrial sector at a low cost. The Modi government provided huge subsidies to Tata for starting Nano factory and other industrial units in Gujarat. The government provided ₹9,570 crore financial assistance at an interest rate of 0.1 per cent to Tata for their investment of ₹2,900 crore in the State. It also provided land for starting industrial firms at a lower rate than the market price (Hensman 2014). It was in this background that the industrial giants appreciated Modi in the Vibrant Gujarat Summit 2013. Ratan Tata said, "Today when investors look for locations to make investments, they would be looking for locations which are investor-friendly. Gujarat stands out distinctly in the country and the credit for it goes to Modi." "In Narendra Bhai, we have a leader with a grand vision ... Gujarat has been a pioneer state in infrastructure giving it an innate advantage," Mukesh Ambani said at the Vibrant Gujarat Summit. His brother Anil Ambani put Modi in the league of Mahatma Gandhi and Sardar Patel. "We began from Gujarat and we come back here again and again to invest. We have committed investment of ₹100,000 crore in Gujarat. We will expand our operations in Gujarat in Jamnagar and Hazira," Ambani said, adding that Reliance is proud to be called a "Gujarati company" (PTI 11 January 2013; *The Hindu* 11–12 January 2013; TNN 11 January 2013).

For the widely acclaimed 'Gujarat Model' the poorest sections paid a heavy price. The Modi government sanctioned land at the cheapest rate for industrialists at the cost of Dalits, adivasis, fishing communities and farmers who were evacuated from their ancestral land. During the reign of Modi, around 16,000 labourers, farmers, agricultural labourers committed suicide. The condition of Muslims became pathetic due to communal violence and exclusions. The Gujarat model was not adhering to human rights dimensions of social progression. Because of pollution caused by heavy industrialisation, the livelihood of the farmers and fishing folks was threatened and it became miserable. In comparison with other states like Kerala, Gujarat was at a lower position in the Human Development Index. The lack of economic discipline caused the heightening of the State's debt from ₹45,301 crore in 2002 to ₹138,978 crore in 2013 (Hensman 2014). The extreme neoliberal version of development in Gujarat under the leadership of Modi made him a national figure and an irresistible candidate in the BJP rank and file. The attempts by national media to hallucinate Gujarat model and Modi were an extension of the changed relationship between Modi and the propertied class in India. The big corporate houses have huge investments in the media sector. The media very much helped Modi to escape from the clutches of negative images on ethnic cleansing by portraying him as the 'champion of development'.

Representation of Modi: A New Icon in National Politics

Narendra Modi, a hardcore member of the RSS and the nationally acclaimed "Vikas Purush" (development man), managed to bury his past, once it was red-inked with anti-Muslim pogroms that killed more than 1,200 Gujaratis. Through the Vibrant Gujarat Summit, "Modi successfully deployed the ancient mercantile and entrepreneurial energy of Gujarat to overhaul his own image" (Jose 2012). By generating an image of the protagonist of development, especially after 'successfully' implementing Tata's

Nano project in Gujarat (before it was forced to shut down in Singur, West Bengal, due to large-scale protest from farmers) Modi succeeded in gathering the trust of the business community in India and across the world, which was once paranoid with the ethnic cleansing. The deal to bring the Nano factory to Sanand attracted worldwide attention and soon after the inauguration of the factory, Ford and Peugeot approached Modi seeking plots to build their own factories. Besides, in the wake of the 2002 riots, Modi employed a different strategy by skilfully pointing any criticism of his government's misdeeds as an attack on Gujarat and Gujaratis. *Caravan* notes:

> Modis … carefully constructed image as an economic miracle-worker has been the result of a well-managed public relations campaign whose false premise is that Gujarat stands head and shoulder above every other Indian state in growth and development—and that anyone who presents data to challenge this narrative is twisting the truth in order to malign Modi and every Gujarati. (Jose 2012)

By generating a pan-Gujarati sentiment, Modi was able to bypass the criticisms pointed against him especially in the background of the post-Godhra violence. This was a general Sangh strategy that any criticisms to their misdemeanour would be perceived as an attack on Hindu civilisational values by the enemies of the Hindu religion and tradition like the religious minorities and the communists. The article in the *Caravan* shows Modi's discomfort towards criticism especially on the post-Godhra violence. Modi never showed any serious regret towards things that happened in Gujarat in the aftermath of the Godhra incident. Many human rights organisations and fact-finding teams as well as Modi's own governmental officials mentioned the role of the Gujarat government in the anti-Muslim riots. Additionally, Modi's rhetoric on the post-Godhra violence invited criticisms across the country. In an interview to Reuters, Modi simplified and caricatured the incidents in the following way:

> if someone else is driving a car and we're sitting behind, even then if a puppy comes under the wheel, will it be painful or not? Of course it is. If I'm a Chief Minister or not, I'm a human being. If something bad happens anywhere, it is natural to be sad. (Colvin and Satarupa 2013)

His comment on Muslim relief camps as "child breeding centres" put even the BJP under pressure. His one decade of rule in Gujarat was based on the principle of 'divisive consolidation' by which the Muslims were totally excluded from the national development. He told the minority community in Gujarat several times, "forget the past, minimize your demands for justice, integrate yourself with the larger populace and drop your religious identity—then you will see progress and improvement" (quoted in Katakam 2012a). In an interview to *Frontline*, Teesta Setalvad of Citizens for Justice and Peace narrated the divisive policy approach of the Narendra Modi government in the post-riot Gujarat in which minorities were fully excluded. According to her

> today Modi's apparent bid to don new clothing is superficial—you only need to check government figures to see how over ₹10,000 crore from the central funds meant for the Prime Minister's scheme for scholarships for Muslim youth was cynically returned. How many of the public prosecutors appointed by the state government to handle cases of crimes are Muslims? You have over 4,000 registered advocates in Gujarat. Is there proportional representation in the appointment of prosecutors, teachers and policemen? (Katakam 2012b)

The media highlighted the picture of economic growth and the image of a development man or a somewhat 'secular figure' who was only focusing on 'national development' and detached from the hardcore ideology of Hindutva as all fake. The very pattern of development that happened in Gujarat in the last decade shows that Muslims were excluded at every sphere of social development. Urban poverty among Muslims in Gujarat is 800 per cent higher than among high-caste Hindus and 50 per cent higher than among OBCs (ibid.). In a secular, multicultural and democratic State like India, 'Gujarat Model' may not be acceptable. In terms of formal economic indicators, Gujarati economy has been growing as like in the past (before even Modi was sworn to office as Chief Minister), but the current social indicators exhibit that Gujarat's position is far behind many other poor states. At the same time, the approach of Narendra Modi towards the Muslim community was always critical. In this background, the media-bombarded image of Modi as a national figure capable of replacing the weak Congress became a 'new product' to the Indian propertied class, a product that had wide market after Nehru.

The 'metamorphic image' of Modi from the communal riot figure in 2002 to a 'development hero' in 2012 was a media-savvy exercise and indeed the media–corporate linkage played a vital role in the remaking of Modi as a national figure. The corporate houses were so interested in Modi because of his strong conviction on the neoliberal policy, smooth governance and no corruption experiences. Besides, what was different in Modi was his 'sales pitch'. He has been telling the story of 'Gujarat success' through the social media as well as print and television channels again and again. As Chief Minister, Modi embraced modern technology and he was very active on social media sites like Facebook and YouTube and maintained 1.8 million followers on Twitter at that time. *New York Times* commented,

> take a look at the raw figures: Among politicians, Mr. Modi ranks second behind only Barack Obama in number of fans of his official Facebook page (Mr. Modi has 21.8 million and counting). No other political leader is even close. His Twitter account and that of his office are among the fastest growing among politicians and elected officials worldwide. Among public figures who have some political sway, he trails only Mr. Obama, the Dalai Lama and Pope Francis in Twitter followers, with 6.62 million. (*New York Times* 25 September 2014)

Thus, by various means, Modi shored up his image. As an energetic practitioner of neoliberal reforms, he received much media attention. Radhika Desai notes that during the reign of Modi in Gujarat

> a repressive ideological and cultural climate, especially towards Muslims and towards critics generally, is maintained in the State in part by a series of fake encounters between police and alleged "terrorists" out to kill Modi; they also bolster Modi's personality cult. He has also devised a strategy for deflection of the criticisms into further favourable attention on himself. (Desai 2014)

With a strong RSS background, Modi took a hard-line position in dealing with the minorities. As a member of the Sangh at the age of nine, Modi imbibed the RSS methodology and became a *pracharak* of the Sangh. "For him, the RSS's Hindu supremacist, pseudo-philosophy and hierarchy, was reassuring, intellectually broadening and a step-up in life, a path out of the social and geographical backwater of small-town genteel poverty and the class and caste barriers it poses for social mobility" (Desai 2014). Modi became a core linking member of RSS with BJP in Gujarat. On 7 October 2001, he became the Chief Minister of Gujarat. The date was decisive, because it was on this day the attack on Afghanistan began and on 13 December terrorists attacked the Indian Parliament and a few months later the Gujarat violence erupted. Modi gently appropriated the currents to consolidate the Hindu votes and divisive politics became an easy task for Modi. Through various measures, Modi was able to sideline and silence the Muslims. Ashis Nandy, a clinical psychologist closely observed that he had identified fascist impulses in Modi (Nandy 2002). The rigorous mental and physical training and the rigidity of the ideological frame especially in terms of its hostility towards other religions and perceptions made Modi a hardcore Hindutva politician. However, this rigidity popularised him in Indian politics. Modi emerged as a national figure when the Indian politics was in a crisis period. The Congress government lost its legitimacy because of acute corruption, the experiment of Aam Aadmi Party was not a complete success at that time, the left parties lost their credentials by repeating age-old slogans and the BJP was struggling without a charismatic leader, which made Modi a new opening in national politics.

Resurgence of Hindutva: 2014 Election

In the 16th Lok Sabha elections, the BJP won 282 seats out of 543 with a voting percentage of 31.34 and it became the largest party in the Indian Parliament. NDA secured 336 seats and UPA got only 59 seats with a voting percentage of 19.52 and faced its worst defeat in its political history. Other major and minor parties secured 148 seats (Election Commission of India 2014). The general elections showed the steady growth of BJP over the years and it was also the reflection of the spread of Sangh Parivar in the social universe. Historically, the growth was perceptible. In the general election to the first Lok Sabha, BJS got only 3.06 per cent votes while the Indian National Congress got 44.99 per cent. In that election, the INC secured 364 seats while the BJS got only four seats. After each election, the voting percentage and the number of seats secured by the BJS/BJP has been increasing. From 3.06 per cent in 1951 elections, it has increased subsequently to 5.97 per cent (1957), 9.31 per cent (1967), 7.35 per cent (1971), 7.74 per cent (1984), 11.36 per cent (1989), 20.11 per cent (1991), 20.29 per cent (1996), 23.75 per cent (1999), 22.16 per cent (2004), 22.16 per cent (2009) and 31.34 per cent in 2014 (Election Commission of India 2014). It is noteworthy that after 1991, India became a full-scale multi-party system. The Party virtually swept the strongholds of northern, western and central India. Besides, it made a significant advancement in many parts of the country where they were not influential in the past. BJP won a large chunk of votes in Jammu and Kashmir (36.4%), West Bengal (16.8%), Assam (36.5%), Manipur (11.9%), Arunachal Pradesh (46.1%) and Orissa (21.5%). In Andhra Pradesh and Tamil Nadu, the BJP made inroads with the help of its alliances (ibid.).

It was the first time in the history of Sangh Parivar that the RSS openly supported a candidate, Narendra Modi, in the 2014 elections. The RSS worked very hard to ensure the victory of Modi. It revealed the fact that the RSS was fascinated by his working style. Ram Madhav, the key spokesperson of the RSS said:

> Starting with just two seats in 1984, the BJP rose quickly to become the ruling party by 1996. There was no looking back after that. Thirty years after its first election, the party has registered a thumping victory in 2014. Undoubtedly, the credit goes to Narendra Modi. (*Indian Express* 17 May 2014)

There is no doubt that the Modi factor was important. Many opinion surveys showed the wider acceptance of Modi among the people, especially youngsters. Certainly the media-bombarded image of Modi as a national icon influenced the voters to a great extent, especially in the background of the political turmoil generated by the Congress. People were looking for a 'Messiah' or 'saviour' to rescue the Indian political system. Besides, the BJP victory was an outcome of an unprecedented coalition of social groups, the upper castes, OBCs, Dalits and Tribals. The poor performance of many caste-based parties like BSP showed that the OBCs, Dalits and Tribals supported the BJP. This was not accidental but an outcome of the planned effort by the Sangh Parivar through their organisations working among them that enabled them to channelise their votes to the BJP.

The RSS gently made its groundwork and with the help of Modi, they have reaped the results.

The Modi factor played a vital role in the election, which mobilised people beyond particularistic and localised interests. At the same time, the Party was able to break social barriers in the elections. So far, the BJP was associated with urban dwellers, upper castes, middle classes and the educated sections of the society. As in the past BJP secured a large percentage of votes and seats from urban constituencies and also its success in the semi-urban and rural constituencies was significant. There was an unparalleled consolidation of the upper caste and middle class votes, but, at the same time, the BJP got warm support from the poorer sections like the Dalits and adivasis. Indeed, it was not the victory for economic reforms or liberalisation policies, but rather it was a response to the pitfalls of the former UPA government (Chhibber and Verma 2014). The electoral victory of the BJP appeared to be the reflection of the rightward shift in society; it was the triumph of Hindutva with neoliberal capitalism (Bidwai 2014).

In the election campaigns, Modi symbolised militarised Hindutva. He started his campaign in the background of the communal riots in Muzzafarnagar, Uttar Pradesh and Kokrajhar in Assam. However, during the campaign, Modi softened his language and used more symbolism in expressions. As Praful Bidwai noted:

> Mr Modi deployed toxic rhetoric about driving out Bangladeshi 'infiltrators' (read, Muslims) while welcoming 'refugees' (read, Hindus), and about the 'Pink Revolution' (beef exports). He brazenly used religious symbols. Six lakh RSS men ran his military-style campaign and cynically used slogans like 'love jihad' and 'bahu bachao, beti bachao' (protect Hindu women from Muslim predators) to polarise opinion communally. (ibid.)

The BJP did not use the Hindutva slogans that much in this election than in previous times. It mainly attacked the UPA government for its inefficiency, corruption and mismanagement and called for a stable and efficient government at the centre under the leadership of Narendra Modi. The anti-incumbent factor obviously came in support of the BJP. At the same time, it also capitalised the large-scale mobilisations by Anna Hazare's team pointing to the corruption scandals. The Aam Admi Party was a political failure. It was in this background that the Hindu Right came to power with a comfortable majority and the representation of the minorities in the government appears to be at stake. It was a victory of the Indian propertied classes who sought a technocratic rule to safeguard their interests. The big corporate houses seem to be in a big hurry to realise their interests without much resistance and legitimacy crisis. The hardcore elements in the Sangh Parivar were already looking upon Modi positively with a great expectation that he could transform India into a Hindu rashtra. A natural consequence is that the liberal–pluralist framework of Indian democracy is being threatened, its long-sustained secular space has been shrinking, and the social polarisation within the system is widened. The State–civil society relations in India thus entered in its most critical-transformative phase with all attendant problems and complexities.

6

Conclusion

State and civil society have been the most widely discussed categories in social sciences. The state–civil society relations have also generated serious debates in developmental discourses and democratic practices. However, the conceptualisation and interpretations of the state and civil society vary across time and space, and between scholars, development practitioners as well as countries and regions. Admittedly, the State as an agency faces critical challenges under neoliberal conditions even as it is compelled to retreat from social security as well as developmental realms. In the liberal tradition, civil society was seen as important in protecting the rights of the individual from the arbitrary power of the State. Over the years, however, civil society has undergone a role transformation—particularly in the era of neoliberal globalism—and has thereby become a necessary partner of the State in the realm of 'development' and 'governance'. Currently, there are also efforts to transpose the State in the Third World from its developmental activities. Though the State in such a scenario may appear to be shrinking in its role and activities, it has also been 'militaristic' in implementing laws and treaties of the market. Consequently, the social dislocations following liberalisation and globalisation tend to generate insecurity complexes, which many right-wing political forces might appropriate to make inroads into societies. The ascendency of the New Right in several countries can, thus, be placed within this paradigm shift in international political economy. The rise of the Hindu Right in India too can be comprehended within this framework.

I

Historically, the concepts of State and civil society have been associated with the development and expansion of capitalism in the West.

The gradual shift from feudalism to capitalist modes of production and the emergence of a new middle class reconfigured the power equations in such societies. The West as a system of states and economies evolved hand in hand. The absolutist/authoritarian states can be considered as the precursors of the modern state. The liberal discourses on State and civil society took progress along with these developments. The Social Contract theorists were, perhaps, the first to offer the basic premises for the development of the concepts of State and civil society. According to them, the individuals created civil society in order to get out of the problem-ridden state of nature. Later, in order to overcome the insecure conditions of civil society, people created the sovereign—the State. The Social Contract theorists agreed on the importance of 'consent' in the making of 'civil/political' society. Giving 'consent' is a rational decision because the individual gets security of his life and property only in a 'civilised' community. J. S. Mill, Tocqueville, Hegel, Max Weber and many other thinkers in the liberal tradition offered insights on the State and civil society. Hegel rejected the classical economist position of the self-regulation of the market and stressed the importance of State in this realm. To him the realm of economy and civil society are the same. The exclusionary nature of the market prevents vast sections of the people from enjoying the freedom of civil society. Hegel's idea of free market and administration of justice resembled that of the classical liberals like Locke and Smith, but he differed from them with respect to the importance of the State in society. To Hegel, the State is necessary to lessen the tension between the general interest and the private interest.

The differences within the liberal discourses were basically on the question of the intensity of the State regulation in society, in accordance with the demands/interests as well as the strategies of the capitalist system. In its classical period, liberalism sought to demand/support for more individual autonomy and very less state regulation. In its welfare capitalist phase, there was more State intervention in societal matters, quintessentially a State-guided society. When it comes to the neoliberal era, the State has been rolling back from the realms of social security and welfare. With the shrinking role of the State as a major 'provider', individual self-regulation and NGO activism became prominent.

The debate on State and civil society assumed a new dimension in the context of the theories of capital accumulation and class domination.

Marx viewed the State as a product of society in a particular stage of its transition. He argued that the State and its officials tend to exploit and oppress the civil society on behalf of certain particular sectional groups. Yet, Marx endorsed a vital role for civil society in the historical development of mankind, and contended that it cut across both the State and the nation. Rejecting the existence of civil society as an independent sphere, Marx saw its origin in the class relations and in the political economy. He claimed that it is the realm of civil society—which is basically exclusionary and exploitative—that caused the total alienation of the working class. This is in contrast to the liberal view, which generally regarded civil society as a realm of high emancipatory potential. Extending the Marxian notion that the State is a coercive instrument of the dominant class, Gramsci said that the very process of domination is not achieved through coercion alone, but also through the active 'consent' of the masses. His theory of the State came out of a proper understanding of the relationship between the State and civil society. However, he rejects the 'economism' of conventional Marxism in all its forms and explains how both the State and civil society have been playing a constitutive role in creating/maintaining the ruling class hegemony. Nicos Poulantzas's analysis on the state is also a departure from the conventional Marxist position. He focuses on political and ideological struggles, and rejects all forms of instrumentalism in analysing the modern State and views that the State is a complex social relation. According to him, classes cannot be seen as simple economic forces existing outside the State and controlling it as a passive instrument for its own interests. The class struggle is not impounded to the civil society but it is reproduced within the State apparatus.

Like Gramsci and Poulantzas, Lukacs also contributed to rethinking of the classical Marxist position on State and civil society. The Critical Theorists of the Frankfurt School had drawn heavily from the perspectives of Lukacs and Gramsci on the relevance of civil society and culture. The focus of their analyses was on the ever-expanding role of the State, alienation, the growing interlocking of the base and superstructure, the spread of culture industry, the development of authoritarianism, human rights violations, social movements, etc. Among the contributions from the Critical Theory tradition, the concept of 'public sphere' developed by Jürgen Habermas stands out. The public sphere, to be located in civil society, is a realm where people could discuss matters of mutual concern, and learn about facts, events, and the opinions, interests and perspectives of others in an environment free of coercion or inequalities. To Habermas, the civil society comprises spontaneously emergent associations, organisations and movements that distil and transmit such reactions in an amplified form to the public sphere. Its core comprises a network of associations that institutionalises problem-solving discourses on questions of general interest inside the framework of organised public spheres.

The State and civil society came in for critical evaluation in the postpositivist traditions of social theory also, as reflected in the postmodern/post-structural literature since 1970s. These writings have thrown open several critical questions concerning the very foundation of modernity, the state and civil society under liberalism and socialism. According to postmodernists, the claims and promises with respect to 'emancipation', 'liberation', 'development', human rights etc. are only grant narratives and therefore they are no longer sustainable. Foucault questioned the statecentric notions of power and stressed the 'capillary flow of power' in the societal body. He insisted that the studies of power should begin from the 'micro-physics of power', which are the specific forms of exercise in different institutional sites.

The revival of the concept of civil society in the last quarter of the 20th century was associated with the 'activist' assertions in many countries, particularly in former socialist countries. The disintegration of the Soviet Union created a conductive atmosphere for the 'minimalist' school to assert its position. This became inevitable for legitimising neoliberal globalism. This situation was gently used by right-wing forces in many countries. They created a general feeling that there was no alternative to the liberal ideology and institutions. This was the time when neoliberal institutions were trying to incorporate the Third World economies into the world capitalist system through aid, loans and assistance.

Long before neoliberalism emerged as a dominant concern of global capitalism, many libertarians had argued for a 'minimal state'. They held that many of the powers of the modern Welfare State are 'morally illegitimate'. According to them, the State violates the rights of citizens when they force, or threaten to force, individuals to transfer their 'legitimately held wealth' to the State in order to provide for pensions, to help the needy or to pay for public goods, etc. Robert Nozick had already asserted that nothing more than the maintenance of peace and the security of individuals and property by the state can be justified. Hayek had also reflected on this theme of 'minimum' dispensation. This gained currency since the 1980s.

The new-found role of the State as a facilitator of global finance has implications for the common people. The changed equation between the State and civil society in a globalised environment has inevitably generated new forms of security threat. Meanwhile there are attempts towards cultural hybridisation and the resulting assertions of New Right forces (like the Hindu Right in India), which tend to undermine the process of democratisation.

II

During the last three decades, there was a proliferation of New Right movements and organisations across the world. The New Right is a term used to denote various forms of conservative, right-wing or self-proclaimed dissident oppositional movements and groups that emerged in the second half of the 20th century who were ideologically committed to neoliberalism as well as being socially conservative. The New Right advocated deregulation of business, dismantling of the Welfare State, privatisation of nationalised industries and restructuring of the national workforce in order to increase industrial and economic flexibility in an increasingly global market. The nature and mobilisation of the New Right groups and organisations vary from country to country. The strategies employed by them for articulation and mobilisation also differ. Religion, race, ethnicity, etc., are the most widely used categories for mobilisation and articulation, and civil society is the terrain of these activities through which the New Right forces attempt to gain legitimacy. Many of them argue that government interference in the market would distort the very balance of demand and supply and emphasised laissez-faire. According to them, the State should only focus on matters of defence, law and order, necessary public works, etc. New Right leaders are also fierce critics of Keynesian policies of economic management and high public expenditure on welfare. They are also known as advocates of 'national discipline and strong defence'. The peculiar feature of the New Right is the convergence of the traditional liberal defence of the free economy with the traditional conservative defence of State authority. As such, the Hindu Right in India shares many of the characteristics of the New Right in other countries.

III

Parallel to the process of re-conceptualisation of State and civil society, there have also been attempts to revisit the notion of security from the neoliberal and Critical Constructivist angles. This has assumed a new dimension with the advent of globalisation. Security has now been re-conceptualised with human beings at the centre of discourses rather than the State. This underlined a shift from the state-centric notion of security to a global, individualistic version of security. The 'human security' approach thus implied that the individual is at the core of any security perspective. Satisfaction of individual needs at different realms of life is central in such an approach. The human security frame acknowledges that the security of citizens is not always bound up with the security of the State. At times, the State itself may threaten its citizens. It also acknowledges that in the 21st century, the State may not always be able to keep its citizens secure, and other actors, at the local, regional and global levels, should share responsibility for human security.

Though security is a core concept in the theory and praxis of national, regional and international politics, it is also viewed in the context of local, inter-local and trans-local relations. In the positivist paradigm, security focuses on power, politics and anarchy as fixed—mainstream IR reads narrowly into the role of ideology as manifested in the concepts of State, national interest and nationalism. However, it does not pay any attention to the ways in which anarchy/insecurity may be constructed or how the roles of ideology, culture, history, or state practices themselves may produce anarchy in IR.

The Critical Constructivists, however, address the above concern and view security as 'representations' of danger. For them, objects of insecurity are not ontologically separate things but mutually constituted in a variety of ways that may privilege a certain conception of identity over others. Operating within a framework of meanings, assumptions and distinctive social identities, the representation of the 'other', their identities and what constitutes insecurity 'imaginaries' are left open to the dynamics of inter-pretation, whereby relations of identity may also be produced, enforced, and reified in a conflictual manner. Critical Constructivists assume that all social (in)securities are culturally produced. Insecurities are inevitably 'social constructions' rather than given—threats do not just exist out there, but have to be produced. Security is also linked closely with identity poli-tics. How we define ourselves depends on how we 'represent' others. This 'representation' is thus integrally linked with how we 'secure' ourselves against the 'other'. Representations of the 'other' as a source of danger to the security of the 'self' in conventional understandings of security are accompanied by an abstraction, dehumanisation and stereotyping of the 'other'. The 'other' gets reduced to being a danger and hence an object that is fit for surveillance, control, policing and possibly extermination. This logic of the discourse of security dictates that the security of the 'self' facilitates and even demands the use of policing and violence against the 'other'. This is demonstrated through the case of the Hindu Right's poli-tics of representation, which legitimises hate campaigns and violence in the name of securing the Hindu 'self' at various levels. This discourse of security has been widely employed through the realm of civil society as illustrated in the previous chapters.

IV

The State and civil society in India are evidently complex domains of socio-political engagement given the very nature of their origin and development under colonial and postcolonial conditions. Perceptibly, the State in India has been undergoing major changes since the colonial days as has been the case with the civil society which had already become vibrant in the context of the challenges of modernity and the rising tempo of nationalism. The State had the pressure of colonial administration and all its requirements, but the civil society in its multitudes developed its own concerns and responses from different vantage points. These concerns and responses were manifested in the anti-colonial struggle, nationalist aspirations, anti-caste/socio-religious reform movements, civil liberty activities, etc. In the postcolonial conditions, the State and civil society went through a variety of experiences largely because of the new challenges of State-building and nation-building.

The nature of the Indian State and its path of development are critical factors in understanding the potential and limitations of the role of civil society. The development of capitalism in India is, therefore, a major factor to be reckoned with. In the course of colonialist expansion, an economic condition was created to facilitate the formation of capitalist relations in India on a massive scale. Meanwhile, way back in the 19th century many Indian trade associations were formed such as the Bombay Mill Owners' Association (1875) and the Ahmedabad Mill Owners' Association (1891). The Congress also started conducting Indian industrial conferences along with its annual sessions. The efforts culminated in the formation of the FICCI. Once the capitalist class strengthened its position, it began to play an active role in the freedom struggle and, by the mid-1930s it became the most influential class on the anti-imperialist front. The capitalist class could easily exercise its influence on the Congress and became a decisive factor at the time of the transfer of power. The Indian business groups drew closer to the Congress, which was emerging as a mass movement aimed at putting an end to British rule. For its part, the Congress was committed to a policy of rapid industrialisation, which it believed would benefit the capitalist class too. The Bombay Plan of 1944 had clearly recognised the necessity of active participation of the State in promoting industry. The post-independent State had followed the proposals of the Bombay Plan. This reflected the Keynesian approach to the role of the state in capitalist development. The notion of Welfare State was thus put in place to legitimise the capitalist path of development. The role of the State was further underlined in India's Industrial Policy Resolutions of 1948 and 1956 by which the State was expected to intervene in the development process.

However, over the years, the Indian economy experienced many difficulties in spite of the planned development and the task of industrialisation. The trends in the economy clearly suggested the slowdown in industrial growth, poor performance of agriculture and unchanged income distribution which constrained the growth of the home market. The pressures resulting from the oil crisis of 1973–74 further upset the tasks of development. This had obviously set the background for economic liberalisation. Thus, by the mid-1970s, the policy of import substitution was relegated to the background and the emphasis shifted to import-led export or export-led growth. The 1980s witnessed the beginning of neoliberalism, which changed the political economy of the Indian state, reoriented industrial production, altered class alignments and prepared the ground for a far-reaching transition.

V

The civil society in India also evolved during the colonial period. It was embedded in the idea of 'nation' and 'nationalism'. There were three 'master narratives' in Indian nationalism: secular nationalism (of the Congress); religious nationalism (consisted of Hindu nationalism as well as Muslim nationalism); and caste-based assertions (of the deprived sections). The national resistance movement spearheaded by the Congress was the main source of civil society activity in the early 20th century. When the Congress developed into a mass movement, large segments of the population were drawn into political and social activism, and while the struggle was basically anti-colonial, the movement held within itself many forms of activities, which would continue as independent sections of civil society, one case in point being the women's movement. Other forms of social movements also gained in strength during the first half of the 20th century. It was a time when the political practices under colonial rule tended to fragment the society along caste and religious lines. The colonial authorities had maintained their hegemony over the inhabitants through various ways. Besides civilian and military superiority, the colonialists also employed the power of rational discourses. Indeed, to the British, the assertion of the native intellectuals was an essential prerequisite for legitimising their regime in the colony. The educational policy of the British was to fulfil the administrative needs of the empire in India and also to sustain an ideological hegemony over the natives.

Meanwhile, from the 19th century onwards, the civil society witnessed struggles by untouchables and other deprived sections against the existing exploitative system. These movements had recognised the modern view of democracy and the equality of man. Though they were basically against the existing social evils of the Hindu belief system, they were also challenging the hegemonic nature of the religious reformist movements in British India. It may be noted that a number of organisations and associations (like AIWC) were formed during this time and were influenced by the 19th-century reform movements. Many of the organisations that addressed social issues were closely associated with the nationalist movement. This trend continued even after independence. A number of organisations and movements mushroomed in different areas of the country. For example, peasant movements were so decisive in the political history of India. During the colonial period as well as in the postcolonial period, the peasants revolted against the existing exploitative system. The movements by the tribals added a new dimension to the existing struggles. The Dalit movements emerged as responses to the socio-economic–cultural differences existing within the system. Indeed, the assertions of the deprived sections in the society were mainly aimed to get a space in the mainstream civil domain, that is, shifting from an exploitative, discriminatory system towards a society based on social equality and justice. This perception was based on the principles of modernity and the deprived sections, on the whole, which anticipated emancipation through modernity. Meanwhile, the minority assertions, especially from the Muslim community, focussed on broader issues like separate electorates, representation, etc. They were, in fact, not the reflection of the will of the whole Muslim population in India; rather they represented the interests of an elite class within the Muslim community. The events since the early 1940s eventually led to partition. The partition riots, in turn, led to polarisations in society.

When India became independent, there already existed a well-developed and relatively mature civil society. The nationalist elite maintained that the objectives of building a modern and prosperous nation guided by the principles of secularism, central planning and democratic socialism could only be attained under the guidance of a strong democratic state. Nehru expected that the ordinary Indians would acquire a democratic consciousness, which would ultimately cease to identify themselves through traditional caste categories and demand greater economic equality. What happened in the political history of India was not a melting away of tradition under the powerful light of modernist enlightenment. Those institutions of modernity, like the State, which had to be accepted as part of the modern condition, have been dealt with through a traditionally intelligible grid of social identity and action. The constitutional system in India, therefore, was consistent with the internal principles of liberal constitutionalism, but inconsistent with the self-understanding of social groups. The State simply assumed that citizens would act as liberal individuals, but failed to set in motion a cultural process, which could provide the great masses of people the means of acquiring such self-understanding. The Congress, in the meantime, relied primarily on the support and cooperation of the local landowning interests—in particular, on the village landlords and the rich and upper strata of the middle peasantry, to organise the party cadres and mobilise the grassroots support for the party. In its effort to win, the Congress adapted to the local power structure. It recruited from among those who had local power and influence. The result was a political system with considerable tension between a government concerned with modernising the society and economy and a party seeking to adapt itself to the local environment to win elections.

However, it became quite clear soon that although the nationalist leaders sought to trigger social change through constitutional democracy, their efforts did not bring forth positive results altogether. This interaction of various social conservatism and economic radicalism in the context of political democracy led to non-elite groups getting organised and they did this through their caste/regional identities. Linguistic states had to be created in response to popular pressure from local elites as well as local middle classes who wanted public jobs and public contracts. Next came the pressure from the rural areas to divert resources to agriculture; this led to the launching of the Green Revolution with input subsidies as well as price guarantees for outputs. But even then the discontent due to slow growth rate continued. This broke into floods of protests from tribal, Dalit and lower caste groups since the 1970s.

The Emergency (1975–77) and the restoration of democracy not only redefined and extended the boundaries of civil society, by redefining the relationship of citizens with the State, it also restructured civil society in a significant way, and made it more alert to the transgression of its boundary hereafter by the State. Understandably, the most important consequence of the Emergency for civil society was the question concerning the collapse of State institutions and their inability to protect the rights of the citizens. The civil rights movement had, until then, remained confined to piecemeal addressing of issues. The Emergency galvanised the movement, as democracy, citizenship and constitutional protection of fundamental rights overnight became important issues for public debate. While the Emergency meant a breach with the Indian democratic practice, and a severe curtailment of civil and political rights, it also had a revitalising effect on civil society, which, after 1977, witnessed an increase of activities within not only traditional social movements such as peasants, workers and students, but also amongst the NSMs, including environmental groups and women's organisations. The emphasis on environmentalism and gender issues was also a global phenomenon of this period. As a consequence, new groups understood the necessity to actively claim their rights and to fight against perceived injustices. State developmentalism as a project was questioned, and from the 1980s the Indian State itself encouraged NGOs to take more responsibility for social development. The liberalisation of the Indian economy facilitated this process. The study thus tried to locate the emergence of the Hindu Right in India within the economic and social dislocations caused by failed developmentalism as well as new discontent triggered off by the State's adoption of neoliberal polices in the era of globalisation.

VI

The emergence and consolidation of the Hindu Right in India almost coincided with the New Right movements in the West. The importance of the Hindu Right emergence in the 1980s and 1990s needs to be understood within a broad framework of the trajectory of Hindutva. Significantly, a major running theme of the evolution and consolidation of the Hindutva has been 'how to secure' the Hindu identity and the 'self' against the perceived threats from 'others'. Plausibly, all ideologues of the Hindutva as well as the organisational programmes of the Sangh Parivar underlined the importance of this 'self/other' dichotomy. This is crucially significant in articulating a political doctrine with 'difference' in order to mobilise people in the civil society.

The emergence of the Hindu Right and its implications for India are often understood as relatively recent phenomena with the decline of the 'Congress System'. In India, the debate surrounding the concept of Hindutva was basically a debate over the viability of cultural nationalism. When political Hinduism is examined in its present variety, one has to look at the movement in its totality. It seems to be very important to look at the transformation that took place in the Hindu society towards more ritualistic patterns of life and how Hindutva has been appropriating these changes. The attempts to invent unity in spite of rich diversity are the peculiar feature of Hindutva. This has been ensured through various organisational networks in the civil society.

The ideology of Hindutva was deployed by the Sangh Parivar organisations such as Jana Sangh, BJP, RSS, VHP, to crystallise the pluralist Hindu identity in their attempt to formulate a Hindu nation. In this process, many 'others' are constructed both within and outside the nation. This provides little room for the dialogue between the 'self' and the 'non-self' because threats and insecurity are the essential pre-requisites of Hindutva. The lineage of the Hindutva can be traced back to the writings and activities of Dayananda Saraswati, Swami Vivekananda, Sri Aurobindo, V. D. Savarkar, M. S. Golwalkar and many others. The 'cow protection movement' led by the Arya Samaj and the Sanatana Dharma Sabha were early attempts to establish an ideological hegemony among the pluralist Hindu folk. The cow protection movement had an impact on the nature of the mental and social space carved out for the emerging civil society, on nationalism and the competing community identities that emerged in the early 20th century. This had produced a dichotomy of 'inside–outside' in which the British, Muslims and the Christians were viewed as 'outsiders' and glorified a native Hindu religious body, which was 'pure' and had originated from the Vedas. Those 'others' were 'polluted'. This was an inception of the religious nationalism in India. Militant Hindu nationalism progressed parallel to mainstream nationalism and the former, in turn, twisted itself towards a more political one, Hindutva, over the years.

The Hindu religious revivalism of the nineteenth century had culminated into an extreme Hindutva posture in the 1920s. V. D. Savarkar was the prime ideologue of this version of politics. Hindutva emerged as a political phenomenon and it had very little to do with the religious practice of the Hindus. Savarkar distinguished Hinduism from Hindutva, the latter being interpreted as the political history of the Hindu people. He tried to securitise the social relations in India on the basis of the 'self' and 'other'. To Savarkar, Indian history is essentially 'antagonistic' and "the Hindus and Muslims were locked in a life and death battle for centuries." Here there were no possibilities of cooperation between the 'self' and the 'non-self'. The defining and distancing of the 'self' possibly led to the caricaturing of the 'non-self'. Savarkar said that unity of the people, "their modernisation and their militarisation are the fundamental dimensions of Hindu nationalism: Every nation should be equipped with up-to-date arms and army so as to be ever prepared to face the danger of civil war within the country and aggression from without." On several occasions, Savarkar gave hints concerning the impossibility of a coexistence of Hindus and Muslims. He accused the Indian Muslims of being "anti-Hindu, anti-Indian with extra-territorial allegiance." According to him, the entire Muslim community in India is communal.

Like Savarkar, M. S. Golwalkar also used the same analytical tools to define the 'Hindu nation'. In an attempt to crystallise a militant Hindu identity, Golwalkar used his own version of 'culture', 'history', 'nation', etc., for securitising the majority community, thereby making a sharp distinction between the Hindu civilisation and other cultures and religious systems. Golwalkar also territorialised the Hindu nation. In an attempt to historicise the Hindu nation, back to thousands of years, he portrayed the history of the Indian Muslims and Christians as 'short' and called them 'aggressors' because they came here to build their empire. So they were 'alien people', 'outsiders'. To Golwalkar, the Muslims and Christians were "outside the boundaries of the nation" who looked to "some foreign land as their holy places." He insisted that the other religions in India must subordinate themselves to the Hindu nation. The nature of the 'Hindu State' Golwalkar conceptualised was not only of an authoritarian type, but it necessarily possessed aggressive characteristics in view of 'threats' and 'dangers of disruption'. Hence, he sought to change the "present ill-conceived federal structure" (of India) to "the only correct form of government, the unitary one." His notion of security was also increasingly associated with 'national defence and military capability'. Thus, by reinforcing an enemy image of the 'other', Golwalkar was trying to politicise and militarise the Hindu identity.

Among all the Sangh Parivar organisations working in the civil society, the RSS has always maintained its hold and acted as the main driving force of Hindu Rashtra. Established in 1925, the RSS had emerged as the largest Hindu organisation in a few years' time and propagated the Hindutva ideology with a view to infusing "new physical strength into the majority community." The RSS has been active throughout India (as well as abroad as the Hindu Swayamsevak Sangh) as the chief motivator and the core organisation of the Sangh family. Each and every organisation of the Sangh Parivar has been inspired by the RSS, which provides an ideological base for their actions. The Sangh consists of BJP (its predecessor, BJS), ABVP, BMS, VHP, Seva Bharati and Kalyan Ashram. The RSS also has a strong influence on various Hindu scholastic centres across the country. The general philosophical outlook of the RSS is cultural nationalism manifesting through "integral humanism, aimed at preserving the spiritual and moral traditions of India." The RSS has been using civil society by engaging itself in social service, charity and relief work; as well as actively participating in the political process after 1948. It is well-organised and has a hierarchical structure with the *Sarsanghchalak* being the highest rank. Over the years, the RSS developed a systematic framework and a very specific modus operandi. The founder of RSS, Hedgewar, called for efforts to work at the grassroots in order to reform Hindu society from below and he set up *shakhas* (local branches) of the movement in towns and villages according to a specified pattern. The work of the Sangh is through personal contact. These contacts lead to close ties, friendship and personal cooperation, mutuality in personal relations and a desire to work together to solve the problems of a particular area. This socialisation process brings forth (bonding) social capital in civil society.

The RSS viewed that the ideal of the Sangh is to carry the nation to the "pinnacle of glory, through organizing the entire society and ensuring protection of Hindu Dharma." Through constant propaganda, the Sangh sought to imagine a nation, 'Hindu Rashtra', by portraying the Muslims and Christians as 'enemies'. This 'enemy' image has been perpetuated through the *shakhas*. To the RSS, the Muslims, Christians and the communists are 'outsiders' who misinterpret history by denouncing the history of Hindu heroism, which had frustrated the invaders. As such they are portrayed as engaged in protecting their 'imperialist interests'. The RSS campaigned that 'the evangelisation' was part of the "uniform world policy to revive Christiandom for re-establishing Western supremacy" and was not prompted by spiritual motives. Establishing a 'Hindu Rashtra' has been the leitmotif of the RSS and hence it has been appropriating various cultural spheres across a wide spectrum of the civil society in India making room for the *swayamsevaks* to work in those organisations and associations, thereby legitimising the RSS ideology.

The Hindu Mahasabha, established in 1915, reorganised itself in 1925 with a view to propagating the Hindutva ideology. When Savarkar became the President of the Hindu Mahasabha in 1937, the organisation assumed new political importance with its aggressive anti-Muslim postures. It took a direct interest in elections and party politics. However, the assassination of Mahatma Gandhi was a setback to both the Hindu Mahasabha and RSS. The RSS was banned and the Sangh lost its credibility among the people. The formation of the BJS in 1951 was another turning point in the history of the Sangh Parivar. The Jana Sangh aimed at re-establishing itself following a party model in the image of the RSS. Indeed, its policies and programmes showed its natural affiliation with the RSS. Contrary to the Nehruvian idealism on matters of national security, the Jana Sangh stood on the RSS position: 'militarise the nation'. In 1958, the Jana Sangh adopted its manifesto and programme, which stated its position on matters of national security: (a) compulsory military training to all young men; (b) nationalisation of all the wings of the armed forces in their inspiration as well as form; (c) immediate establishment of defence industries; and (d) organisation of the vast territorial army. The Jana Sangh also emphasised the necessity of manufacturing nuclear weapons.

The Sangh stood for a unitary State, contrary to the Indian federal system. It also severely criticised the special status granted to Jammu and Kashmir and called for enacting a common civil code for both the Hindus and Muslims. However, the Jana Sangh, over years, lost its influence because of its tie-up with the RSS. The increase in communal rioting and the number of people killed during the late 1960s and 1970s and the allegations against the Hindu nationalists as shown in the reports on various communal riots put the Jana Sangh in a defensive position. Meanwhile the failure of the Jana Sangh to promote the RSS ideology prompted them to think about a new organisation, which culminated in the formation of the VHP in 1964. The leitmotif of this was to unite the pluralist Hindu on a single platform for the safeguarding of their common interest. Through its wide networks all over India and abroad, the VHP had been mobilising Hindus on a wide range of issues from cow protection, Ram temple, jihadi terrorism to the use of Sanskrit. It has also networks among the backward castes and Dalits. The VHP has offices and activities in foreign countries too.

The Sangh Parivar's aim was not merely to penetrate into the civil society through *shakhas*. It also sought to establish organisations working within specific social categories. The ABVP, the students' wing, the BMS, its workers' union, the VKA, its Adivasi wing were some of them. VKA sought to counter the influence of Christian movements among the *adivasis*. The VKA developed a counter-strategy by imitating missionary methods and thus accomplished a number of reconversions. The other Sangh organisations that began to make headway in the civil society were 'Vidya Bharati' (Indian Knowledge) established in 1977 to coordinate a network of schools, first developed by the RSS in the 1950s on the basis of local initiatives and Seva Bharati (Indian Service) created in 1979 to penetrate India's slums through social activities such as free schools, low-cost medicines, etc. Perhaps the most controversial organisation in the Sangh family is the recently emerged BD. The VHP was instrumental in the creation of the BD, which is a militant organisation based on the ideology of Hindutva. Established in October 1984 in Uttar Pradesh in the background of the Ayodhya movement, it began to grow in size. The BD, like VHP and RSS, generated fear psychosis about Islamic jihad in India and declared that they were engaged in the campaign across the nation. In sum, the Sangh organisations had already established wide networks in the civil society and the persistent theme of mobilisation was securitisation of the society by reinforcing the 'self/other' images.

VII

State and civil society came under critical challenges since the 1980s. This period was also marked by momentous changes within the country and across the world. There was an unprecedented economic crisis in India in the late 1980s, which affected the country's position very badly. The disintegration of the socialist bloc, the ascendency of neoliberal/New Right forces and market economy, ever-expanding global capital, the formation of the WTO, 9/11 attacks and the 'war on terror' were the other major developments of this period. The economic crisis led India to substantially revise its development paradigm and the economic/industrial policies pursued for more than four decades. When India launched neoliberal policies in the 1990s, many critical questions emerged with respect to the role of State and civil society, long-held policies of self-reliance, import substitution, etc. This period also witnessed new trends and patterns within the political system such as aggressive communal mobilisation, regionalism, shifting electoral strategies of political parties, governmental instability, etc. Coalition experiments also became an accepted reality.

The State and civil society in India began to experience new forms of challenges against the backdrop of a new political economy regime, which was gradually emerging in the 1980s. Its main objective was to ensure a slow but steady rollback of the State, deregulation of industries, decontrol of prices, liberalisation of imports, tax reductions, etc. With the proclamation of a new economic policy by the Rajiv government, the development paradigm of the Indian State experienced a new shift. Following this, the Narasimha Rao government embarked on a wave of economic reforms in 1991 under the macroeconomic stabilisation and the structural adjustment policy.

Meanwhile the relative failure of the Indian state created feelings of exclusion amongst large segments of the population, and there were allegations that the State was not neutral, but biased on the basis of class and caste interests. These biases created sentiments of apathy and also facilitated negative mobilisation and manipulation of various primordial identities such as religion and caste. This ultimately led to demands and actions, which seriously undermined the democratic system by the strengthening of exclusivist identities. These were based on religion or caste and were at the centre of political mobilisation, which involved political parties as well as other parts of Indian civil society. This resulted in the cementing of the community-based identities. The ascendency of the Hindu Right was most evident during this time when the BJP in the 1980s and 1990s grew from a marginal party to a dominant force in Indian politics.

Meanwhile, as a result of the extremely personalised rule of Indira Gandhi, especially after the Emergency, the 'Congress System' went into decline, creating a political vacuum, which was filled by competing regional, caste and linguistic interests. Indira Gandhi's government could not alleviate poverty in the ways that it had promised and the people became disillusioned with the Congress and turned to alternatives.

Consequently, the divisions that characterised the Indian politics in the 1980s and 1990s were marked by a more competitive electoral environment in which coalition-building and the support of consistent vote banks became the hallmark of a successful political strategy.

It is here that the rise of Hindutva has been analysed within the larger context of the struggle and debate over the secularism of the postcolonial Indian State, on the one hand, and the emerging social issues and tensions following the introduction of liberalisation and privatisation, on the other. This became significant since the 1990s—the decade that saw the end of Congress's dominance and the rise of BJP. The discourse of violence that the BJP and other Hindu Right organisations carried on during the period included the hate campaign against the minorities, which was facilitated and justified in the name of achieving 'security' for the 'Hindu Self' at individual, community, national and international levels. The will to secure the 'self' has as its corollary the will to make insecure the 'other', the desire to control and use violence. The new discourse of security/insecurity that Hindutva unleashed enabled extreme violence to be normalised, systematised and institutionalised. The 'politics of hate' spawned by Hindutva was a good example that fed upon, as well as shaped, civil society's conceptions of security/insecurity. The global environment with its own dynamic politics of representation of dangers had a direct impact on civil society.

The 1980s and 1990s were marked by the growing fear generated by the Hindu Right that the minority Muslim population was "increasing its presence in India," "challenging Indian sovereignty and rule of law" and "controlling the politics of the country." The 'insecurity' of the Hindus was blown out of proportion, and the BJP, RSS, VHP and other Hindu Right organisations had worked hard within the civil society in the task of securitisation of the Hindu identity. Thus, BJP's emergence as the most dominant Hindu Right force in India in the 1980s was the culmination of a sustained effort on the part of its predecessor, Jan Sangh, VHP and the RSS to bring Hindutva into mainstream politics. The BJP and other Hindu Right organisations played on "the fears of the Hindu majority" that the "Muslim population posed a threat to Hindus in India." This was based on the "changing demographics of the Muslim population" and the political mobilisation in the 1980s and 1990s such as the growth of Islamic fundamentalism and the changing voting patterns of the Muslim population. This has also been linked with 'terrorism' and 'Islamism'. The Sangh leaders said that the ideological basis of terrorism in India was "anti-national in its intent and pan-Islamic in its appeal." It was called the manifestation of a deeper malaise of the spread of extremism in most parts of the Muslim world, funded by fundamentalist groups. According to them, the "murderous campaign" of jihad and the terrorists had a definite objective—to "establish worldwide domination of political Islam." Naturally, India's multi-faith society, the constitutional principle of secularism and the cultural–spiritual ethos of Hinduism "are anathema to Islamism," they said. Throughout this period, the Hindu Right organisations and their leaders persistently talked about the 'threats' to the Hindus. The themes of this campaign included illegal immigration from neighbouring Bangladesh, the plight of the Kashmiri Pandits, demolition of temples in Kashmir, conversion, etc.

The Jana Sangh, which spearheaded the cause of 'Hindu nationalism' for long, merged with other non-communist parties to form the Janata Party in 1977 and assumed power at the centre. But the Janata experiment failed when it was caught up in conflicts among its constituent units. The Jana Sangh faction finally left the Janata Party. One of the main causes of the collapse of the Janata experiment was 'the dual membership'—the loyalty of the Jana Sangh faction to the RSS. The new party, BJP, faced two main problems: first, how the new party could be distinguished from the former BJS, in order to exhibit its 'newness' and to "broaden their electoral reach on both a geographic and demographic basis"; secondly, how it could be placed as an alternative to the Congress. As a strategy, the BJP declared itself committed to a programme of 'Gandhian Socialism' and introduced a new set of policy documents to become a counterforce to the Congress. Its leadership criticised the Congress for its 'denial of democracy by imposing emergency in 1975', 'minority appeasement', and 'distortion of secularism', 'corruption', 'unprincipled pursuit of power', 'unbridled consumerism', 'disregard of India's cultural traditions', etc.

However, the attempts to broaden its support base in the 1984 parliamentary elections failed to attain the expected results. The BJP got only two seats with 7.86 per cent votes in the election. This was a setback to the party. The RSS during this time indicated that the remedy to the crisis lay in the restoration of the leadership's rapport with a sizeable section of its 'selfless cadres' still alienated since the Janata rule. It also argued that 'positive secularism' and 'Gandhian Socialism' had alienated the party. In the wake of this, the BJP appointed a high power Working Group to study the results of the elections, which later came out with a remedial action. Meanwhile, two events in early 1986 provided considerable leeway for BJP's re-emergence, which it skilfully utilised through its mobilisation in the civil society with the help of the RSS, VHP and BD. The first one was the opening of the gates of the Babri Masjid in Ayodhya. The second was in February, when the Rajiv Gandhi government passed the Muslim Women's Bill in Parliament to override the Supreme Court's verdict in the Shah Bano case. The BJP and the Sangh Parivar organisations decided to appropriate these issues, thereby mobilising the majority Hindu community for drawing political mileage. It was during this time that the BJP held its plenary in May 1986, with L. K. Advani assuming the leadership of the party. The change in leadership had rejuvenated the hardcore members of the Sangh who were motivated by the principles of 'Hindu nationalism' rather than 'Gandhian Socialism'.

BJP's aggressive nationalism and its strategy of electoral alliance brought 86 seats to the party and it became the third largest party in Parliament. The BJP and the left parties gave support to the V. P. Singh-led National Front government. However, this was seen as the victory of a new wave of politics played by L. K. Advani. The BJP's strategy of gaining popularity needs to be understood in the context of its politics of mobilisation and securitisation since the mid-1980s. The Uniform Civil Code (in the context of the Shah Bano case), Article 370 (in the context of the Kashmir question), Ayodhya dispute (in the context of Ram Janmabhoomi–Babri Masjid issue), Mandal Commission recommendations (reservations for backward classes) and ban on cow slaughter were some of the prominent issues that the BJP, VHP, BD and other Sangh organisations took up for mobilisation in the civil society. The BJP also understood that the Rajiv government was playing both minority and majority cards simultaneously. While appeasing the Muslims in the Shah Bano case, the government also decided to authorise the Hindus to conduct prayers at the site of Babri Masjid by opening the gate of the premises in an attempt to woo the Hindus.

The Ram Janmabhoomi movement began to gather momentum when the Hindu Right organisations like the RSS, VHP and BD, with the BJP's blessings and participation, launched a series of powerful mobilisations using religious symbols and gestures such as a campaign to collect bricks for the temple, carrying *Ram-Jyotis* (lamps in processions), and holding special *pujas* (worship) in cities and towns. Highly politicised *sadhus* and upper-caste cadres of the Sangh Parivar constituted the most committed participants in the movement. Very soon, it also began to gather the support of the low and middle-caste Hindus. For them, the movement's main attraction was that it sought to provide a homogenous, respectable and 'Sanskritised' pan-Indian or pan-Hindu identity to them, as distinct from the subaltern, marginal and oppressive reality of their (typically rural or semi-urban) existence.

In 1983, the VHP became the central figure in the Sangh family with its 'sacrifice for unanimity'. It launched three processions throughout India with the 'Sacred Water' from the river Ganges. It also launched another programme named *Ram Puja*. It was a ceremony in which the bricks (*shila*) inscribed with the words 'Shri Ram' were consecrated locally and, then, they were collected and taken to Ayodhya in special chariots for building the proposed Ram temple. There was another organisation, which was in the forefront of the Ayodhya agitation, the BD, the militant youth wing of the VHP. The name of BD invoked the imagery of the army of monkey warriors in the epic Ramayana. This organisation was primarily seen as an instrument of other organisations.

Yet another opportunity for the BJP–RSS–VHP–BD combine to gain further political leverage occurred during 1989–1990 when the National Front government decided to implement the recommendations of the Mandal Commission. The BJP formally supported the Mandal recommendations at the national level and undermined it locally, especially in places where it relied on upper caste support. Advani's Rath Yatra from Somnath to Ayodhya affected a sea change in the political scene. The BJP itself admitted that "Mandal had divided the people, Ayodhya united the people." The success of the Sangh combine was its strategic approach to mobilise the pluralistic Hindu folk towards a particular end, the 're-construction' of the Ram temple in Ayodhya.

However, Advani's Rath Yatra was accompanied by massive bloodshed, and several communal riots broke out throughout India. The long years of communal mobilisation through more than 84 organisations controlled by the RSS finally culminated in the destruction of the Babri Masjid on 6 December 1992. The provocations for the demolition were outlined by the BJP: The general and growing "Hindu resentment against pseudo-secularism" and "minority appeasement," the allergy of most political parties to Hinduism and the consequent "loss of national identity," the political effect implicit in the Babri structure, which is an "invader's victory monument," etc. The Liberhan Commission, which enquired into the whole episode came to the conclusion that "the mobilisation of the Kar-sevaks and their convergence to Ayodhya and Faizabad was neither spontaneous nor voluntary. It was well-orchestrated and planned."

The demolition of the Masjid and the accompanying communal violence helped the BJP to securitise the whole issue, thereby polarising the population into groups. The party very skilfully utilised the issue for electoral gains. From 1989 onwards, the BJP had made considerable progress in terms of the number of seats that it won in various elections as well as the percentage of votes that they secured. Meanwhile, the demolition of the Babri Masjid had invited widespread criticisms against the BJP and its support organisations from all over the world. The BJP was, therefore, in a defensive posture for some time. Yet, the increase in the voting percentage of the BJP was amazing. It had risen from 7.7 per cent in 1984, 11.3 per cent in 1989, 20 per cent in 1991, 20.2 per cent in 1996 to 25.4 per cent in 1998. In the 1999 Lok Sabha elections, the BJP secured 298 seats and became the ruling party at the centre with a clear-cut majority in parliament. Apparently, the common factor in the increase in the popularity of the Jana Sangh and the BJP was their indebtedness to Hindutva and cultural nationalism. L. K. Advani, later, acknowledged that the "BJP's subsequent trajectory of meteoric growth was due to the Ayodhya movement." He also admitted that the movement had changed his "profile in Indian politics."

The ascendency of the BJP as the ruling party of India during 1998–2004 represented the revival of Hindutva. Communal sentiments continued to echo in the writings and campaigns of the BJP, which tended to see Hindutva as a unifying force that would create a national identity and ensure social cohesion for India. A manifestation of this ideological prejudice in the nation-building process could be seen in the Election Manifesto of BJP in 1996. There were several instances in which the BJP–VHP–RSS combine had indulged in the constructions of 'self' and 'other' on the basis of religious identity. The VHP and other Sangh leaders consistently called for "a fight for the preservation of a civilization, for Indianness, for national consciousness" and they even suspected alleged "treachery on the part of the Muslims against India" because the former "rooted for Pakistan during the two Indo-Pakistan wars." The BJP claimed that its national-ism has been based on "one nation, one people, one culture." Thus the concept of Hindu Rashtra becomes virtually essential to Hinduism as the dominant religion in India. Muslims have been constructed as "invaders and foreign transplants." The Sangh openly said:

> Muslims, led by the Islamic clergy and Islamic society have innate unwill-ingness to change, did not notice the scars that Hindus felt from the Indian past. It is admirable that Hindus never took advantage of the debt Muslims owed Hindus for their tolerance and non-vengefulness.

While Hindutva sought to carve out a cultural space during this period, the BJP as a ruling party began to face a serious dilemma in the realm of economy. Initially, its economic policy was caught between two contradictory tendencies: 'pragmatism and ideological purity'. The party later on talked about 'calibrated globalisation'. It suggested that although internal liberalisation would continue, the State would intervene to protect Indian industry from foreign competition and regulate external influence in the economy. The notion of Swadeshi was again deployed to appeal to intra-party elements and find an electoral space in response to the liberalising agenda of the opposition. However, after assuming office, the BJP leadership switched positions to appeal to the middle class, which embraced globalisation.

The BJP-led NDA government's decision to test nuclear weapons in May 1998 strengthened the hands of the reform faction. The nuclear explosions were greeted with euphoria within the Sangh Parivar for having displayed Indian power and assured its status in the world. The RSS, VHP and other organisations celebrated the Pokhran-II and unleashed a nationwide campaign to legitimise nuclear weapons to meet the threat from Pakistan, the traditional rival of India. This was given a hyper-realist dimension by deploying the discourse of security along cultural lines. This gave the pragmatists within the BJP considerable leverage to proceed with neoliberal reforms. The VHP projected the nuclear weapons as a "symbol of militarised Hindu revivalism" and celebrated the blasts with the cry of *Jai Shri Ram*. The BJP's nationalist agenda constructed an internal othering vis-à-vis Islam/Pakistan, thereby justifying India's nuclearisation. The VHP leader Ashok Singhal said:

> Hindu Sadhus and religious leaders, in a bid to 'immortalise' the recent nuclear tests at Pokhran, are planning to set up a shakti peeth (seat of divine power) near the blasts' site. India intends to be powerful in the interest of world peace, in keeping with the preaching of Lord Buddha. (*The Pioneer* 18 May 1998; Joshy and Seethi 2010:169)

He quipped, adding that there could be no peace without power. "Look at the Hindu deities, they all bear weapons in their hands," Singhal remarked. Other Sangh leaders said that "this singular historic feat has aroused the dormant self-respect of the nation." The 'consensus' behind the BJP's dangerous nuclear adventure was obviously an attempted consensus behind Hindutva. The security adventurism had in fact satisfied the hardcore elements in the Sangh.

NDA government's education policy also sought to legitimise the cultural logic of Hindutva. There were allegations of saffronisation of education designed to promote bigotry and religious fanaticism in the name of inculcating knowledge of culture in the young generation. Even school children were indoctrinated in religious intolerance, the inferiority of non-Hindus, and the collective blame of Muslims and Christians for wrongs against Hindus at various points in Indian history, as interpreted by Hindu nationalists. In the textbooks the West and its culture were projected as "enemies of Hindu culture." Religions such as Islam and Christianity were depicted as "alien to India," as they were the religions of foreign invaders—the Mughals and the British. The historical reconstruction of "Muslim and Christian atrocities" and their projection onto the present as a 'threat' to the integrity and security of India were powerful weapons in legitimising the violence against Christians and Muslims, later on.

In 2002, the State of Gujarat experienced a traumatising episode of communal violence in which Muslims were aggressively targeted. Gujarat was even called a "Hindutva Laboratory." In February–March 2002, hundreds of people—mostly Muslims—were killed in Gujarat, apparently aided and abetted by the BJP-ruled state government headed by Narendra Modi. Intermittent violence against Muslims continued in the months that followed. In the aftermath, thousands of people were rendered homeless and internally displaced. Numerous inquiries and commissions—such as the NHRC of India—held that Narendra Modi, as the Chief Minister of the State, had complete command over the police and other law enforcement machinery during the period. They all condemned the role of the government in providing leadership and material support in the politically motivated attacks on minorities in Gujarat. The NHRC pointed out that "there was a comprehensive failure on the part of the State Government to control the persistent violation of the rights to life, liberty, equality and dignity of the people of the State." Chief Minister Narendra Modi and other leaders belonging to the Hindu Right organisations alleged that the Godhra tragedy had been a pre-planned Muslim conspiracy to attack Hindus, subvert the State and damage the economy. In addition, Modi further sought to stoke religious passions of the majority Hindu community by taking the decision to bring the charred remains of the victims of the tragedy to Ahmedabad in a public ceremony.

Advani, however, defended the role of Narendra Modi in the whole episode saying that "Gujarat made spectacular progress" under him. He said that "people of all castes and communities in Gujarat have benefitted" from his "commitment to security, development and clean administration." He went a step further and said that "Modi's re-election highlighted several lessons, which were relevant not only for Gujarat but for the whole country." Thus, the anti-Muslim violence in Gujarat in 2002 was cloaked by the Hindutva organisations as 'inevitable' and 'understandable' acts to secure the Hindu 'self'. The discourse of security offered the Hindu Right organisations a tool to legitimise violence as non-violence, killers as defenders, rape as understandable lust and death as non-death.

The NDA government continued to exploit the rhetoric surrounding the global 'war against terrorism' in order to target religious minorities and political opponents. Most notably, the long debated anti-terrorism legislation, the POTA, was pushed through parliament in March 2002. This logic of the discourse of security dictated that the security of the 'self' facilitated and even demanded the use of policing and violence against the 'other'. This was exemplified in the case of Hindutva's politics of representation, which legitimised anti-Muslim/anti-Pakistan stance in the name of 'securing' the Hindu body politic at various levels. Here 'the Muslim' was seen as a 'threat' to national, state and international security. These representations of 'Muslim' as a danger to the 'security' of Hindu body politic facilitated the politics of hate campaign against the Muslims in India (and inevitably against Pakistan too). While the Gujarat carnage was an example of this campaign of Hindutva in the realm of domestic politics, Pokhran-II (1998) and Kargil War (1999) represented two other major instances in the realm of national security/defence whereby representations did play a major role in legitimising the logic of cultural nationalism.

The Kargil war in May–July 1999 provided a huge boost to the campaign of Hindutva forces, and thereby the electoral future of the BJP. The war generated a "unifying response of binding a nation together as never before" claimed the NDA government. The public saw for themselves that the Indian military personnel assigned to winkle out the infiltrators entrenched in commanding heights with clear lines of fire performed heroically. It was also the first experience of war as a spectacle and war as infotainment. Even the media endowed militarism with a nobility of purpose and defined nationalism as patriotic flag waving, dangerously intolerant and demonising of the 'other'—in this case, all Pakistanis. Pakistan and the people of Pakistan became the enemy, fused in the media-shaped popular imagination with rogue states and Talibanised terrorists. Following the outbreak of the war, the BJP and other Sangh organisations unleashed a violent campaign across the nation. Political leaders, strategic analysts and sections of the media in India called for a more aggressive war and the opening of new fronts. There were also calls in India for the bombardment of Pakistani supply routes to Kargil. The BJP leaders argued that unilateral ceasefires against militants and 'Pakistani mercenaries' would be signs of weakness and softness before 'a duplicitous adversary' and difficult for (the BJP) cadre to swallow.

Having won the Kargil war, the NDA predictably played heavily on its national security credentials during the 1999 general elections. Its 1999 manifesto expounded the war leadership shown by the caretaker administration. The manifesto also was very specific in noting the high ratio of national security pledges made in 1998 and their achievements in just 13 months of government, including exercising the nuclear option, successfully testing a second-generation Agni ballistic missile, increasing the defence budget and creating an NSC to advise the government on all matters of national security. In October 1999, the NDA headed by the BJP won a comfortable majority in the 13th Lok Sabha and came back to power. The December 2001 terrorist attacks on the Indian Parliament further helped the Sangh organisations to launch aggressive campaigns.

The Sangh cadres felt that their past appeals to the Prime Minister not to negotiate with Pakistan had been vindicated with "yet another betrayal." Calls for declaration of war on Pakistan drawing parallels with America's war on the Taliban after 9/11 were made regularly by the RSS and other Sangh organisations.

In sum, the Hindutva mobilisation during the last three decades resulted in aggressive campaigns and violent incidences—from the demolition of the Babri Masjid to Gujarat carnage, from Pokhran nuclear explosions to the Kargil war. The Hindu Right assertions were fuelled by the structural changes in the Indian State and civil society since the 1980s. The BJP's mobilisational tactics leading to its capture of power in the 1990s can be explained in terms of its strategic intervention following the social dislocations caused by the economic liberalisation and neoliberal policies. The failure of the UPA dispensation during the last decade (2004–14) notwithstanding its populist policies, the decline of the Congress party and the changing dimension of the state politics in India all helped facilitate the return of the BJP. During the 2014 parliament elections, the BJP, under the leadership of Narendra Modi, registered a decisive victory. The principal means of achieving political power was its consolidation of communal votes through its persistent campaign in civil society. Thus, a new era of State–civil society relations began in India with much greater emphasis on militarism and securitisation.

Bibliography

Primary Sources

Government Documents/Reports

CSO (1989). *National Accounts Statistics: Sources and Methods.* New Delhi: Central Statistical Organisation.

Election Commission of India (2010). *Election Results: Full Statistical Reports: Statistical Reports of Lok Sabha Elections, Assembly Elections,* http://eci.nic.in/eci_main/StatisticalReports/ElectionStatistics.asp (accessed on 14 March 2010)

Election Commission of India: Election Reports (1951, 1957, 1967, 1971, 1984, 1989, 1991, 1996, 1999, 2004, 2009, 2014). New Delhi: Election Commission of India.

Government of Gujarat (2008). *Report by The Commission of Inquiry Consisting of Mr Justice G. T. Nanavati and Mr Justice Akshay H. Mehta PART-I (Sabarmati Express Train Incident at Godhra).* Ahmedabad: Government of Gujarat.

Human Rights Watch (1999). *Human Rights Watch Report (September 1999),* www.hrw.org/press/1999/sep/christians.htm (accessed on 20 March 2010)

——— (2002). *Report on Gujarat Carnage,* www.hrw.org/press/2002/04/gujrat.htm (accessed on 08 September 2009).

Hussain, A. (1984): *Report of the Committee on Trade Policies.* New Delhi: Government of India.

——— (1989). *Report of the Committee on Trade Policies.* New Delhi: Government of India.

Jha L. K. (1985). *Report of the Economic Administration Reforms Commission on Government and Public Enterprises.* New Delhi: Government of India.

Kargil Review Committee (2000). *From Surprise to Reckoning.* New Delhi: SAGE Publishers.

MEA (1998). *Foreign Affairs Record,* 45(5). New Delhi: Ministry of External Affairs, Government of India.

——— (1999). *Annual Report 1998–1999.* New Delhi: Ministry of External Affairs, Government of India.

——— (2000). *Annual Report 1999–2000.* New Delhi: Ministry of External Affairs, Government of India.

——— (2001). Statement made by Shri L. K. Advani, Union Home Minister on Tuesday, the 18th December, 2001 in Lok Sabha in Connection with the terrorist attack on Parliament House,' http://www.mea.gov.in/articles-in-indian-media.htm?dtl/16856/Statement+made+by+Shri+LK+Advani+Union+Home+Minister+on+Tuesday+the+18th+December+2001+In+Lok+Sabha+in+Connection+with+the+terrorist+attack+on+Parliament+House (accessed on 10 September 2014).

MF (1985). *Long Term Fiscal Policy.* New Delhi: Ministry of Finance, Government of India.
———— (1986). *Economic Survey 1985–1986.* New Delhi: Ministry of Finance, Government of India.
———— (1989). *Economic Advisory Council, Report on the Current Economic Situation and Priority Areas for Action.* New Delhi: Ministry of Finance, Government of India.
———— (1991). *Economic Survey 1990–1991.* New Delhi: Ministry of Finance, Government of India.
MHA (2002). *Annual Report 2001–2002*, New Delhi: Ministry of Home Affairs, Government of India.
———— (2004). *Annual Report 2003–2004.* New Delhi: Ministry of Home Affairs, Government of India.
———— (2009). *Report of the Liberhan Ayodhya Commission of Inquiry.* New Delhi: Ministry of Home Affairs, Government of India.
Ministry of Defence (1999). *Annual Report 1998–1999.* New Delhi: Ministry of Defence, Government of India.
———— (2000). *Annual Report 1999-2000*, New Delhi: Ministry of Defence, Government of India.
———— (2005). *Annual Report 2004–2005.* New Delhi: Ministry of Defence, Government of India.
Narasimham, M. (1985). *Report of the Committee to Examine Principles of Possible Shift from Physical to Financial Controls.* New Delhi: Government of India.
NHRC (2002). *Annual Report 2001–2002*, New Delhi: National Human Rights Commission, Government of India.
———— (2003). *Proceedings of the National Human Rights Commission on the Situation in Gujarat (1 March–July 2002).* New Delhi: National Human Rights Commission, http://nhrc.nic.in/Old_Files/gujarat.htm (accessed on 3 February 2010).
———— (2004). *Annual Report 2002–2003.* New Delhi: National Human Rights Commission.
PUCL (2002). *An Interim Report to the National Human Rights commission.* Vadorara: People's Union for Civil Liberties, http://www.pucl.org/ Topics/Religion-communalism/2002/gujarat-nhrc-submission.htm (accessed on 9 July 2010).
RBI (1976). *Report on Currency and Finance, 1975–1976*, Vol. I. Mumbai: Reserve Bank of India.
———— (1988). *Report on Currency and Finance, 1987–1988*, Vol. 1. Bombay: Reserve Bank of India.
Sengupta A. (1984). *Report on the Committee to Review Policy for Public Enterprises.* New Delhi: Government of India.
South Asia Human Rights Documentation Centre (SAHRDC) (28 August 2000). www.hri.ca/partners/sahrdc/hrfeatures/HRF 25.htm (accessed on 08 September 2009).

International Organisations: Documents/Reports

Awaaz South Asia Watch Limited (26 February 2004). "In the name of charity, British people is funding Hindutva Extremism," (press release). London: Awaaz South Asia Watch Limited. www.awazasaw.org (accessed on 08 September 2009).

South Commission (1990). *The Challenge to the South: Report of the South Commission*. New Delhi: Oxford University Press.

UNDP (1992). *Human Development Report 1992*. New York: Oxford University Press.

——— (1994). *Human Development Report 1994*. Oxford: Oxford University Press.

World Bank (1991). *India: Structural Loan/Credit*. Washington, D.C.: World Bank.

——— (1997). *The State in Changing World*. Oxford: Oxford University Press.

——— (1999). *Nongovernmental Organizations in World Bank Supported Projects: A Review*. Washington, D.C.: World Bank.

——— (2000). *The Quality of Growth*. Oxford: Oxford University Press.

——— (2003). *World Development Report 2003*. Oxford: Oxford University Press.

Writings, Speeches, Memoirs and Autobiographies

Advani, L. K. (1986). "Government must not capitulate." *Indian Express*, January 7.

——— (1989a). "Reported in Bangalore." *Organiser*, Vol. 40, No. 42, April 23.

——— (1989b). *Ram Janmabhoomi: Honour People's Sentiments*. Delhi: Bharatiya Janatha Party.

——— (1990a). "BJP is good only because of its Association with the Sangh." *Organiser*, Vol. 41, No. 41, May 13.

——— (1990b). *Why Rathyatra?* Bangalore: Jagarana Prakashana.

——— (1992). *Ayodhya Before and After*. Delhi: Janadhikar Samiti.

——— (2007). *My Country My Life*. New Delhi: Rupa & Co.

——— (2009). "BJP condemns the 'Leak': Shocked" in BJP (ed.), *Liberhan Commission Report: Not a Report, but Just a New Controversy*. New Delhi: Bharatiya Janata Party.

——— (2010a). *Vision Document 2004,*http://www.lkadvani.in/eng/content/view/448/293/ (accessed on 03 February 2010).

——— (2010b). "*Hindutva,*" http://www.lkadvani.in/eng/content/view/378/344/ (accessed on 08 February 2010).

——— (2010c). "*Indian Muslims,*" http://www.lkadvani.in/eng/content/view/374/345/ (accessed on 08 February 2010).

——— (2010d). "*Communal Violence in Gujarat,*" http://www.lkadvani.in/eng/content/view/596/365/ (accessed on 08 February 2010).

——— (2010e). "*Politics of Minorityism,*" http://www.lkadvani.in/eng/content/view/375/347/ (accessed on 08 July 2015).

Bhagwat, Mohan (2009). Speech by Mohan Bhagwat Vijayadashimi Mahotsva, Nagpur, Yugabda-5111, 27 September (Sara-Sanghchalak RSS).

Deoras, Balasaheb (1990). "The public speech delivered on the occasion of Nagpur Shakha's Vijayadashimi Mahotsav, held on 29th of September" *Organiser*, Vol. XLII, No. 10, 14 October.

Goel, Sita Ram (1984a). *Perversion of India's Political Parlance*. New Delhi: Voice of India.

Goel, Sita Ram (1984b). *History of Heroic Hindu Resistance to Muslim Invaders (636–1206 AD)*. New Delhi: Voice of India.

Golwalkar, M. S. (1939). *We or Our Nationhood Defined*. Nagpur: Bharat Publications.

——— (1968). "The answer to All Questions" An English rendering of the Speech (Original in Hindi) delivered by Shri M. S. Golwalkar, Sarsanghachalak of the RSS at the closing function of a camp held near Delhi on 8–10 November.

Golwalkar, M. S. (2000). *Bunch of Thoughts*. Bangalore: Sahitya Sindhu Prakasana.

———— **(2008)**. A Malayalam translated version of the work "Shri Guruji Drishti or Dharshan" (Hindi), *Shri Guruji Drishtiyum Dharshanavum* (Malayalam). Kochi: Kurukshetraprakashan.

Kurushethra Prakashan (2008). *M. S. Golwalkar: His Vision and Mission*. Nagpur: Dr Hedgewar Smarak Samithi.

Madhok, Balraj (1966). "Presidential Address to the 13th All India session of the BJS," on 30 April, 1–2 May 1966, at Jallander (Punjab).

MIB (1983a). *Jawaharlal Nehru's Speeches 1949–1953*, Vol. 2. New Delhi: Ministry of Information and Broadcasting, Government of India.

——— (1983b). *Jawaharlal Nehru's Speeches 1953–1957*, Vol. 3. New Delhi: Ministry of Information and Broadcasting, Government of India.

——— (1983c). *Jawaharlal Nehru's Speeches: 1946–1949*, Vol. 1. New Delhi: Ministry of Information and Broadcasting, Government of India.

——— (1983d). *The Years of Endeavour: Selected Speeches of Indira Gandhi, August 1969– August 1972*. New Delhi: Ministry of Information and Broadcasting.

——— (1987). *Rajiv Gandhi: Selected Speeches and Writings, 31 October 1984–1931 December 1985*, Vol. 1. New Delhi: Ministry of Information and Broadcasting, Government of India.

Mishra, Dina Nath (1980). *RSS: Myth and Reality*. UP, India: Vikas Publishing Home.

Navalgundkar, S. N. (n.d.). "Hindus, Unite, Modernise and Militarise" in Sudhakar Raje (ed.), *Savarkar*. Bombay: Savarkar Darshan Pratisthan Trust.

——— (n.d.). "Aryan Invasion: Historical Theory or Political Myth," *Madra*, a public opinion Forum.

Sastry, Shripaty (1983). *A Retrospect: Christianity in India (An Exposition of the RSS View on the Relevance of Christianity in India Today)*. Pune: Bharatya Vihar Sadhana.

Sastry, Shripaty (n.d.). "Shri Gurujiyum Christian Sabakalum" (Malayalam), *Shri Guruji and Cathelic churches*. Kerala: Sree Guruji Janmasthabdi Akhoshasamithi.

Savarkar, V. D. (1940). *Hindu Sangatan: Its Ideology Immediate Programme*. Bombay: Hindu Mahasabha Presidential Office.

——— (1942). *Hindu Padashahi or A Review of the Hindu Empire of Maharashtra*. Poona: Manohar Mahadeo Kelkar.

——— (1967). *Historic Statements*. Bombay: B. G. Fhawale, Karnatak Printing Press .

——— (1971). *Hindu Pad Padashati: Story of the Maratha Struggle to Re-establish Sovereign Hindu Power*. New Delhi: Bharati Sahitya Sadan.

——— (1984). *Hindu Rashtra Darshan*. Bombay: Veer Savarkar Prakashan.

——— (1989). *Hindutva: Who is a Hindu*. New Delhi: Bharati Sahitya Sadan.

——— (1993a). "Nehru's Nightmare—Hindu Raj? Carpet Knights" in V. Grover (ed.), *V. D. Savarkar: Political Thinkers of Modern India-14*. New Delhi: Deep and Deep.

Savarkar, V. D. (1993b). "Problems before Hindudom after Bloodless Vivisection" in V. Grover (ed.), *V. D . Savarkar: Political Thinkers of Modern India-14*. New Delhi: Deep and Deep.

——— (1998). "A Dangerous Cult of Absolute Nonviolence" in Sharma, S.D (ed.), *100 Best Pre–Independence Speeches 1870–1947*. New Delhi: Harper Collins. (1998).

——— (2007). "Presidential Address, Akhil Bharatiya Hindu Mahasabha," 1937, in Batabyal, Rakesh (ed.), *The Penguin Book of Modern Indian speeches: 1877 to the present*. New Delhi: Penguin Books.

Sheshadri, H. V. (1984). *Hindu Renaissance under Way*. Bangalore: Jagarana Prakashana.
———— (1985). *Christian Missions in Bharat: Some Questions to Pope*. Bangalore: Jagarana Prakashana.
———— (ed.) (1988). *A vision in Action*. Bangalore: Jagarana Prakashana.
———— (1998). "India can no more be treated as a Second rate nation." *Organiser*, Vol. XLIX, No. 43, May 24.
———— (1999), "Hindutva at the centre stage of Bharatiya politics." *Organiser*, Vol. XLIX, No. 24, January 11.
Tirtha, Swami Bharati Krishna (1985). *Sanatana Dharma*. Bombay: Bharatiya Vidya Bhavan.
Togadia, Pravin (n.d.). *The conspiracy for Universal Christian Conversion*. Gujarat: Samskriti Raksha Manch.
Upadhyaya, Deenadayal (1989). *Integral Humanism*. Translated by Ramesh Sheth. Bombay: Bharatiya Jana Sangh.
Vajpayee, Atal Bihari (1992). *Speeches on Ayodhya Issue*. New Delhi: Bharatiya Janata Party.
Vivekananda (2007). "Assertion of Universality," in Batabyal (2007).

Party/Organisational Documents and Reports

Akhil Bharatiya Vanavasi Kalyan Ashram (n.d.). *Worshiping Motherland*. Chhattisgarh.
Bajrang Dal (2001). "Bajarangis-Do not become Hindu Jihadis," http:// www. hindutva.org/ bajrang.html (accessed on 9 February 2010).
BJP, Bharatiya Janata Party: http://www.hvk.org/specialrepo/bjpwp/index.html
BJP (1993). *White Paper on Ayodhya and the Rama Temple Movement*. New Delhi: Bharatiya Janata Party.
———— (1996). *For a Strong and Prosperous India: Election Manifesto 1996*. New Delhi: Bharatiya Janata Party.
———— (1998). *Election Manifesto*. Delhi: Bharatiya Janata Party Office.
———— (1999). *Foreign Policy Resolutions 1980–1999*. Delhi: Bharatiya Janata Party.
———— (2001). National Executive Resolution 2–3 November 2001. Resolution on Terrorism, http://www.bjp.org/content/view/2598/394/ (accessed on 12 February 2010).
———— (2004a). 'Vision Document,' Manifesto of the Bharatiya Janata Party.
———— (2004b). Meeting of the National Executive Ranchi, November 24–26, 2004, Resolution on Internal Security.
———— (2006). *"Foreword"* 18 May 2006, http://www.bjp.org/Publication/CE.pdf (accessed on 12 February 2010).
BJP (2009a). 'Good Governance, Development, Security,' Manifesto of the Bharatiya Janata Party.
———— (2009b**). *Liberhan Commission Report: Not a Report, but Just a New Controversy*. New Delhi: Bharatiya Janata Party.
———— (2010a). "Hindutva: The Great Nationalist Ideology," http://www.bjp.org/ (accessed on 12 February 2010)
———— (2010b)."BJP History: Its Birth and Early Growth," http://www.bjp.orgcontent/ view/432/284/ (accessed on 29 June 2010).

BJS (1961). *Manifesto and Programme of the Bharatiya Jana Sangh, as Adopted by the Bhartiya Pratinidhi Sabha, at its Bangalore Session in December 1958*. Delhi: Bharatiya Jana Sangh Publications.

——— (1965). "Principles and Policy", adopted by Bharatiya Pratinidhi Sabha at Vijaya wada (Andra) on January 25 and 26.

Dalits Intellectual Collective and Vikas Adyayan Kendra, Mumbai (2009). Manuscript provided as a part of "Dalit Women's Capacity Building Workshop: 16–19 October 2009 at Asha Sadan, Vagamon, Kerala.

Dr Hedgewar Birth Contrary Celebrations (1989). *Heralding a New Era: A Bird's Eye View of Dr Hedgewar Birth Centenary Celebrations*. Bangalore: Jagarana Prakashana.

NDA (2004). *An Agenda for Development, Good Governance, Peace, and Harmony Elections to the 14th Lok Sabha April–May 2004, National Democratic Alliance*. New Delhi: National Democratic Alliance.

Pragana Bharati (n.d.). *Temple in Ayodhya: A Must*. AP Cell: Pragana Bharati.

RSS (1964). *Not Socialism but Hindu Rashtra*. Banglore: RSS Prakashan Vibhag.

——— (2010a). "Home," http://rssonnet.org/index.php (accessed on 12 February 2010)

——— (2010b). *Annual Report 2009–2010*. New Delhi: RSS.

Sahitya Sangama (1992). *RSS: Widening, Horizons*. Bangalore: Sahitya Sangama.

Sangh Parivar (2010). "Rashtriya Swayamsevak Sangh," http://www.sanghparivar. org/ (accessed on 29 June 2010).

Shiv Sena (2010). http://www.shivsena.org/ (accessed on 12 April 2010)

Swadeshi Jagarn Manch (1997). *Rebuilding the Nation: A Swadeshi Outline, Integrated Development: The Concept and the Plan of Action* (draft circulated for national debate/ Mathan). New Delhi: Asgha National Action Group on Development, Swadeshi Jagaran Manch.

VHP (1991). Vishwa Hindu Parishad: The Great Evidence of Shri Ram Janmabhoomi Mandir. Delhi: Vishwa Hindu Parishad.

——— (2003). "Tenth Dharma Sansad in Delhi on 22–23 February 2003," http://vhp.org/ dharma-sansad-10/ (accessed on 12 February 2010)

——— (2010a). "Shri Ram Janmabhoomi Movement–Frequently Asked Questions," http:// vhp.org/faqs/faq-ramjanmabhoomi/ (accessed on 12 February 2010)

——— (2010b). "Summary of the Evidence Proving Destruction of Shri Ram Janmabhoomi Temple in 1528 AD," http://vhp.org/faqs/faq-ramjanmabhoomi-append/ (accessed on 25 June 2010).

Vivekananda Kendra (n.d.). *Guidelines for Branch Centres*. Kanyakumari.

VKA (2010a). "Vanavasi Kalyan Ashram: Glimpses of Social Activity," http://www.vanavasi-kalyan.org/socialprogram.html (accessed on 24 June 2010).

——— (2010b)."Vanavasi Kalyan Ashram: Homepage," http://www.vanvasi.org/ aboutus. php (accessed on 1 April 2010)

BOOKS

Ahluwalia, Sashi (1987). *Spiritual Masters from India*. Delhi: Manas Publications.

Ahluwalia, I. J. (1985). *Industrial Growth in India*. New Delhi: Oxford University Press.

Ahmed, Akbar S. (1993). *Postmodernism and Islam: Predicament and Promise.* New Delhi: Penguin Books.

Aiyar, Mani Shankar (2004). *Confessions of a Secular Fundamentalist.* New Delhi: Penguin/ Viking Group.

Alam, Javeed (2004). *Who Wants Democracy?* Hyderabad: Orient Longman.

Alexander, Jeffery, Raymond Boudon, and Mohamed Cherkaoui (eds.). (1997). *The Classical Tradition in Sociology: The American Tradition,* Vol. I. New Delhi: SAGE Publications.

Amin, Samir (1997). *Capitalism in the Age of Globalization.* Delhi: Madhyam Books.

Anderson, James (ed.). (1986). *The Rise of the Modern State.* London: Wheat sheaf Books Ltd.

Anderson, Perry (1979). *Lineages, of the Absolutist State.* London: Verso Books.

Anderson, Walter K. and Shridhar D. Danle (1987). *The Brotherhood in Saffron: The Rashtriya Swayam Sevaks Sangh and Hindu Revivalism.* New Delhi: Visitar Publications.

Arulanantham, David P. (2004). *The Paradox of the BJP's Stance Towards External Economic Liberalisation: Why a Hindu Nationalist Party Furthered Globalisation in India.* London: Royal Institute of International Affairs, Chatham House.

Aurobindo (1965). *On Nationalism.* Pondicherry: Sri Aurobindo Ashram.

Bagchi, Amiya Kumar (1982). *The Political Economy of Underdevelopment.* Cambridge: Cambridge University press.

Baran, Paul and Paul M. Sweezy (1966). *Monopoly Capitalism.* New York: Modern Reader.

Bardhan, Pranab (1998). *The Political Economy of Development in India.* Delhi: Oxford University Press.

Barrow, Clyde W. (1993). *Critical Theories of the State: Marxist, Neo-Marxist, Post-Marxist.* Madison: University of Wisconsin Press.

Batabyal, Rakesh (ed.) (2007). *The Penguin Book of Modern Indian Speeches: 1877 to the Present.* New Delhi: Penguin Books.

Beiser, Frederick (2008). *Hegel.* New York: Routledge.

Below, Walden (1995). *Rolling Back the south, Rolling Back the State: US Corporate Interests and Structural Adjustment in the Third World in 'Just World Trust' (JUST).* Malaysia: Vinlin Press.

Benoist, Alain de and Charles Champetier (2000). *The French New Right in the Year* 2000, http://foster.20megsfree.com/index_en.htm (accessed on 7 February 2009)

Berglund, Henrik (2009). *Civil Society in India: Democratic Space or the Extension of Elite Domination?* Working Papers 2009:1. Stockholm: Department of Political Science, Stockholm University.

Berti, Daniela, Nicolas Jaoul and Pralay Kanungo (eds.) (2011). *Cultural Entrenchment of Hindutva: Local Mediations and Forums of Convergence.* New Delhi: Routledge.

Bhagwati, Jagdish (1993). *India in Transition: Freeing the Economy.* Oxford: Oxford University Press.

Bhargava, Rajeev (ed.) (1998). *Secularism and its Critics.* New Delhi: Oxford University Press.

Bhargava, Rajeev and Helmut Reifeld (2005). *Civil Society, Public Sphere and Citizenship: Dialogues and Perceptions.* New Delhi: SAGE Publications.

Bidwai, Praful and Achin Vanaik (2001). *South Asia on a Short Fuse: Nuclear Politics and the Future of Global Disarmament.* New Delhi: Oxford University Press.

Boundeon, Raymon, Mohammed Cherkaoni, and Jeffrey Alexander (eds.) (1997). *The Classical Traditions in Sociology: The European Tradition,* Vol. I. New Delhi: SAGE Publications.

Brass, P. (1997). *Theft of an Idol: Text and Context in the Representation of Collective Violence.* Princeton, NJ: Princeton University Press.

Brass, Paul R. (2003). *The Production of Hindu-Muslim Violence in Contemporary India*. Seattle: University of Washington Press.

Buchanan, D. H. (1934). *The Development of Capitalist Enterprise in India*. New York: Macmillan.

Budhoo, Davison L. (1990). *Enough is Enough*. Delhi: The Other India Press.

Burchill, Scott and Andrew Linklater (1996). *Theories of International Relations*. New York: St. Martin Press.

Buzan, Barry (1987). *People states and fear: The National Security Problem in International Relations*. New Delhi: Transasia Publishers.

Buzan, Barry, Ole Waever, and Jaap de Wilde (1998). *Security: A New Framework for Analysis*. Boulder, CO: Lynne Rienner.

Campbell, D. (1998). *Writing Security: United States Foreign Policy and the Politics of Identity*. Minneapolis: University of Minnesota Press.

Carr, E. H. (1946). *The Twenty Years' Crisis, 1919–1939: An Introduction to the Study of International Relations*. London: Macmillan.

Chandhoke, Neera (1995). *State and Civil Society: Explorations in Political Theory*. New Delhi: SAGE Publications.

———— (2002). *Beyond Secularism—The Rights of Religions Minorities*. New Delhi: Oxford University Press.

———— (2003). *The Conceits of Civil Society*. New Delhi: Oxford University Press.

Chandra, Bipan (1984). *Communalism in Modern India*. New Delhi: Vikas.

Chatterjee, Partha (1986). *Nationalist Thought and the Colonial World: A Derivative Discourse?* Delhi: Oxford University Press.

———— (1994). *The Nation and Its Fragments: Colonial and Post Colonial Histories*. Delhi: Oxford University Press.

Chen L., S. Fukuda-Parr, and E. Seidensticker (eds.) (2003). *Human Insecurity in a Global World*. Cambridge, MA: Harvard University Press.

Cheyl, Welch (1997). *De Tocqueville*. Oxford: Oxford University Press.

Clark, Ian (1999). *Globalisation and International Relations Theory*. Oxford: Oxford University Press.

Cohen, Jean L. and Andrew Arato (1992). *Civil Society and Political Theory*. Cambridge Massachusetts: MIT Press.

Corbridge, Stuart and John Harriss (2000). *Reinventing India: Liberalisation, Hindu Nationalism and Popular Democracy*. New Delhi: Oxford University Press.

Crook, Nigel (ed.) (1996). *The Transmission of Knowledge in "South Asia."* Delhi: Oxford University Press.

Curran, J. A. (1951). *Militant Hinduism in Indian Politics—A Study of the RSS*. N.P.: Institute of Pacific Relations.

Czempiel E-O. and J. N. Rosenau (2004). *Global Changes and Theoretical Challenges, Approaches to World Politics for the 1990s*. Lexington: Quoted in George Sorensen, *The Transformation of the State: Beyond the Myth of Retreat*. New York: Palgrave.

Dalton, Dennis (1982). *Indian Idea of Freedom: Political Thought of Swami Vivekānanda, Aurobindo Ghose, Mahatma Gandhi and Rabindranath Tagore*, Gurgaon: Academic Press.

Deakin, Nicholas (2001). *In Search of Civil Society*. New York: Palgrave.

Della Porta, Donalella and Mario Diani (2000). *Social Movements: An Introduction*. UK: Blackwell.

Desai, A. R. (ed.). (1986). *Violation of Democratic Rights in India*. Bombay: Popular Prakashan.

Deshpande, B. V. and S. R. Ramaswamy (1981). *Dr Hedgewar the Epoch Maker*. Bangalore: Sahitya Sindhu.

De Souza, Peter Ronald and E. Sridharan (2006). *India's Political Parties* New Delhi: SAGE Publications.

Diamond S. (1995). *Roads to Dominion: Right Wing movements and Political Power in the United States*. New York: Guilford.

Diaz, Victor M. Perez (1993). *The Return of Civil Society: The Emergence of Democratic Spain*, Cambridge: Harvard University Press.

Dillon, Michael (1996). *Politics of Security: Towards a Political Philosophy of Continental Thought*. London and New York: Routledge.

Dumont, Louis (1970). *Homo Hierarchicus: The Caste System and Its Implications*, translated by Mark Sainsbury, Louis Dumont, and Basia Gulati. Delhi: Oxford University Press.

Edwards, Michael (2004). *Civil Society*. London: Polity Press.

Elliott, Carolyn M. (2003). *Civil Society and Democracy: A Reader*. New Delhi: Oxford University Press.

Elst, Koenraad (1997). *Bharatiya Janata Party Vis-a-Vis Hindu Resurgence*. New Delhi: Voice of India.

Engels, Frederic (1884). *The Origins of Family, Private Property and the State*. New York: Internal Publishers (1942).

Engineer, Asghar Ali (1985). *Lifting the Veil: Communal Violence and Communal Harmony in Contemporary India*. Hyderabad: Sangam Books.

———— (1990). *Babri Masjid Ramajanmbhoomi Controversy*. Delhi: Ajanta Publications.

———— (ed.) (1992). *Politics of Confrontation: The Babri Masjid/Ram Janmabhoomi Controversy Runs Riot*. Delhi: Ajanta Publications.

———— (1995). *Lifting the Veil: Communal Violence and Communal Harmony in Contemporary India*. Hyderabad: Sangam Books.

Esteves, Satro (1996). *Nationalism, Secularism and Communalism*. Delhi: South Asia Publications.

Falk, Richard (1999). *Predatory Globalization: A Critique*. London: Polity Press.

Femia, Joseph V. (1981). *Gramsci's Political Thought: Hegemony Consciousness, and the Revolutionary Process*. Oxford: Oxford University Press.

Foucault, Michel (1979). *Discipline and Punish: The Birth of the Prison*. New York: Vintage.

Frank, A. G. (1985). *Crisis: In the Third World*. London: Grower.

Frankel, Francine R. (2008). *India's Political Economy 1947–2004*, Second Edition. New Delhi: Oxford University Press.

Friedman, Milton (1980). *Free to Choose*. New York: Harcourt Brace Jovanovich.

———— (1962). *Capitalism and Freedom*. Chicago: The University of Chicago Press.

———— (1963). *A Monetary History of the United States, 1867–1960*. Princeton: Princeton University Press and National Bureau of Economic Research.

Froerer, Peggy (2007). *Religious Division and Social conflict: The Emergence of Hindu Nationalism in Rural India*. New Delhi: Social Science Press.

Fukuyama, F. (1992). *The End of History and the Last Man*. London: Hamish Hamilton.

Fukuyama, Francis (1995). *Trust*. New York: The Free Press.

———— (1999). *The Great Disruption: Human Nature and the Reconstitution of Social Order*. New York: Free Press.

Gamble, Andrew (1988). *The Free Economy and the Strong State*. London: Macmillan.

Gandhi, M. K. (1938). *Hind Swaraj or Indian Home Rule*. Ahmedabad: Navajivan Trust.

Gaus, Gerald F. (1983). *The Modern Liberal Theory of Man*. New York: St. Martin's Press.

Gellner, Ernest (1983). *Nations and Nationalism.* Oxford: Blackwell Publishers.

——— (1994a). *Encounters with Nationalism.* Oxford: Blackwell Publishers.

——— (1994b). *The Conditions of Liberty: Civil Society and Its Rivals.* New York: Penguin.

Gerth, H. H. and C. W. Mills (eds.) (1972). *From Max Weber.* New York: Oxford University Press.

Ghosh, Partha S. (2001). *BJP and the Evolution of Hindu Nationalism.* New Delhi: Manohar.

Giddens, Anthony (ed.) (1986). *Durkheim on Politics of the State.* London: Polity Press.

——— (2001). *The Global Third Way Debate.* Cambridge: Polity.

Glasius, Anheier M. and Mary Kaldor (eds.) (2001). *Global Civil Society 2001.* Oxford: Oxford University Press.

Glasius, Marlies, Mary Kaldor, and Helmut Anheier (eds.) (2002). *Global Civil Society 2002.* New York: Oxford University Press.

——— (2006). *Global Civil Society 2005/06.* London: SAGE Publications.

Goodin, Robert E of Philip Petlit (eds.) (1997). *Contemporary Political Philosophy: An Anthology.* Oxford: Blackwell.

Gopal, Sarvepalli (ed.) (1993). *Anatomy of a Confrontation: The Babri Masjid Ram Janmabhoomi Issue* New Delhi: Penguin.

Gore, M. S. (ed.) (1991). *Secularism in India.* Allahabad: Indian Academy of Social Sciences.

Graham, Bruce (1990). *Hindu Nationalism and Indian Politics: The Origins and Development of Bharatiya Jana Sangh,* Cambridge: Cambridge University Press.

——— (1993). *Hindu Nationalism and Indian Politics: The Origins and Development of the Bharatiya Jana Sangh.* New Delhi: Foundation Books.

Graham, David T. and Nana K. Poku (eds.) (2005). *Migration, Globalisation and Human Security.* London: Routledge.

Gramsci, Antonio (1971). *Selections from the Prison Notebooks,* edited and translated by Q. Hoare and G. Nowell. Smith London: Lawrence and Wishart.

——— (1998). *Selections from the Prison Notebooks,* edited and translated by Quintin Hoare and Geoffrey Novell Smith. Hyderabad, India: Orient Longman Ltd.

Green, D. (1987). *The New Right: The Counter Revolution in Political, Economic and Social Thought.* London: Wheatsheaf Books.

Gujarat Carnage (2002). "A Report to the Nation by an Independent Fact Finding Mission," http://www.sacw.net/Gujarat2002/GujCarnage.html (accessed on 12 February 2010)

Gunn, S. (1989). *The Revolution of the Right: Europe's New Conservatives.* London: Transnational Institute/Pluto Press.

Gupta, Dipankar (2005). *Anti-Utopia: Essential Writings of André Beteille.* New York: Oxford.

Habermas, Jürgen (1975). *Legitimation Crisis,* translated by Thomas McCarthy. Boston: Beacon Press.

——— (1989). *Structural Transformation of the Public Sphere.* Cambridge, Mass: MIT Press.

——— (1997). *Between Facts and Norms: Contributions to a Discourse Theory of Law and Democracy.* Cambridge: Polity Press.

Hall, John A. (ed.). (1995). *Civil Society: Theory, History, Comparison.* Oxford: Polity Press.

Hall, Stuart, David Held, Don Hubert, and Kenneth Thompson (1996). *Modernity: An Introduction to Modern Societies.* USA: Blackwell.

Hansen, Thomas Blom (1999). *The Saffron Wave.* New Delhi: Oxford.

Hansen, Thomas Blom and Christophe Jaffrelot (eds.) (2001). *The BJP and the Compulsions of Politics in India.* New Delhi: Oxford University Press.

Hardgrave, Robert and Stanley Kochanek (2000). *India: Government and Politics in a Developing Nation.* Orlando: Harcourt Press.

Harvey, David (1989). *The Condition of Postmodernity*. Oxford: Basil Blackwell.
——— (2005). *A Brief History of Neoliberalism*. Oxford: Oxford University Press.
Hasan, Mushirul (1997). *Legacy of a Divided Nation-India's Muslims since Independence*. New Delhi: Oxford University Press.
——— (2004). *Will Secular India Survive?* Haryana: Imprint One.
Hasan, Zoya (2000). *Politics and State in India*. New Delhi: SAGE Publications.
——— (ed.) (2002). *Parties and Party Politics in India*. New Delhi: Oxford University Press.
Hayek, F. A. (1960). *The Constitution of Liberty*. London: Routledge and Kegan Paul.
Hegel (1897). "The philosophy of Right (Third part)," www.marxist.org (accessed on 1 March 2008)
Heimsath, C. H. (1964). *Indian Nationalism and Hindu Social Reform*. Princeton: Princeton University Press.
Held, David (1980). *Introduction to Critical Theory: Horkheimer to Habermas*. London: Hutchinson.
——— (1998). *Political Theory and the Modern State*. New Delhi: Maya Polity.
Hobbes, Thomas (1651). *Leviathan*. Cambridge Revised Student Edition Edited by Richard Tuck, 1996. First five chapters in www.marxist.org (accessed on 12 February 2008)
——— (1991). *Leviathan,* edited by Richard Tuck. Cambridge: Cambridge University Press.
——— *De Cive* in www.marxist.org (accessed on 11 February 2008)
Hobson, Jon M. (2000). *The State and International Relations*. Cambridge: Cambridge University Press, http://home.alphalink.com.au/~radnat/ defendnationalism/defend13.html (accessed on 20 June 2010).
Horkheimer, Max (1972). *Critical Theory*. New York: Herder & Herder.
Indian Express (2005). "Increase population: Togadia Tells Hindus" December 09, 2005 at http://www.expressindia.com/news/fullstory.php?newsid=59779 #compstory
Jacob, Margaret C. (2000). *The Enlightenment: Brief History with Documents (Bedford Series in History and Culture)*. London: Palgrave Macmillan.
Jaffrelot, Christophe (1996). *The Hindu Nationalist Movement in India*, New York: Columbia University Press.
——— (2005). *The Sangh Parivar*. New Delhi: Oxford University Press.
——— (ed.) (2007). *Hindu Nationalism: A Reader*. Princeton: Princeton University Press.
Jalan, Bimal (1991). *India's Economic Crisis—The Way Ahead*. Delhi: Viking.
James P. J. (2004). *Global Funding and NGO Network: The True Mission*. Thrissur, Kerala: New Spring Publications.
Jameson, Fredric (1992). *Postmodernism or the Cultural Logic of Late Capitalism*. London: Verso.
Jennings, Jeremy and Anthony Kemp-Welch. (1997) *Intellectuals in Politics: From the Dryfus Affair to Salman Rushdie*. London: Routledge.
Jessop, Bob (1990). *State Theory: Putting Capitalist States in their Place*, Cambridge: Polity Press.
Jogdand, P. G. (ed.). (2000). *New Economic Policy and Dalits*. Jaipur: Rawat Publications.
Joshi, Shastri and Bhagavan Josh (1994). *Struggle for Hegemony in India: 1920–1947*. New Delhi: SAGE Publications.
Kaldor, Mary (2004). *Global Civil Society: An Answer to War*. UK: Polity Press.
Kaldor, N. (1978). *Further Essays on Economic Theory*. London: Cambridge University Press.
Kanungo, Pralay (2002). *RSS's Tryst with Politics: From Hedgewar to Sudarshan*. Delhi: Manohar Publications.

Kanungo, Pralay (2011). "Casting Community, Culture and Faith: Hindutva's Entrenchment in Arunachal Pradesh" in Berti, Daniela, Nicolas Jaoul and Parlay Kanungo (eds.) *Cultural Entrenchment of Hindutva: Local Mediations and forms of Convergence*, UK: Routledge.

Kapur, Anup Chand (1989). *Select Constitutions*. New Delhi: S. Chand & Company.

Kapur, Ashok (2003). *Pokhran and Beyond: India's Nuclear Behavior*. New Delhi: Oxford University Press.

Kaviraj, Sudipta (ed.) (1997). *Politics in India*. Delhi: Oxford University Press.

Kaviraj, Sudipta and Sunil Khilnani (eds.) (2001). *Civil Society: History and Possibilities*. Cambridge: Cambridge University Press.

Keane, John (ed.) (1998). *Civil Society and the State: New European Perspectives*. London: Verso.

Keynes, J. M. (1957). *The General Theory of Employment, Interest and Money*. London: Macmillan.

King, Christopher R. (1994). *One Language Two Scripts: The Hindi Movement in Nineteenth Century North India*. Bombay: Oxford University Press.

Kleinberg, Remonda Bensabat and Jamine A. Clark (2000). *Economic Liberalization, Democratization and Civil Society in the Developing World*. New York: Palgrave.

Kohli, Atul (2002). *The Success of India's Democracy*. New Delhi: Foundation Books.

Kothari, Rajni (2006). *Politics in India*. Hyderabad: Orient Longman.

Kozlov, G. A. (1977). *Political Economy: Capitalism*. Moscow: Progress.

Krause, K. and M. Williams, (eds.) (1997). *Critical Security Studies*. Boulder, CO: Lynne Rienner.

Krishna, Sankaran (1999). *Post-colonial Insecurities: India, Sri Lanka and the Question of Nationhood*. Minneapolis: University of Minnesota Press.

Kumar, Krishna (2001a): *Prejudice and Pride: School histories of the freedom struggle in India and Pakistan*, Delhi: Viking.

Kumar, Sunil (2001b). *Communalism and Secularism in Indian Politics Study of the BJP*. New Delhi: Rawat Publishers.

Kurien, C. T. (1994). *Global Capitalism and the Indian Economy*. New Delhi: Orient Longman.

Kuruvachira, J. (2006). *Hindu Nationalists of Modern India: A Critical Study of the Intellectual Genealogy of Hindutva*. New Delhi: Rawat Publications.

Kymlicka, Will (1989). *Liberalism, Community and Culture*. Oxford: Clarendon Press.

Lajpat Rai (1991). *Swami Dayananda Saraswati: His Biography and Teachings*. New Delhi: Reliance Publishing Company.

Larbeer P. Mohan (2003). *Ambedkar on Religion: A Lacerative Perspective*. New Delhi: ISPCK.

Leonard, Peter (1997). *Postmodern Welfare: Restructuring an Emancipatory Project*. London: SAGE.

Levitas, Rus (1986). *The Ideology of the New Right*. Cambridge: Polity Press.

Lipschutz, R. D. (1995). *On Security*. New York: Columbia University Press.

Locke, John (1960). *Two Treatises of government*, in Peter Laslette. Cambridge: Cambridge University Press.

Low, D. A. (ed.). (1977). *Congress and the Raj*. London: Arnold-Heinemann.

Ludden, David (2005). *Making India Hindu: Religion, Community, and the Politics of Democracy in India*. New Delhi: Oxford University Press.

Lukacs, G. (1993). *History and Class Consciousness*. Bombay: Rupa.

Lyotard, Jean Francis (1984). *The Postmodern Condition: A Report on Knowledge*. Minneapolis: University of Minnesota Press.

Mac Ewan, Arthur (1999). *Neo-liberalism or Democracy? Economic Strategy Markets and Alternatives for the 21st Century.* Australia: Pluto Press.

Majumdar, R. C. (1981). *British Paramount and Indian Renaissance.* Bombay: Bharatiya Vidhya Bhavan.

Malik, Yogendra K. and V. B. Sing (1995). *Hindu Nationalists in India: The Rise of the Bharatiya Janata Party.* New Delhi: Vistara Publications.

—— (1996). *Hindu Nationalists in India.* Boulder: Westview.

Manchanda, Rita (2002). *Militarized Hindu Nationalism and the Mass Media.* Kathmandu: South Asia Forum for Human Rights.

Mann, Michael (1986). *The Sources of Social Power,* Vol. 1. England: Cambridge University Press.

Markovitz, Claud (1985). *Indian Business and Nationalist Policies 1931–1939: The Indigenous Capitalist Class and the Rise of the Congress Party.* Cambridge: Cambridge University Press.

Marx, Karl (1843). *Contribution to the Critique of Hegel's 'Philosophy of Right,'* in Karl Marx and Frederik Engels (1975): *Collected Works,* Vol. 3. London: Lawrence and Wishart.

—— (1857). *Introduction to Contribution to the Critique of Political Economy,* in Karl Marx. *Grundrise,* Harmandsworth: Penguin (1973).

Marx, Karl and Fredrick Engels (1848). *Manifesto of the Communist Party.* Moscow: Progress Publishers (1969).

—— (1962). *Selected Works,* Vol. 1. Moscow: Foreign Language Publishing House.

Mattoo, Amitabh and Kanti Bajpai (eds.) (2001). *Kargil and Beyond.* New Delhi: Har Anand.

Mc Clellan, David (1979). *Marxism after Marx: An Introduction.* London: The Macmillan Press Ltd.

Mc Clelland, J. S. (1996). *A History of Western Political Thought.* London: Routledge.

McGirr, Lisa (2001). *Suburban Warriors: The Origins of the New American Right (Politics and Society in Twentieth-century America).* Princeton: Princeton University Press.

McGuire, John and Ian Copland (2008). *Hindu Nationalism and Governance.* New Delhi: Oxford University Press.

Mc Lellan, David (1995). *The Thought of Karl Marx.* London: Macmillan Press.

Mc Lennan, Gregor, David Held, and Stuart Hall (1993). *The Idea of the Modern State.* Philadelphia: Open University Press.

McSweeney, Bill (1999). *Security, Identity and Interests: A sociology of International Relations.* Cambridge: Cambridge University Press.

Mehra K, Ajay, D. D. Khanna, and Gert W. Kneck (2003). *Political Parties and Party Systems.* New Delhi: SAGE Publications.

Merrington, John (1977). *Theory and Practice in Gramsci's Marxism'* in *New Left Review* (ed.) *Western Marxism: A critical Reader.* London: New Left Review.

Michael, Dillon (1996). *Politics of Security: Towards a Political Philosophy of Continental Thought,* London: Routledge.

Migdal, Joel S. (2001). *State in Society: Studying in How States and Societies Transform and Constitute One Another.* Cambridge: Cambridge University Press.

Migdal, Joel S, Atul Kohli, and Vivienne Shue (eds.) (1994): *State Power and Social Forces: Domination and Transformation in the Third World.* Cambridge: Cambridge University Press.

Miller, Roland E. (1976). *Mappila Muslims of Kerala: A Study in Islamic Trends.* Bombay: Orient Longman.

Mill, John Stuart (1991). *On Liberty and Other Essays*. Oxford: Oxford University Press.

Mitra A. (1977). *Terms of Trade and Class Relations*. London: Frank Cass.

Mohanty, Bijaya Kumar (2006). *The Growing role of Civil Society Organisations in Contemporary India: A Case Study of the Mazdoor Kisan Shakti Sangathan*. Kolkata: Centre for Studies in Social Sciences.

Moore, Andrew (1995). *The Right Road?' A History of Right-wing Politics in Australia*. Melbourne: Oxford University Press.

Morgenthau, H. J. (1985). *Politics Among Nations*. New York: Alfred A. Knopf.

Mukherjee, Aditya (2002). *Imperialism, Nationalism and the Making of the Indian capitalist Class: 1920–1947*. New Delhi: SAGE Publications.

Mukherjee, Subrata and Sushila Ramaswamy (2000). *A History of Socialist Thought: From the Precursors to the Present*. New Delhi: Sagar Publications.

Nag, Sajal (1999). *Nationalism, Separatism and Secessionism*. New Delhi: Rawat Publishers.

Nandy, Ashis (1983). *The Intimate Enemy: Loss and Recovery of Self Under Colonialism*. Oxford: Oxford University Press.

———— (1998). *Exiled at Home*. Oxford: Oxford University Press.

Nandy, Ashis, Shikha Trivedy, Shail Mayaram, and Achyut Yagnik (1995). *Creating a Nationality: The Ramajanmabhumi Movement and Fear of the Self*. Delhi: Oxford University Press.

Narayan, Badri (2009). *Fascinating Hindutva: Saffron Politics and Dalits Mobilisation*. New Delhi: SAGE Publications.

Nash, June (ed.) (2005). *Social movements: An Anthropological Reader*, USA: Blackwell.

Nayar, Baldev Raj (1989). *India's Mixed Economy*. Bombay: Popular Prakashan.

———— (2001). *Globalization and Nationalism: The Changing Balance in India's Economic Policy, 1950–2000*. New Delhi: SAGE Publications.

Nayyar, Deepak (1996). *Economic Liberalisation in India*. Calcutta: Orient Longman.

Nehru, Jawaharlal (1983a). *Jawaharlal Nehru's Speeches*, Vol. 1. New Delhi: Publication Division, Ministry of Information and Broadcasting.

———— (1983b). *Jawaharlal Nehru's Speeches*, Vol. 3. New Delhi: Publication Division, Ministry of Information and Broadcasting.

———— (1983c). *Jawaharlal Nehru's Speeches* Vol. 4. New Delhi: Publication Division, Ministry of Information and Broadcasting.

———— (1993). *Discovery of India*. New Delhi: Oxford University Press.

Noorani, A. G. (1986). *The Muslims of India: A Documentary Record*. New Delhi: Oxford University Press.

———— (2000). *The RSS and BJP: A Division of Labour*. Delhi: LeftWord Books.

———— (2001). *The RSS and the BJP: A Division of Labour*. New Delhi: Leftword Books.

Nordlinger (1989). *On the Autonomy of the Democratic State*. Massachusetts: Harward University Press.

Nozick, Robert (1974). *Anarchy, State and Utopia*. New York: Basic Books.

Ohmae, K. (1996). *The End of the Nation State: The Rise of Regional Economics*. London: Harper Collins.

Olivelle, Patrick (2005). *Manu's Code of Law: A critical Edition and Translation of the Manava Dharmasastra*. New Delhi: Oxford University Press.

Overbeek, H. W. (1990). *Global Capitalism and National Decline: The Thatcher Decade in Perspective*. London: Unwin and Hyman.

Pandey, Gyanendra (ed.) (1993). *Hindus and Others: The Question of Identity in India Today*. New Delhi: Penguin Books.

Panikkar, K. N. (1995). *Culture, Ideology, Hegemony: Intellectuals and Social Consciousness in Colonial India*. New Delhi: Tulika.

——— (ed.). (2001). *Vargeeyatayude Adiverukal Thedi* (Malayalam). *The Concerned India's Guide to Communalism*. Calicut: Olive Publications.

Parameswaran, P. (1990). Hindu; Matham Samskaram Deshiyatha (in Malayalam) *Hindu; Religion Culture and Nationalism*. Kochi: Kurukshethra.

Patnaik, Utsa (ed.) (1990). *Agrarian Relations and Accumulation: The 'Mode of Production' Debate in India*. Bombay: Oxford University Press.

Pavlov, V. I. (1999). *The Indian Capitalist Class: A Historical Survey*. New Delhi: Peoples Publishing.

Peet, R. (2010). "Neoliberalism, Inequality and Development," in Ahmed, Waquer, Amitabh Kundu, and Richard Peet (eds) *India's New Economic Policy: A Critical Analysis*, London: Routledge.

Piccone, Paul (2006). "Confronting the French New Right: old prejudices or a new political paradigm?" http://www.new-right.org/?p=46 (accessed on 12 February 2010)

Pierson, Christopher (1996). *The Modern State*. London: Routledge.

Pillai, Mohanan B. and L. Premashekhara (ed.) (2010). *India's Foreign Policy: Continuity and Change*. New Delhi: New Century Publications.

Pilling, Geoffrey (1986). *The Crisis of Keynesian Economics: A Marxist Review*. London/Sydney: Croom Helm.

Poulantzas, Nicos (1968). *Political Power and Social Classes*. London: NLB.

——— (1974). *Classes in Contemporary Capitalism*. London: NLB.

Punyani, Ram (2009). *Fascism of Sangh Parivar*. Thiruvananthapuram: Mythri Books.

Raghuramraju, A. (2006). *Debates in Indian Philosophy: Classical Colonial and contemporary*. New Delhi: Oxford University Press.

Rasul, M. A. (1974). *A History of All India Kisan Sabha*. Calcutta: National Book Agency.

Ray, Rajat K. (1979). *Industrialisation in India: Growth and Conflict in the Private Corporate Sector 1914–1947*. Bombay: Oxford University Press.

——— (1997). *Industrialisation in India: Growth and Conflict in the Private Corporate Sector 1914–1947*. Bombay: Oxford University Press.

Rhoads, John K. (1990). *Critical Issues in social Theory*. Pennsylvania: The Pennsylvania State University Press.

Rodrigues, Valerian (ed.) (2003). *The Essential Writings of B.R. Ambedkar*. New Delhi: Oxford University Press.

Ronald de Souza, Peter and E. Sridharan (eds.) (2006). *India's Political Parties*. New Delhi: SAGE Publications.

Rosenau J. N. and E. O. Czempiel (eds.) (1993). *Governance Without Government. Order and Change in World Politics*. Cambridge: Cambridge University Press.

Roy, Virendra K., and Ramesh C. Sarikwal (eds.) (1979). *Marxian Sociology*. Delhi: Ajanta Publications.

Rudolph, Lloyd and Susanne Rudolph (1987). *In Pursuit of Lakshmi: The Political Economy of the Indian State*. Chicago: Chicago University Press.

Russell, Bertrand (1979). *A History of Western Philosophy*. London: Unwin Paperbacks.

Sacchi, Franco "Italian New Right," http://es.geocities.com/sucellus 23/telos9.htm (accessed on 12 February 2010)

Sachs, Jeffrey D. Ashutosh Varshney and Nirupam Bajpai (eds.) (1993). *India in the Era of Economic Reforms*. Oxford: Oxford University Press.

Saleam, Jim (2010). "On the History of 'New Right' Ideas in Australia," http://es.geocities.com (accessed on 12 February 2010)

Samel, Swapna H. (2004). *Dalit Movement in South India: 1857–1950*. New Delhi: Serials Publications.

Scholte, Jan Aart (2000). *Globalisation: A Critical Introduction*. Basingstoke: Macmillan.

Shah, Ghanshyam (1990a). *Social Movements in India—A Review of the Literature*. New Delhi, Newbury Park and London: SAGE Publications.

**———— (ed.) (1990b). *Capitalist Development: Critical Essays*. Bombay: Popular Prakashan.

Sharma, Jyotirmaya (2003). *Hindutva: Exploring the Idea of Hindu Nationalism*. New Delhi: Penguin.

Sharma, R. S. (1990). *Communal History and Rama's Ayodhya*. Delhi: People's Publishing House.

Sharma, S. D. (ed.). (1998). *100 Best Pre–Independence Speeches 1870–1947*. New Delhi: Harper Collins.

Sharma, Shalendra D. (2003). *Development and Democracy in India*. New Delhi: Rawat Publications.

Shaw, Martin (1999). *Civil Society on a Global Scale in Encyclopedia of Violence, Peace, Conflicts*, Vol. I. USA: Academic Press.

Shonfield, A. (1965). *Modern Capitalism: The Changing Balance of Public and Private Power*. London: Oxford University Press.

Shrivastava, Sushil (1991). *The Disputed Mosque: A Historical Inquiry*. Delhi: Vistaar Publications.

Smith, Brian (1989). *Reflections on Resemblance, Ritual, and Religion*, New York: Oxford University Press.

Sorensen, George (2004). *The Transformation of the State: Beyond the Myth of Retreat*. New York: Palgrave.

Stavos, D. Mavroudeas and Demophanes Papadatos (2005). *Neoliberalism and the Washington Consensus*, http://www.econ.voa.gr/VA/files/1435329852.pdf (accessed on 14 August 2009).

Strange, Susan (1996). *The Retreat of the State: The Diffusion of Power in the World Economy Series: Cambridge Studies in International Relations (No. 49)*. Cambridge: Cambridge University Press.

Susan, George A. (1990). *Fate Worse than Debt: The World Financial Crisis and the Poor*. Delhi: Grove Press.

Swamy, Dilip S. (1994). *The Political Economy of Industrialisation: From Self Reliance to Globalisation*. New Delhi: SAGE.

Sweezy, Paul M. (1966). *Monopoly Capitalism*. New York: Monthly Review Press.

———— (2002). *Essays on Keynesian Economics and the Crisis of Capitalism*. Kharagpur: Cornerstone.

Tandon, Rajesh and Ranjitha Mohanty (eds.) (2003). *Does Civil Society Matter? Governance in Contemporary India*. New Delhi: SAGE Publications.

Taylor, Charles (1989). *Sources of the Self: The Making of the Modern Identity*. Cambridge: Cambridge University Press.

Tetreault, Mary Ann and Robert A. Denemark (eds.) (2004). *Gods, Guns and Globalization: Religious Radicalism and International Political Economy*. London: Boulder.

Thakurdas, Purshotamdas and J. R. D. Tata et al. (1944). *A Brief Memorandum Outlining a Plan or Economic Development for India*. Bombay. New York: Penguin

Thakur, Ramesh (1994). *The Politics and Economics of India's Foreign Policy*. Delhi: Oxford University Press.

Tocqueville, Alexis de (1997). *Democracy in America:* Vol. I. New York: Longmans, Green & Co. (Extracted in Jeffery Alexander, Raymond Boudon, Mohamed Cherkaoui (eds.)).

———— (2000). *Democracy in America*, section four, chapter VI. New York: Bantam Books.

———— (n.d.). *Democracy in America*, Book 2; Chapter 5: 'Of The Use Which the Americans Make of Public Associations in Civil Life' in www.marxist.org (accessed on 10 May 2009).

———— (n.d.): *Democracy in America*, Book 2; Influence of Democracy on the Feelings of Americans; Chapter 4, 'That The Americans Combat The Effects Of Individualism By Free Institutions' in www.marxist.org (accessed on 10 May 2009).

Törnquist, Olle (1999). *Politics and Development—A Critical Introduction*. London: SAGE, New Delhi: Thousand Oaks.

UNCTAD (1995). *Trade and Development Report*. New York and Geneva: UNCTAD.

United Nations (1970). *International Development Strategy: Action Programme of the General Assembly of the Second United Nations Development Decade*. New York: UN.

Vanaik, Achin (1990). *The Painful Transition: Bourgeois Democracy in India*. London: Verso.

Van der Veer, Peter (1994). *Religious Nationalism*. Berkeley: University of California Press.

———— (1996). *Religion Nationalism: Hindus and Muslims in India*. Delhi: Oxford University Press.

Varshney, Ashutosh (2002). *Ethnic Conflict and Civic Life*. New Delhi: Oxford University Press.

Vincent, Andrew (1995). *Modern Political Ideologies*. UK: Blackwell.

Vohra, N. N. (ed.). (2003). *History Culture and Society in India and West Asia*. New Delhi: India International Centre.

Vora, Rajendra and Suhas Palshikar (eds.) (2004). *Indian Democracy: Meanings and Practices*. New Delhi: SAGE Publications.

Warren, Mark E. (2001). *Democracy and Association*. Oxford: Princeton University Press.

Wayper, C. L. (1974). *Political Thought*. New Delhi: B.I. Publications.

Weber, Max (1958). *Essays in Sociology,* translated and edited by H. H. Gerlt and C. Wright Mills. New York: Oxford University Press.

Weiner, Myron (1967). *Party Building in a New Nation: The Indian National Congress*. Chicago: University of Chicago Press.

Welch, Cheryl B. (2001). *De Tocqueville*. Oxford: Oxford University Press.

Weldes, J., M. Laffey, H. Gusterson, and R. Duvall (eds.) (1999). *Cultures of Insecurity: States, Communities, and the Production of Danger*. Minneapolis: University of Minnesota Press.

Wilkinson, Stephen I. (2005). *Religious Politics and Communal Violence*. New Delhi: Oxford University Press.

William, Connolly (ed.) (1984). *Legitimacy and the State*. New York: York University Press.

Williams, David (ed.) (1999). *The Enlightenment (Cambridge Readings in the History of Political Thought*. Cambridge: Cambridge University Press.

Wilson, A Jeyaratnam and Dennis Dalton (eds.) (1982). *The States of South Asia: Problems of national Integration*. New Delhi: Vikas Publishing House.

Zelliot, Eleanore (2001). *From Untouchable to Dalit: Essays on the Ambedkar Movement*. New Delhi: Manohar Publishers.

ARTICLES

Acharya, A. (2001). Human Security. *International Journal*, Vol. 56, No. 3, Summer: 442–60.

Adlakha, Hemanta Kumar (2001). *Issues and Themes in the Civil Society Discourse in Fifty Years of India and China Crossing a Bridge of Dreams*, G. P. Deshpande and Alka Acharya (ed.). New Delhi: Tulika.

Advani, L. K. (2001). 'Advani hints at joint action with USA,' Tribune News Service, Sept 14 in Lahttp://www.tribuneindia.com/2001/20010915/nation.htm#1tin," (accessed on 13 September 2014); http://www.milligazette.com/Archives/2004/01-15May04-Print-Edition/0105200475.htm (accessed on 20 September 2014).

Ahamad, Aijaz (1997). 'Tryst with Destiny'-Free but divided, *The Hindu port folio*, August 15.

———— (1998). "The Hindutva Weapon." *Frontline*, Vol. 15, No. 11, May 23–June 5.

Alam, Javeed (2005). "A look at theory: Civil Society, Democracy, and Public Sphere in India" in Bhargava and Reifeld (2005).

———— (2007). "Democracy in India and the Quest for Equality." *Bharatiya Samajik Chintan*, Vol. VI, No. 3, October–December.

Alavi, Hamza (1975). "India and the Colonial Mode of Production." *Economic and Political Weekly*, Special Number, August.

Ali, Amir (2001). "The Evolution of the Public Sphere in India". *Economic and Political Weekly*, June 30, 2419–25.

Anand, Dibyesh (2005). "The Violence of Security: Hindu Nationalism and the Politics of Representing 'the Muslim' as a Danger." *The Round Table*, 94(379) April: 203–15.

Anderson, James and Stuart Hall (1986). "Absolutism and Other Ancestors" in J. Anderson (ed.), (1986). *The Rise of the Modern State*. London: Wheathsheaf Books Ltd.

Asian Age (2002). "Gujarat Used as Hindutva Laboratory," 25 March.

Ayers, Alison J. (2006). "Demystifying democratisation: the global constitution of (neo) liberal Polities in Africa." *Third World Quarterly*, Vo. 27, No. 2: 321–38.

Bagchi, Amiya Kumar (1991). "Reflections on the Nature of the Indian Bourgeoisie." *Social Scientist*, Vol. 19, Nos. 3–4, March–April: 8-9.

Bajpai, Kanti (2011). "Born Again Patriot—an Anti-Corruption Movement and the rise of Illiberalism." *The Telegraph*, 25 August.

Banaji, Jairus (1972). "For a Theory of Colonial Mode of Production." *Economic and Political Weekly*, Vol. 7, No. 52, December: 498–502.

Bandhyopadhyaya, D. (2001). "Tebhga Movement in Bengal: Retrospect." *Economic and Political Weekly*, Vol. 36, No. 41, Oct 13–14, pp. 3901–07, http://www.jstor.org/stable/4411230 (accessed on 7 May 2009)

Baru, Sanjaya (1983). "Self-Reliance to Dependence in Indian Economic Development." *Social Scientist*, Vol. 12, No. 5, November: 34–35.

Baruah, Amit (1999). "The South Asian Nuclear Mess." *Frontline*, Vol. 16, No. 10, May: 8–21.

Basu, Amrita (1996). "Caste and class: the rise of Hindu nationalism in India." *Harvard International Review*, Vol. 18, No. 3, June 22.

———— (2002). "The Dialectics of Hindu Nationalism" in Kohli (2002).

———— (2005). "Mass Movement or Elite Conspiracy: The Puzzle of Hindu Nationalism"' in Ludden (2005).

Baviskar, B. S. (2001). "NGOs and Civil Society in India." *Sociological Bulletin*, Vol. 50, No. 1: 3–15.

Berger, Mark T. (2001). The Rise and Demise of National Development and the Origins of Post-Cold War Capitalism in *Millennium: Journal of International Studies*, Vol. 30, No. 2: 211–34.

Beteille, Andre (1996). "Civil Society and its Institutions," *Economic and Political Weekly*, 15 May.

———— (1999). "Trials of Indian Democracy." *Times of India*, 29 April.

———— (2005). "The Conflict of No-rms and Values," in Gupta (2005).

Beveridg, Annette Susannae (1922). *The Babur-nama in English (Memoirs of Babur) (1922)*, Vol. 1, https://archive.org/details/baburnamainengli01babuuoft (accessed on 10 May 2009)

Bhattacharya, Budhadev (1990). "Dominant Mode of Production and the Character of the State in India," in Ghanshyam Shah (ed.)

Bidwai, Praful (2014). " A Nightmare Materializes in India: Hindutva-Capitalism takes Power." *Mainstream Weekly*, Vol. LII, No. 23, 31 May.

Blaney, David L. and Mustapha Kamal Pasha (1993). "Civil Society and Democracy in the Third World: Ambiguities and Historical Possibilities." *Studies in Comparative International Development*, Vol. 28, issue 1: 3–24.

Bleiberg, Remonda Bensabat and Jamine A. Clark (2000). "Conclusions Politics of Democratization, the Force of Civil Society," in Clark (2000).

Bowie, Katharine A. (2005). "The state and the right Wing: The Village scout Movement in Thailand," in June Nash (ed.), *Social Movements: An Anthropological Reader*. USA: Blackwell.

Buchan, Bruce (2002). Explaining War and Peace: Kant and Liberal International Relations Theory. *Alternatives*, 27 (4): 407–28.

Chandhoke, Neera (2002a). "Exploring the Mythology of the Public Sphere." in Chandhoke (2002).

———— (2002b). "The limits of global civil society," in Marlies Glasius, Mary Kaldor and Helmut Anheier (eds.), *Global Civil Society 2002*. New York: Oxford University Press.

———— (2003). "Exploring Composite Culture in India" in N.N. Vohra (2003).

———— (2004). "Re-presenting the secular Agenda for India," in Hasan (2004).

———— (2007a). "Civil Society." *Development in Practice*, Vol. 17, Numbers 4–5, August, 607–14.

———— (2007b). "Global Civil Society and Global Justice." *Economic and Political Weekly*, July, Vol. 42, No. 29: 3016–26.

Chandler, David (2004). "Building Global Civil Society 'From Below'?" *Millennium*, Vol. 33, No. 2.

Chatterjee, I. (2010). "From Red Tape to Red Carpet? Violent Narratives of Neoliberalising Ahmedabad" in Waquar Ahmed, Amitabh Kundu, and Richard Peet (eds.), *India's New Economic Policy: A Critical Analysis*. London: Routledge.

Chatterjee, Manini (1992). "Seeds of Fascism." *Seminar*, 399, November I.

———— (1993). "Strident Sadhur: Contours of a Hindu Rashtra." *Frontline*, Vol. 10, No. 2, January: 16–29.

Chatterjee, Partha (2000). "Development Planning and the Indian State" in Zoya Hasan (2000).

———— (2002). "On Civil and Political Society in Postcolonial democracies," in Kaviraj and Khilnani (2002).

Chattopadhyay, Paresh (1972). "On the Question of the Mode of Production in Indian Agriculture: A Preliminary Note." *EPW*, Vol. 7, No. 13, March.

Chaulia, Sreeram S. (2002). BJP, India's Foreign Policy and the 'Realist Alternative' to the Nehruvian Tradition. *International Politics*, 39 (June): 215–34.

Cha, Victor D. (2000). Globalisation and the Study of International Security. *Journal of Peace Research*, 37(3): 391–403.

Chhibber, Pradeep and Rahul Verma (2014). "It is Modi not BJP Won this Election." *The Hindu*, http://www.thehindu.com/opinion/op-ed/it-is-modi-not-bjp-that-won-this-election/article6070375.ece (accessed on 15 Januray 2015).

Chidambaram, R. (1998). "An interview by TS Subramanian." *Frontline*, Vol. 15, No. 11, May 23–June 5.

Chowdhury, Neeraja (1986). "Shortsighted Move to Appease Communities." *The Statesmen*, in Noorani (1986).

Clark, Janine A. and Remonda Bensabat Kleiberg (2000). "Introduction: The Impact of Economic Reform on Civil Society, Popular Participation and Democratization in the Developing World," in Kleinberg & Clark (2000).

Coalition Against Genocide (2005). "Genocide in Gujarat: The Sangh Parivar, Narendra Modi, and the Government of Gujarat," www.coalitionagainst genocide.org (accessed on 11 May 2010)

Colvin, Ross and Satarupa Bhatacharjya (2013). "The Remaking of Narendra Modi: Spaecial Report." *Reuters*, July 12, http://www.reuters.com/article/2013/07/12/us-india-modi-idUSBRE96B02320130712 (accessed on 15 January 2015).

Czempiel, Ernst-Otto (2004). "Internationalizing Politics: Some Answers to the Question of Who Does What to whom," in Czempiel and Rosenau (2004).

Das, Runa (2002). Engendering Post-Colonial Nuclear Policies Through the Lens of Hindutva: Rethinking the Security Paradigm of India. *Comparative Studies of South Asia, Africa and the Middle East*, XXII (1 and 2): 76–89.

Datta, Pradip Kumar (1993). "VHP's Ram: The Hindutva Movement in Ayodhya," in Pandey (1993).

Davis, Richard H. (2005). "The Iconography of Rama's Chariot," in Ludden (2005).

Desai, Meghnad (2005). "Democracy and Development in India: 1947–2002" in Desai (ed.), *Development and Nationhood: Essays in the Political Economy of South Asia*. New Delhi: Oxford University Press.

Desai, Radhika (2011). Gujarat's Hindutva of Capitalist Development. *South Asia: Journal of South Asian Studies*, XXXIV (3): 354–81.

——— (2014). "A Latter-Day Fascism?" *Economic and Political Weekly*, XLIX (35): 48–58.

Dev, Arjun (n.d.). New Social Science Text Book of NCERT: Publishing in Parivar View, in Safdar Hashmi Memorial Trust (SAHMAT) (n.d.).

Dirks, Nicholas (1997). "The Study of State and Society in India," in Kaviraj (1997).

Dulton, Dennins (1982). "The concepts of Politics and Power in India's Ideological Tradition," in Wilson and Dalton (1982).

Dumont, Louis (1997). "Power and Territory," in Kaviraj (1997).

Eatwell, Roger (1989). "The Nature of the Right, 2: The Right as a Variety of "Styles of Thought" in R. Eatwell and N. O'Sullivan (eds), *The Nature of the Right*. London: Pinter Publishers Limited.

Edelman, Marc (2001). Social Movements: Changing Paradigms and forms of Politics. *Annual Review of Anthropology* 30: 285–317.

Elliott, Carolyn M. (2003): "Civil Society and Democracy: A Comparative Review Essay," in Elliott (2003).

Engineer, Asghar Ali (1985a). "Forces behind the Agitation." *Deccan Herald*, 10 December.
———— (1985b). "Vacillating and Weak Leadership." *Decan Herald*, 11 December.
———— (1990). "Introduction," in Engineer (1990).
Engineer, Asghar Ali (2001). "Srikrishna Commission Report—Will it be Implemented?" *Centre for Study of Society and Secularism*, February 16–28, http://www.csss-isla.com/arch%20208.htm (accessed on 1 August 2010)
———— (2002). "Gujarat Riots in the Light of the History of Communal Violence." *Economic and Political Weekly*, Vol. XXXVII, No. 50: 5047–54.
Etzioni, Amitai (2004). "The Capabilities and Limits of the Global Civil Society." *Millennium*, Vol. 33, No. 2: 341–53.
Falk, Richard (1991). "Reflections on Democracy and the Gulf War." *Alternatives*, Vol. 16, No. 2: 263–74.
Femia, Joseph (2001). "Civil Society and the Marxist Tradition," in Kaviraj and Khilnani (2001).
———— (2003). "Civil Society and the Marxist Tradition," in Kaviraj and Khilnani (eds.).
Foley, Michael W. and Bob Edwards (1996). The paradox of Civil Society. *Journal of Democracy*, Vol. 7, No. 3: 38–52.
Foster, John Bellamy (1999). "Contradictions in the Universalization of Capitalism." *Monthly Review*, Vol. 50, No. 11, : 29–39.
Foucault, Michel (1988). "Critical theory/intellectual history," in Lawrence D Kritzm (ed.), *Michel Foucault: Politics, Philosophy, Culture: Interviews and Other Writings*. New York: Routledge.
Fox, Richard G. (2005). "Communalism and Modernity", in Ludden (2005).
Freitag, Sandria B. (2005). "Contesting in Public: Colonial Legacies and Contemporary Communalism," in Ludden (2005).
Frevert, Ute (2005). "Civil Society and Citizenship in Western Democratic Historical Developments and Recent Challenges," in Bhargava and Reifeld (2005).
Friedman, Milton (1968). "The Role of Monetary Policy." *The American Economic Review*, Vol. 58, No. 1: 1–17.
Fukuyama, Francis (2001). Social Capital, Civil Society and Development in *Third World Quarterly*, XXII (1).
Ghosh, Jayati (1999). "Liberalization Debates," in Terence J. Byres (ed.), *The Indian Economy: Major Debates Since Independence*. New Delhi: Oxford University Press.
Ghosh, Partha S. (2003). "The Congress And the BJP: Struggle for the Heartland," in Mehra K, Khanna and Kneck (2003).
Gold, Daniel (1991). "Organized Hinduism: From Vedic Truth to Hindu Nation" in Martin E. Marty and R. Scott Appelby (eds), *Fundamentalisms Observed*, vol. 1 of the *Fundamentalism Project*, 531–59. Chicago: University of Chicago Press.
Gopalakrishnan, Shankar (2008). "Neoliberalism and Hindutva—Fascism, Free Markets and the Restructuring of Indian Capitalism" 29 October, http://radicalnotes.com/content/view/77/39/ (accessed on 19 June 2010)
Gough, Kathleen (1974). "Indian Peasant Uprisings." *Economic and Political Weekly*, Vol. 9, No. 32/34, accessed from http://www.jstor.org/ stable/4363915 (accessed on 15 May 2009).
Graham, B. D. (2002). "The Leadership and Organization of the Jana Sangh 1951 to 1967," in Hasan (2002).
Graham, Bruce D. (2006). "The Challenge of Hindu Nationalism: The Bharatiya Janata Party in Contemporary Indian Politics," in Ronald de Souza and Sridharan (2006).

Guillebaud, Christine (2011). "Music and Politics in Kerala: Hindu Nationalists versus Marxists," in Daniela Berti et al. (eds.), *Cultural Entrenchment of Hindutva: Local Mediations and Forums of Convergence.* New Delhi: Routledge.

Gupta, Charu (2002). "Anxieties of Hindu Right in Everyday Realm." *Economic and Political Weekly*, Vol. XXXVII, No. 3.

Gwin, Catherine (1983). "Financing India's Structural Adjustment," in John Williamson (ed.), *IMF Conditionality.* Washington, DC: Institute for International Economics.

Habermas, Jurgen (1984). "What does a Legitimation crisis mean today? Legitimation Problems in Late capitalism," in Connolly (1984).

Hansen, Thomas Blom (1996). "Globalisation and Nationalist Imaginations: Hindutva's Promise of Equality through Difference." *Economic and Political Weekly*, Vol. XXXI, No. 10, March 9: 603–16.

——— (2001a). "Hindutva and Capitalism," in Hansen and Jaffrelot. New Delhi: Oxford University Press.

——— (2001b). "The Ethics of Hindutva and the Spirit of Capitalism," in Hansen and Jaffrelot (2001).

——— (2007). "Neoliberalism as Creative Destruction." *ANNALS, AAPSS*, 610, March.

Hasan, Zoya (2000). "Introduction: The Political Career of the State in Independent India," in Hasan (2000).

Health, Liver (2002). "Antomy of BJP's Rise to Power: Social, Regional and Political Expansion in 1990s," in Hasan (2002).

Hegel, G. W. F. (1952). "The Philosophy of Right," edited and translated By T. M. Knox. Oxford: The Clarendon Press, http://www.marxists.org/ reference/ archive/hegel/index. htm (accessed on 7 April 2009)

Held, David (1993). "Central perspectives on the modern State," in Mc Lennan, David Held and Stuart Hall (1993).

——— (1996). "The Development of the Modern State," in Hall, David Held, Don Hubert, (1996 Kenneth Thompson).

Hensman, Rohini (2014). "The Gujarat Model of Development: What would it do to the Indian Economy." *Economic and Political Weekly*, Vol. XLIX, No. 11.

Houtart, Francois and Genevieve Lenercinier (1978). "Socio-Religious Movements in Kerala: A reaction to the capitalist Mode of Production," Part 1. *Social Scientist*, Vol. 6, No. 11, June, pp. 3–34, http://www.jstor.org/ stable/3516609 (accessed on 10 August 2009).

Hua, Han (1998). "Sino-Indian Relations and Nuclear Arms Control," in *Nuclear Weapons and Arms Control in South Asia After The Test Ban*, SIPRI Research Report No.14, ed. Eric Arnett, pp. 37–41. New York: Oxford University Press.

Islam, Shamsul (2004). "The History and Politics of Vande Mataram." *The Millie Gazette*, May 15.

Jaffrelot, Christophe (1993). "Hindu Nationalism: Strategic Syncretism in Ideology Building, "*Economic and Political Weekly*, March 20–27: 517–24.

——— (2001). "The Vishva Hindu Parishad: A Nationalist but Mimetic Attempt at Federating the Hindu Sects," in Vasudha Dalmia, Angelika Malinar, and Martin Christof (eds.), *Charisma and Canon: Essays on the Religious History of the Indian Subcontinent.* Delhi: Oxford University Press.

——— (2002). "A Specific Party Building Strategy: The Jana Sangh and the RSS Network," in Hasan (2002).

——— (2008). Hindu Nationalism and (Not so Easy) Art of being Outraged: The Ram Sethu Controversy in *South Asia Multi-disciplinary Academic Journal*, http://samaj.revues. org/1372 (accessed on 11 May 2014)

Jayaraman, T. (1993). "Facing up To Fraud: On Science and Secularism." *Frontline,* Vol. 10, No. 3, January 30–February 12.

Jean-Marie Guehenno (1998–1999). The Impact of Globalisation on Strategy. *Survival,* Vol. 40, No. 4, 5–19.

Jogdand P. G. (2000). "Introduction," in Jogdand (2000).

Jones, Gareth Steadman (2001). "Hegel and the Economics of Civil Society" in Sudipta Kaviraj and Sunil Khilnani (eds.), *Civil Society—History and Possibilities.* Cambridge: Cambridge University Press.

Jose, K. Vinod (2012). "The Emperor Uncrowned: The Rise of Narendra Modi," Caravan Magazine, March 1, http://caravanmagazine.in/reportage/emperor-uncrowned?page=0,10 (accessed on 15 January 2015).

Joshy, P. M. (2010). Perils of "Security": Identity and Nation-building in South Asia with Special Reference to India and Pakistan. *International Journal of South Asian Studies,* Vol. 4, No. 2, 345–59.

———— (2011). State, Civil Society and the Process of Democratisation: A Study on Vanavasi Kalyan Ashram. *Indian Journal of Politics and International Relations,* 44(1 and 2) 63–73.

———— (2012). Old Elite are Co-opted, Subdued or Oppressed? The Politics of Anti-corruption Crusade in India in Perspective. *Indian Journal of Public Administration,* Vol. LVIII, No. 1, 1–14

Joshy, P. M. and K. M. Seethi (2010). Interrogating Security: The Hindu Right and the Nuclear Question. *South Asian Journal of Diplomacy,* Vol. 1, No. 1, 163–74.

Joshy, P. M. and Mohanan B. Pillai (2010). "Nation-building and Foreign Policy Behaviour of India" in the Regional Setting of South Asia, in Mohanan B Pillai and L Premashekhara (2010).

Juergensmeyer, Mark (1996). "The Debate Over Hindutva." *Religion,* 26: 129–36.

Kanungo, Pralay (2008). "Hindutva's Furry against Christians in Orissa." *Economic and Political Weekly,* September 13, pp. 16–19

———— (2010). "Hindutva's Discourse on Development" in Gurpreet Mahajan and Surinder S Jodhka (eds.), *Religion, Community and Development: Changing Contours of Politics and Policy in India.* New Delhi: Routledge.

Kapur, Anurudha (1993). "Deity to Crusader: The Changing Iconography of Ram," in Pandey (1993).

Karat, Prakash (1998). "A lethal link." *Frontline,* Vol. 15, No. 2, June 6–19.

Katakam, Anupama (2011). "The Fall of Guys." *Frontline,* Vol. 28, No. 3, Jan 29–Feb 11.

———— (2012a). "From Lab to Field." *Frontline,* Vol. 29, No. 3, February 11–24: 25.

———— (2012b). "Divisive Consolidation," an interview with Teesta Setalvad. *Frontline,* Vol. 29, No. 3, February 11–24, pp. 26–27.

Katzenstein, Mary F. (1989). "Towards Equality? Cause and Consequence of the Political Prominence of Women in India," in Minault, G. (ed.), *The Extended Family: Women and Political Participation in India and Pakistan.* Delhi: Chanakya Publications.

———— (1989). "Organising Against Violence: Strategies of the Indian Women's Movement." *Pacific Affairs,* Vol. 62, No. 1, pp. 53–71, http://www.jstore.org/stable/2760264 (accessed on 10 May 2009).

Kaviraj, Sudipta (1995). "Religion, Politics and Modernity," in Upendra Baxi and Bhikhu Parekh (eds.), *Crisis and Change in Contemporary India.* New Delhi: SAGE Publications.

———— (1997). "Caste and Class (Introductory note)," in Kaviraj (1997).

———— (2000). "The Modern State in India" in Hasan (2000).

Kaviraj, Sudipta (2003). "A State of Contradictions: The Post-colonial State in India," in Quentin Skinner and Bo Strath (eds.), *States and Citizens: History, Theory, Prospects.* Cambridge: Cambridge University Press.

Keane, John (1998). "Civil Society: Old Images new visions," in Edwards (2004).

Keane, John (2001). "Global Civil Society in Global Civil Society 2001, in Anheier, M. Glasius and M. Kaldor (2001).

Kothari, Rajni (1990). "Capitalism and the Role of the State," in Ghanshyam Shah (ed.).

—— (2002a). "Masses, Classes and the State," in Ghanshyam Shah (ed.), *Social Movements and the State.* New Delhi: Saga Publications.

—— (2002b). The Congress 'System' in India," in Hasan (2002).

Lal, Vinay (1995). Hindu 'Fundamentalism' Revisited. *Contention,* 5: Fall, 79–112.

Lankala, Srinivas (2006). "Mediated Nationalisms and 'Islamic terror': The articulation of Religious and Postcolonial Secular Nationalisms in India." Westminister papers in Communication and Culture, University of Westminister, London, Vol. 3, No. 2: 86–102.

Lele, Jayant (1996). "Hindutva as Pedagogic Violence" in Nigel Crook (1996).

Lochtefeld, James G. (1996). "New Wine, Old Skins: The Sangh Parivar and the Transformation of Hinduism," *Religion,* 26, 101–18.

Low, D. A. (1977). "Introduction: The Critical Years, 1917-47," in Low (1977).

Luke, Timothy (1991). The Discipline of Security Studies and the Codes of Containment: Learning from Kuwait. *Alternatives,* Vol. 16, No. 3, 315–44.

Madan, T. N. (1991). "The Concept of secularism," in Gore (1991).

—— (1997). "Secularism in its Place," in Kaviraj (1997).

—— (1999). "Secularism in its place," in Bhargava (1999).

Mahajan, Gurpreet (1999). "Civil Society and Its Avtars: What Happened to Freedom and Democracy." *Economic and Political Weekly,* Vol. 34, No. 20, May 15–21: 1188–96.

Marx, Karl (1967). "On the Jewish Question," in L. D. Easton and K. H. Guddat (eds.), *Writings of the Young Marx on Philosophy and Society.* New York: Doubleday.

McCarthy, Thomas (1984): "Legitimation Problems in Advanced 'Capitalism,'" in Connolly (1984).

McChesney, Robert W. (1999). Noam Chomsky and the Struggle Against Neoliberalism. *Monthly Review,* Vol. 40, No. 11: 40–47.

Mehta, Pratab Bhanu (2003). "Where is the strong defence?" *The Hindu,* June 26.

Migdal, Joel S. (1994). "The State in Society: An Approach to Struggles for Domination" in Migdal, Atul Kohli, Vivienne Shue (1994).

Mohanty, Manoranjan (2011). "People's Movements and Anna Upsurge." *Economic and Political Weekly,* Vol. XLVI, No. 38: 16–19.

Mookerjee, Syama Prasad (2007a). "On the National Language," in Batabyal (2007).

—— (2007b). "On Jammu and Kashmir," in Batabyal (2007).

Mukherjee, Aditya and Mridula Mukherjee. (1990). "Imperialism and Growth of Indian Capitalism in the Twentieth Century," in Ghanshyam Shah (1990).

Mukherji, Partha (1987). Study of Social Conflicts: Case of Naxalbari Peasant Movement. *Economic and Political Weekly,* 22 (38): 1607–1617, http://www.jstor.org/stable/4377512 (accessed on 13 June 2009).

Muppidi, Himadeep (1999). "Post-Coloniality and The Production of International Insecurity," in Jutta Weldes (eds.) *Cultures of Insecurity: States, Communities, and The Production of Danger.* Minneapolis: University of Minneapolis.

Muralidharan, Sukumar (1992–1993). "Shame at Ayodhya: On the Road to Fascism." *Fortline,* Vol. 9, No. 26, December 19–January 1.

Nadadur, Anuj (2006). The 'Muslim Threat' and the Bharatiya Janata Party's Rise to Power. *Peace and Democracy in South Asia*, Vol. 2, No. 1 and 2: 88–110.

Nag, Sajal (2001). "Nationhood and Displacement in Indian Subcontinent." *Economic and Political Weekly*, Vol. XXXVI, No. 51, December 22: 4753–60.

Nanda, Meera (2009). "Postmodernism, Hindu Nationalism and 'Vedic science.'" *Frontline*, December 20, 2003–January 02.

Nandy, Ashis (2002). "Obituary of a Culture." *Seminar*, http://www.india-seminar.com/2002/513/513%20ashis%20nandy.htm (accessed on 15 January).

Narayan, Jayaprakash (2003). "The Crisis of Governance" in Tandon and Mohanty (2003).

Narayanan, K. R. (2005). "Gujarat riots a BJP conspiracy." *The Hindu*, March 02, http://www.hinduonnet.com/thehindu/ holnus/001200503022152.htm (accessed in March 2005).

Narula, Smita (2003). "Overlooked Danger: The Security and Rights Implications of Hindu Nationalism in India." *Harvard Human Rights Journal*, 16: 41–68.

Nehru, Jawaharlal (1955). "A Socialist Pattern of Society, a Speech Delivered at the 60th annual session of the Indian National Congress on 21 January, in Batabyal (2007).

Nigam, Aditya (2005). "Civil Society And Its 'Underground': Explanations in the Nation of Political Society" in Bhargava and Reifeld (2005).

Niva, Steve (1999). "Contested Sovereignties and Post-colonial Insecurities in the Middle East," in Jutta Weldes et al. (eds.), *Cultures of Insecurity: States, Communities and the Production of Danger*. Minneapolis: University of Minneapolis.

Noorani, A. G. (1990). "Babri Masjid Ram Janmabhoomi Question" in Engineer (1990).

———— (1992–93). "The Battles Ahead." *Frontline*, Vol. 9, No. 26, December 19–January.

———— (1993). "Article 370: Broken Pledges and Flawed Secularism," in Panday (1993).

Omvedt, Gail (1971). "Otirao Phule and the Ideology of Social Revolution in India." *Economic and Political Weekly*, Vol. 6, No. 37, Sep 11, http://www.jstor.org/stable/4382505 (accessed on 18 May 2009).

———— (1994). Peasants, Dalits and Women: Democracy and India's New Social Movements. *Journal of Contemporary Asia*, Vol. 24, No. 1, pp. 35–48.

Padmanabhan, R. (1998). "Assault on Art." *Frontline*, Vol. 15, No. 10, May 9–22.

Palshikar, Suhas (2004). "Whose Democracy are we Talking About?" in Vora and Palshikar (2004).

———— (2009). "Between Fortuna and Virtu: Explaining the Congress Ambiguous Victory." *Economic and Political Weekly*, Vol. XLIV, No. 39, September 26, pp. 33–46.

Palshiker, Suhas and CSDS Team (2004). "Vajpayee's Popularity Alone was not Enough." *The Hindu*, May 20.

Pandey, Gyanendra (1977). "A Rural Base for Congress: The United Provinces, 1920–40," in Low (1977).

———— (1993). "The Civilized and the barbarian: The 'New' Politics of Late Twentieth century India and the World" in Panday (1993).

Parajuli, Pramod (1991). Power and Knowledge in the Development Discourse: New Social Movements and the State in India. *International Social Science Journal*, Vol. 43, No. 1, pp. 173–90.

Parker, Priya (2008). Reconciliation in Gujarat. *Peace Prints: South Asian Journal of Peace Building* 1.1. http://www.abstract.xlibx.com/a-history/93003-1-reconciliation-gujarat-priya-parker-abstract-while-there-are-m.php (accessed on 20 June 2009).

Pasha, Mustapha Kamal (2004). "Modernity, Civil Society, and Religious Resurgence in South Asia," in Mary Ann Tetreault, Robert A. Denemark (eds.), *Gods, Guns and Globalization: Religious Radicalism and International Political Economy*. London: Boulder.

Pasha, Mustapha Kamal and David L. Blaney (1998). "Elusive Paradise: The Promise and Peril of Global Civil Society." *Alternatives*, Vol. 23, No. 4, October–December: 417–50.

Patel, S. 2010. "Seva, Sangathans and Gurus: Service and The Making of the Hindu Nation", in Gupreet Mahajan and Surinder S. Jodhka (eds.), *Religion, Community and Development: Changing Contours of Politics and Policy in India*. New Delhi: Routledge.

Patnaik, Arun Kumar (1990). "Relative Autonomy." *Seminar* 367, March.

Patnaik, Prabhat (1979). "Industrial Development in India since Independence." *Social Scientist*, June.

——— (1986). "New Turn in Economic Policy Context and Prospect." *Economic and Political Weekly*, Vol. 21, No. 23: 1014–19.

——— (1988). A Perspective on the Recent Phase of India's Economic Development. *Social Scientist*, No.177, 16(2), February 3–16.

——— (1992). "A Note on the Political Economy of the Retreat of the State." *Social Scientist*, Vol. 20, No. 11: 44–57.

——— (1994a). "Macro-economic Policy in Times of Globalisation." *Economic and Political Weekly*, Vol. 29, Nos. 16–17, April 16–23.

——— (1994b). "International Capital and National Economic Policy: A Critique of India's Economic Reforms." *Economic and Political Weekly*, Vol. 29, No. 12.

——— (2000). "The State in India's Economic Development," in Hasan (2000).

——— (2011). "Premodern Project," http://www.frontlineonnet.com/fl2813/stories/20110701281312900.htm (accessed on 08 November 2012).

Patnaik, Prabhat and S. K. Rao (1977). "Towards an Explanation of Crisis in a Mixed Underdeveloped Economy." *Economic and Political Weekly*, Vol. XII, Nos. 6–7–8, February, Annual number.

Patnaik, Utsa (1971). "Capitalist Development in Agriculture: A Note." *Economic and Political Weekly*, Vol. 6, No. 39, September, 123–30.

Persaud, Randolph B. (2002). "Situating Race in International Relations: The Dialectics of Civilizational Security in American Immigration," in Geeta Chowdhry and Sheila Nair (eds.), *Power, Post-colonialism and International Relations*. New York: Routledge.

Pinch, William R. (2005). *Soldier Monks and Militant Sadhus*, in Ludden (2005).

Poku, Nana K. Neil Renovick and John Glenn (2005). "Human Security in Globalising World" in Graham and Poku (2005).

K.B. (1985). Indira Gandhi: An Attempt at A Political Appraisal, *Economic and Political Weekly*, March 23: Vol. XX, No. 12: 496–499+502–503.

——— (1995). "The Indian Economy under Structural Adjustment." *Economic and Political Weekly*, Vol. 30, No. 47, pp. 3001–13. November.

Pranab, Bardhan (1991). "Dominant Proprietary Classes and India's Democracy" in Atul Kohli (ed.), *India's Democracy: An Analysis of Changing State–Society Relations*. Hyderabad: Orient Longman.

Puniyani, Ram (2007). "Secularization Process, Caste and gender Equality in India," Bharatiya Samajik Chintan, Vol. VI, No. 3, October–December.

——— (2012). "Globalisation, Rise of Fundamentalism and Roots of Terror" in Sajad Ibrahim (ed.), *Globalisation, Fundamentalism and Terrorism: Issues in South India*. New Delhi: Abhijeeth Publications.

Puniyani, Ram (2013). "Hindutva Agenda and the Elections 2014." *Social Action*, Vol. 63, July–September.

Ramakrishnan, A. K. (2004). "Conceptualising Security" in Purusottam Bhattacharya, Tridib Chakraborti and Shibashis Chatterjee (eds.), *Anatomy of Fear*. New Delhi: Lancers Books.

Ramakrishnan, Venkitesh (2004). "A Party's Predicament." *Frontline*, Vol. 21, No. 17, August 14–27.

——— (2011). "Swami's Confession." *Frontline*, Vol. 28, No. 3, Jan–Feb 11.

Ram, Mohan (1973). "The Telengana Peasant Armed Struggle, 1946–1951." *Economic and Political Weekly*, Vol. 8, No. 23, June 9, http://www.jstor.org/stable/4362720 (accessed on 1 May 2008).

Ram, N. (1998). "From Nuclear Adventurism to Appeasement." *Frontline*, Vol. 15, No. 2, June 6–19.

Raychaudhuri, Tapan (1995). Shadows of the Swastika: Historical Reflections on the Politics of Hindu Communalism. *Contention*, 5: Fall, pp. 141–62.

Roy, Arundhati (2011a). "Jan Lokpal Bill Regressive," http://www.thehindu.com/news/national/article2412518.ece (accessed on 08 November 2012).

——— (2011b). "While His Means May be Gandhian, His Demands Are Certainly Not," http://www.thehindu.com/opinion/lead/article2379704.ece?homepage=true (accessed on 08 November 2012).

Rudolph, Susanne Hoeber (2000). "Civil Society and the Realm of Freedom." *Economic and Political Weekly*, Vol. 35, No. 20, pp. 1762–69.

Saberwal, Satish (2001). "Democracy and Civil Society in India: Integral or Accidental." *Sociological Bulletin*, Vol. 50, No. 2: 33–57.

Sacchi, Franco (2006). "The Italian New Right," http://www.new-right.org/?p=49 (accessed on 19 August 2009).

Sarkar, Sumit (1993). "The Fascism of the Sangh Parivar." *Economic and Political Weekly*, XXVIII (5), January 30, 163–67.

——— (2005). "Indian Nationalism and the Politics of Hindutva," in Ludden (2005).

——— (n.d.). Class IX social Science textbook: Errors and Howlers, in SAHAMAT.

Sarkar, Tanika (1993). "Women's Agency within Authoritarian communalism: The Rashtrasevika Samiti and Ramajanmabhoomi," in Gyanendra Panday (1993).

——— (2002). "Semiotics of Terror: Muslim Children and Women in Hindu Rashtra." *Economic and Political Weekly*, Vol. XXXVII, No. 28, July 13: 2872–76.

——— (2005). "Imagining Hindurashtra: The Hindu and the Muslim in Bankim Chandra's Writings," in David Ludden (2005).

Satyamurthy, T. V. (1994). "India's International Role: Economic Dependence and Non-alignment (1947–1991)," in T. V. Satyamurthy (ed.), *State and Nation in the Context of Social Change* Vol. 1. New Delhi: Oxford University Press.

Sau, Ranjit (1979). "India's Economic Crisis: Dialectics of Sub-Imperialism." *Economic and Political Weekly*, March 3.

Seethi, K. M. (2001). Postmodernism, Neoliberalism and Civil Society: A Critique of the Development Strategies in the Era of Globalisation. *Indian Journal of Political Science*, Vol. 62, No. 3, September: 307–20.

——— (2005). "India's CTBT Policy: From the Text to the Testing Times," in Rajan Harshe and K. M. Seethi (eds.), *Engaging with the World: Critical Reflections on India's Foreign Policy*. New Delhi: Orient Longman.

Seethi, K. M. (2009a). Reinventing Public Sphere. *Indian Journal of Politics and International Relations*, Vol. 2, No. 1: 174–91.

——— (2009b). "Contested Terrains of State and Civil Society." *Indian Journal of Politics and International Relations*, Vol. 2, No. 2: 271–90.

Sen, Pranab (1985). "The 1966 Devaluation in India: A Reappraisal." *Economic and Political Weekly*, Vol. XXI, No. 30, 1322–28.

Setalvad, Teesta (2001). " Rathyatra Retraced." *Communalism Combat,* April.

Sharma, Ashok (1990a). "Caste-based reservation for OBCs are Unconstitutional." *Organiser,* Vol. XLII, No. 7, September 23: 14.

———— (1990b). "Free Indians Worst Brutalities Perpetrated in Ayodhya." *Organiser,* Vol. XLII, No. 15, and November 18.

Sharma, Hari P. (1991). "The Green Revolution in India: Prelude to a Red One," in Gough and Sharma (1991).

Sheshadri, Kandadai (1979). " From Civil Society to Human Society," in Virendra K. Roy of Ramesh C. Sarikwal (eds.), *Marxian Sociology.* Delhi: Ajanta Publications.

Shrivastava, Sushil (1990). "The Ayodhya Controversy: Where Lies the Truth," in Engineer (1990).

Singha, Anup Kumar (1998). "ICHR Reconstituted: Marxists Dethroned." *Organiser* Vol. XLIX, No. 47, June 21.

Singh, Jaswant (1998). "Against Nuclear Apartheid." *Foreign Affairs,* Vol. 77, No. 5: 41–52.

Singh, Kirti (1993). "Women's Rights and the Reform of Personal Laws" in Panday (1993).

Singh, N. K. and Uday Mahurkar (1999). "Bajrang Dal: Loonies at Large." *India Today,* 8 February.

Singh, Pritam (2005). "Hindu Bias in India's 'Secular' Constitution: Probing Flaws in the Instruments of Governance." *Third World Quarterly,* Vol. 26, No. 6: 909–26.

Sobhan, Rehman (1984). "The State and Development of Capitalism: Third World Perspective," in Krishna Bharadwaj and Sudipta Kaviraj (eds.), *Perspectives on Capitalism.* London: Zed Press.

Sridharan, E. N. (2004). "Electoral Coalitions in 2004 Elections: Theory and Evidence." *Economic and Political Weekly,* December 18, Vol. 39, No. 51, pp. 5418–25.

Srikanth, H. (1994). "Industrial Development in India," in Kuttan Mahadevan et al. (eds.), *Society and Development in China and India.* Delhi: B.R. Publishing Corporation.

Srinivasan T. N. and N. S. S. Narayanan (1977). "Economic Performance Since the Third Plan and Its Implications for Policy." *Economic and Political Weekly,* Annual number, February.

Stammers N. (1999). Social Movements and the Social Construction of Human Rights. *Human Rights Quarterly,* Vol. 21, No. 4.

Subramanyan, Mngala (2004). The Indian Women's Movement in *Contemporary Sociology,* Vol. 33, No. 6, http://www.justor.org/ stable/3593826 (accessed on 22 May 2009).

Suri, K. C. (2004). "Democracy, Economic Reforms and Election Results in India." *Economic and Political Weekly,* December 18, Vol. 39, No. 51, pp. 5404–11.

Talbot, Strobe (1999). Delink with the Bomb in South Asia. *Foreign Affairs,* Vol. 78, No. 2: 110–22.

Taneja, Nalini (2002): BJP's Assault on Education and Educational Institutions in South Asian Documents, http://www.indowindow.com/sad/article.php?child=29&article=27. (accessed on 27 June 2013).

Taylor, Charles (1997). "Invoking Civil Society" in Goodin and Petlit (1997).

Thapar, Romila (2001). "Vargheekaranathinte Prashnangal" (Malayalam), *The problems of Classification,* in Panikkar (2001).

Tinker, Hugh (1982). "South Asia at Independence," in Wilson and Dalton (1982).

Tocqueville, Alexis De (1889). *Democracy in America,* Vol. I. New York: Longmans, Green & Co., extracted in Alexander, Raymond Boudon, Mohamed Cherkaoui (1997).

Vanaik, Achin (1990). "The Enemy Within." *Times of India,* 16 December.

———— (2001). "The New Indian Right," *The New Left Review,* May–June, http://sacw.insaf. net/2002/achin_NewIndianRight.html (accessed on 3 July 2009).

Vanaik, Achin (2006). "Communalization of the Indian Polity," in Ronald de Souza and Sridharan (2006).
—— (2008). "Making India Strong: The BJP-led government's Foreign Policy Perspectives," in John McGire and Ian Copland (eds.).
Viswanath, L. S. (1990). "Peasant Movements in Colonial India: An Examination of Some Conceptual Frame works." *Economic and Political Weekly*, Vol. 25, No. 2, January 13, pp. 118–22, http://www.jstor.org/stable/43958039 (accessed on 10 May 2009).
Vyas, K. K. (1969). "Incendiary Hand of the RSS and Jana Sangh Behind Communal Riots," Communist Party Publication, No. 3, January 1969.
Vyas, Neena (2009). "Behind the BJP's Defeat: All Noise and Negativism." *The Hindu*, May 21.
Wallerstein, Immanuel (1986). "The Incorporation of the Indian Subcontinent into the Capitalist World-Economy." *Economic and Political Weekly*, Vol. 21, No. 4, January 25.
Walzer, Michael (2003). "The Idea of Civil Society: A Path to Social Reconstruction," in Elliot (2003).
Wickramasinghe, Nira (2005). "The Idea of Civil Society in the South: Imaginings, Transplants, Designs." *Science and Society*, Vol. 69, No. 3: 458–86.
Williams, David and Tom Young (1994). "Governance, the World Bank and liberal theory." *Political Studies*, Vol. 42, No. 1: 84–100.
Wolpert, Stanley (1993). Resurgent Hindu Fundamentalism, *Contention*, 2(Spring).
Xaxa, Virgina (2009). "Tribes, Conversion and the Sangh Parivar" in Dharmendra Kumar and Yemuna Sunny (eds.), *Proselytisation in India: The Process of Hinduisation in Tribal Societies*. Delhi: Aakar Books.
Yadav, Yogendra (2004). "The Elusive Mandate of 2004." *Economic and Political Weekly*, 18 December 2004, pp. 5383–95.

Index

About the Authors

P. M. Joshy is Assistant Professor at the Postgraduate Department and Research Centre of Political Science, Sree Narayana College, Kollam affiliated to the University of Kerala. Earlier, he served as Deputy Director, Indian Council of Social Science Research (ICSSR) project at the Department of Politics and International Studies, Pondicherry University. He has also worked as a Lecturer (ad hoc) at the School of International Relations and Politics (SIRP), Mahatma Gandhi University, Kottayam, Kerala. He has contributed research articles to many national and international journals such as *South Asian Journal of Diplomacy, International Journal of South Asian Studies, Indian Journal of Politics and International Relations, Indian Journal of Politics,* and *Indian Journal of Public Administration* as well as in many edited volumes. His research interests include political theory, state and society in South Asia, and security studies.

K. M. Seethi is Professor and Director of the School of International Relations and Politics (SIRP) and former Dean, Faculty of Social Sciences, Mahatma Gandhi University (MGU), Kerala. He served in SIRP for nearly three decades and became Chairman, Centre for Cross-National Communication in South Asia, MGU in 2009. He also serves as the Honorary Director of the KN Raj Centre, MGU. The books authored by Professor Seethi include *Coastal Security: Needed A New Look* (2010), *Engaging with the World: Critical Reflections on India's Foreign Policy,* edited with Rajen Harshe (2005/2009) and others. He has contributed several articles in national and international journals such as *Millennium, South Asian Journal of Diplomacy, Economic and Political Weekly, Indian Journal of Political Science, Indian Journal of Politics and International Relations* and others. He is also the Editor of *South Asian Journal of Diplomacy, Indian Journal of Politics and International Relations* and *Journal of Political Economy and Fiscal Federalism.* His research interests include issues of security, foreign policy, human rights, environment and political theory.